REICHERT The Human Edifice

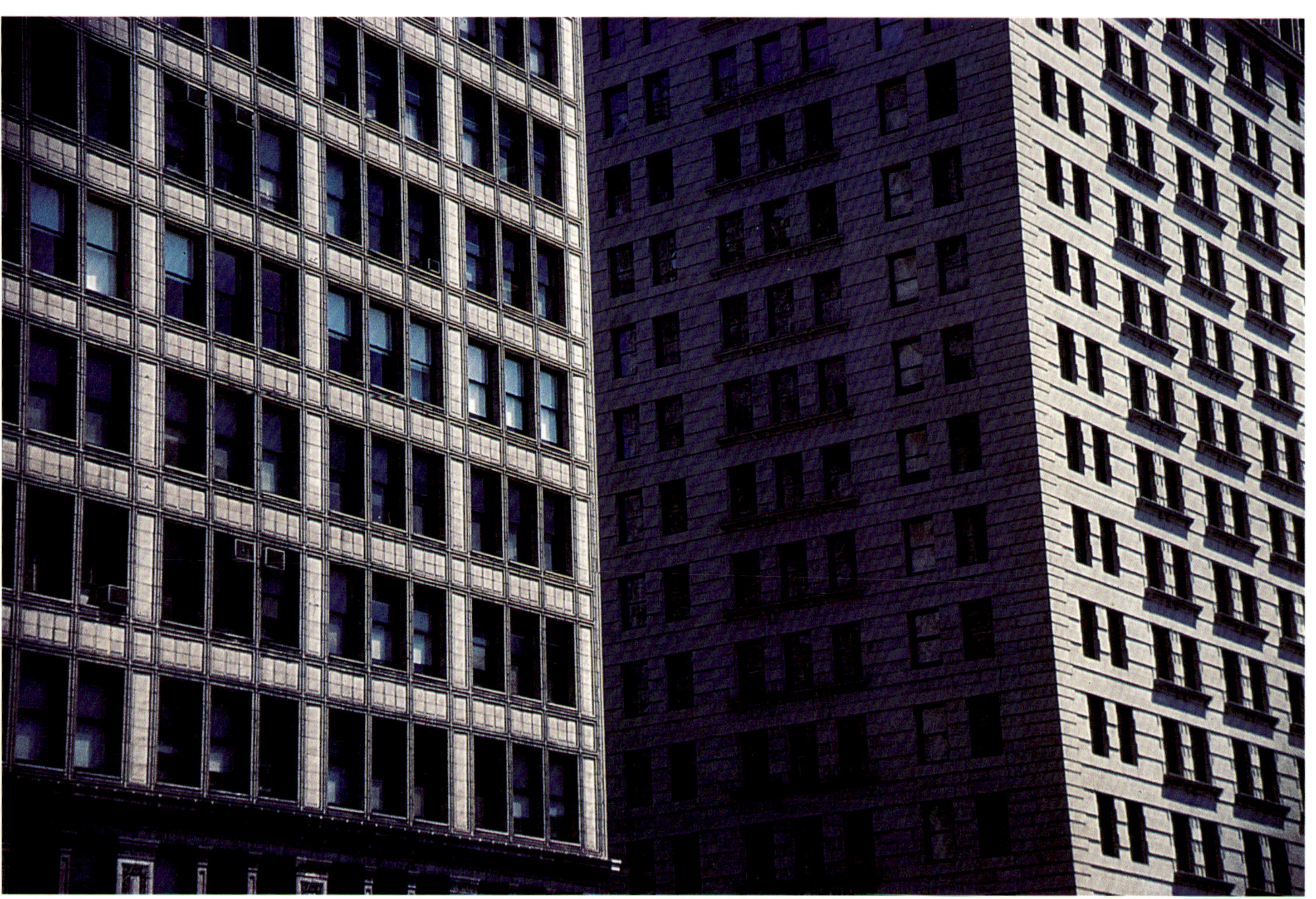

NEW YORK, AUGUST 2002

REICHERT The Human Edifice

MEL GOODING

ARTMEDIAPRESS

For Sal

With grateful acknowledgement

The JUDSON H. BLOUNT III and MARY MARGARET McDADE Fund for the Visual Arts

I would like to thank everyone who has so graciously allowed me to photograph them over the years, especially as represented in this book, including Armande Altai, Sally MacLeod, Anya Varda, and Katherine Zuber. I would also like to thank all those people who allowed me to photograph them in their anonymity. MR

Front cover: Benson, Vermont, July 1981

Published in Great Britain in 2003 by ARTMEDIA PRESS
Culvert House
Culvert Road
London SW11 5AP

ISBN: 1 902889 07 X

Printed and bound in Italy

Contents

Thirteen texts for the photographs

'It is as though beautiful things have been placed here and there throughout the

world to serve as small wake-up calls to perception, spurring lapsed alertness back

to its most acute level.' (Elaine Scarry)

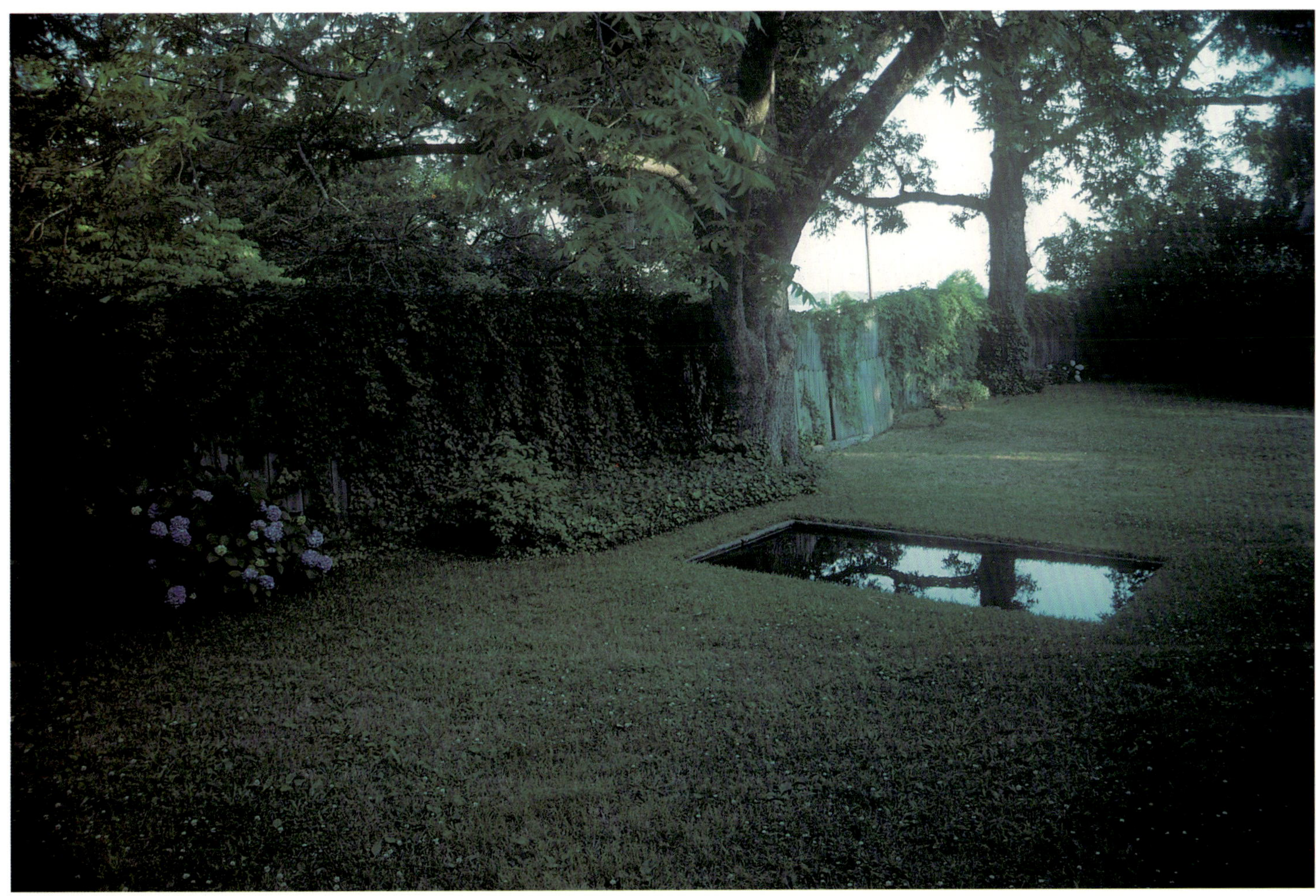

WASHINGTON, NORTH CAROLINA, JUNE 1997

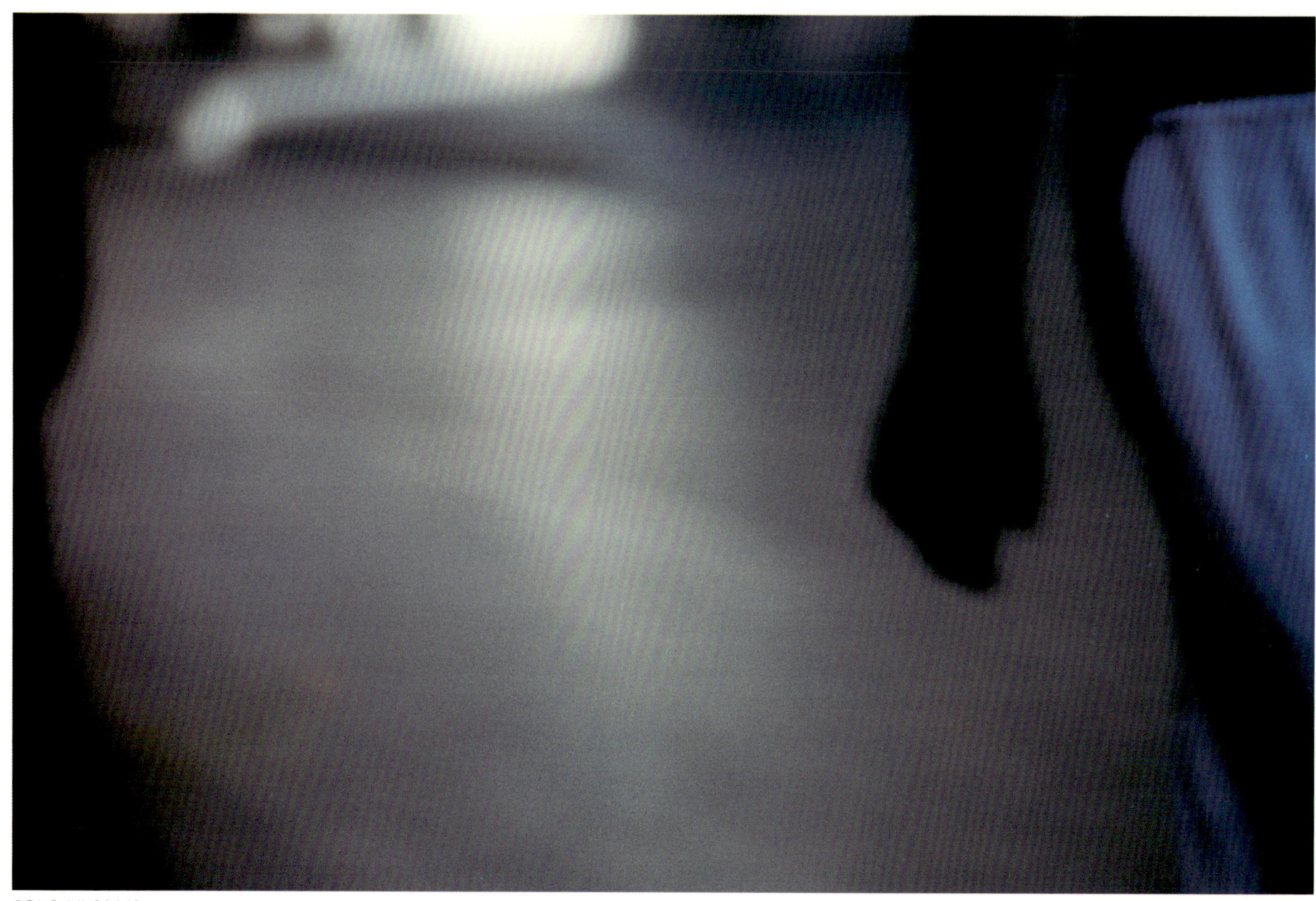

ROME, JUNE 2003

1 eye and mind

The eye looks: at what? The camera records: what? The first question is unanswerable, because every act of looking involves countless operations of the subjective mind, and the eye is itself constantly constructively on the move. What is seen is the secret we all carry with us at every waking moment: it is a mental secret. The second question is answered by the photograph. At what do we look when we look at the photograph? An object in the world that is an image of a portion of it. A trace of light, a register of light and shadow, an approximation of colour. Leonardo described painting as *cosa mentale*: it was 'a thing of the mind'. He meant that the act of painting involved the complexly artful (cunning, knowing) coordination of hand and eye at the service of thought and memory; it was a constructive and transformative process analogous to the work of the mind upon the world. No painting without premeditation and intent. No such process attends upon the creation of the photographic image. The camera has no eye, and no mind: it does not act upon the world, the world acts upon it. Reichert accepts the logic of this; he takes photographs without premeditation, without intent.

2 absence

Reichert's photographs have a quality of the uncanny, as if he had not been there to take them.

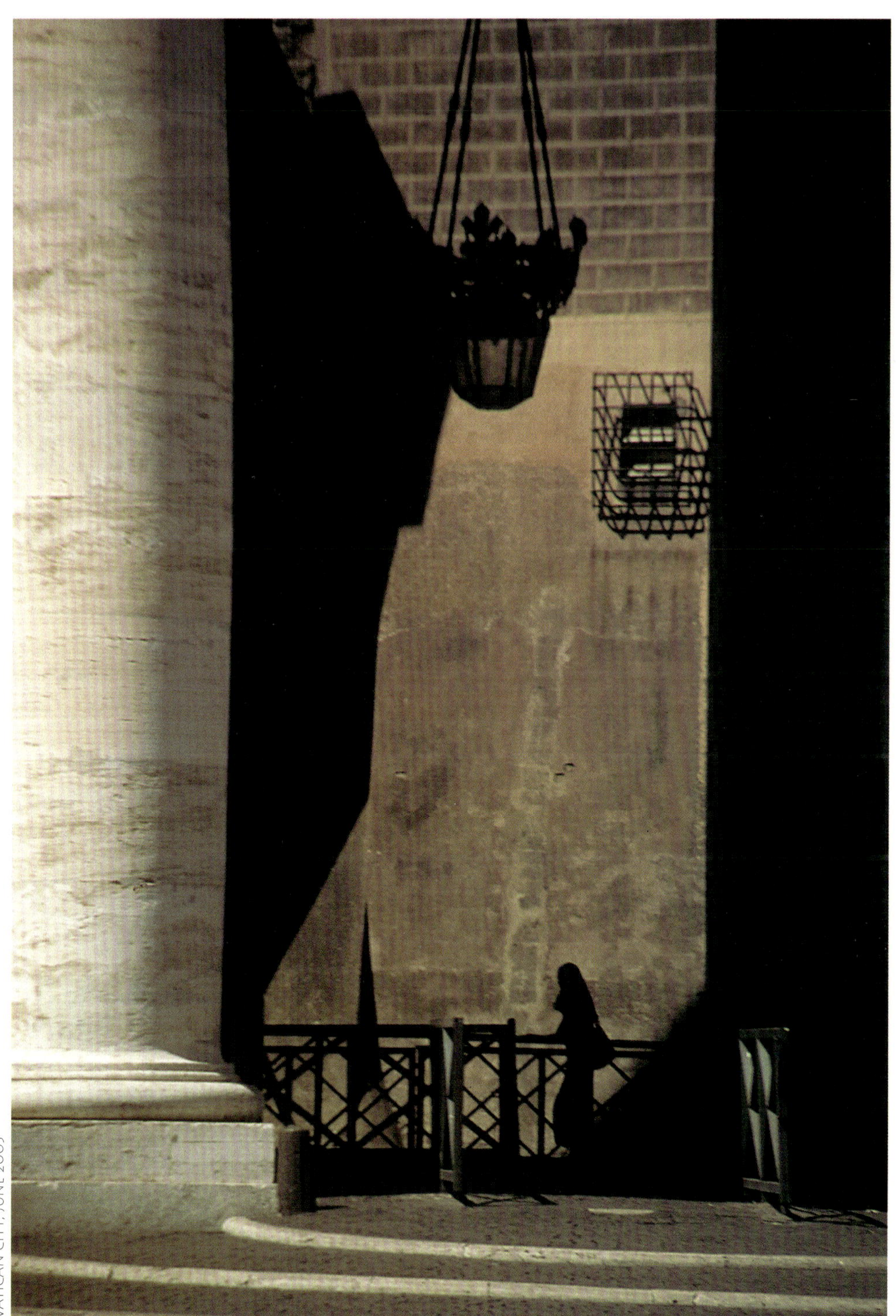

VATICAN CITY, JUNE 2003

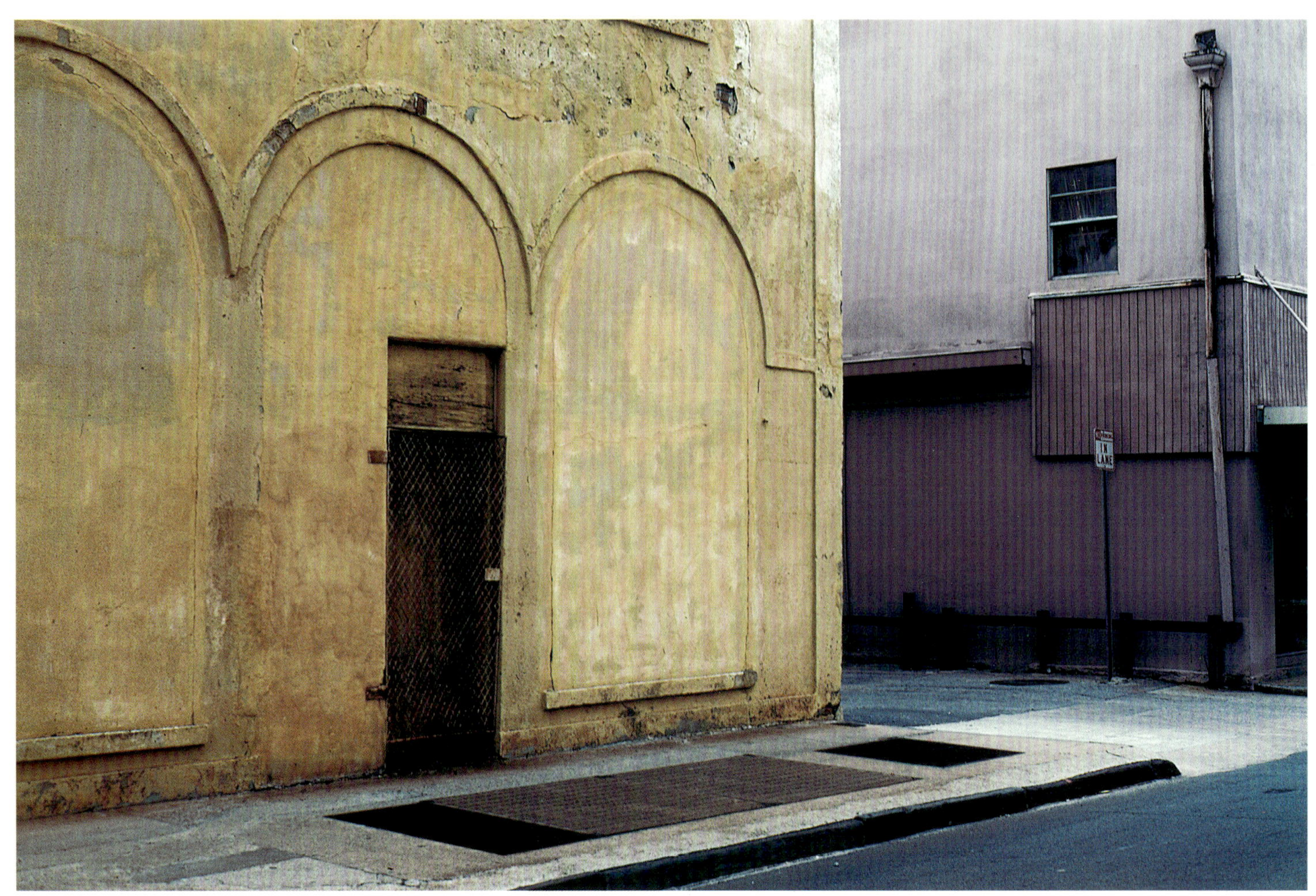

SAVANNAH, GEORGIA, JANUARY 1997

3 corners

Why are corners of buildings, which are seen so often out of the corner of our eye, here so central? It is a motif insistent enough to disconcert. These photographs are not interested in architecture, or architectural detail: they are too arbitrary for that. The eye behind the camera *likes* architecture, for sure. But that's not a motive for these images. The eye behind the camera *looks* at architecture. But not with historical or aesthetic intent, still less with sociological or analytical intent, at least not when the moment is seized, and the picture shot. These corners are just there. Sometimes there are more than one in eyeshot: all the better, says the eye behind the camera. To say 'the moment is seized' suggests action, but these corners are not going to move. The 'moment' is in the mind of the eye behind the camera. The corner is seen, and in a moment, taken. The moment in the mind is secret. We are presented with another corner. It joins all the other corners. It does not in itself disconcert. It is the insistence of corners that disconcerts. As if instead of buildings the built world was full of corners. Or as if Reichert's world is a world of corners. Or as if the architectural beauty of his world, or the beauty of his architectural world, is discovered most often in corners.

4 intents and purposes

This angular aesthetic is purely photographic. The beauty that the eye seeks and the camera registers is found only in the photograph, an object in the world. The reproductions in this book are also objects in the world. The photographs exist to become the reproductions in this book. They have no other purpose. I mean by this that they are not documentary, neither technical, nor descriptive nor illustrational; neither poetic, nor atmospheric, nor commemorative. Neither are they rhetorical; they have no intent upon us, emotional, moral, political. To adapt Roland Barthes' terms, they are denotative without apparent connotation. They are without implication. Why are they here? Why is this book here? Leaving aside the circumstantial, there is only one answer: to be looked at. What do we see? Photographic reproductions of photographs. Images of a registered light at one remove.

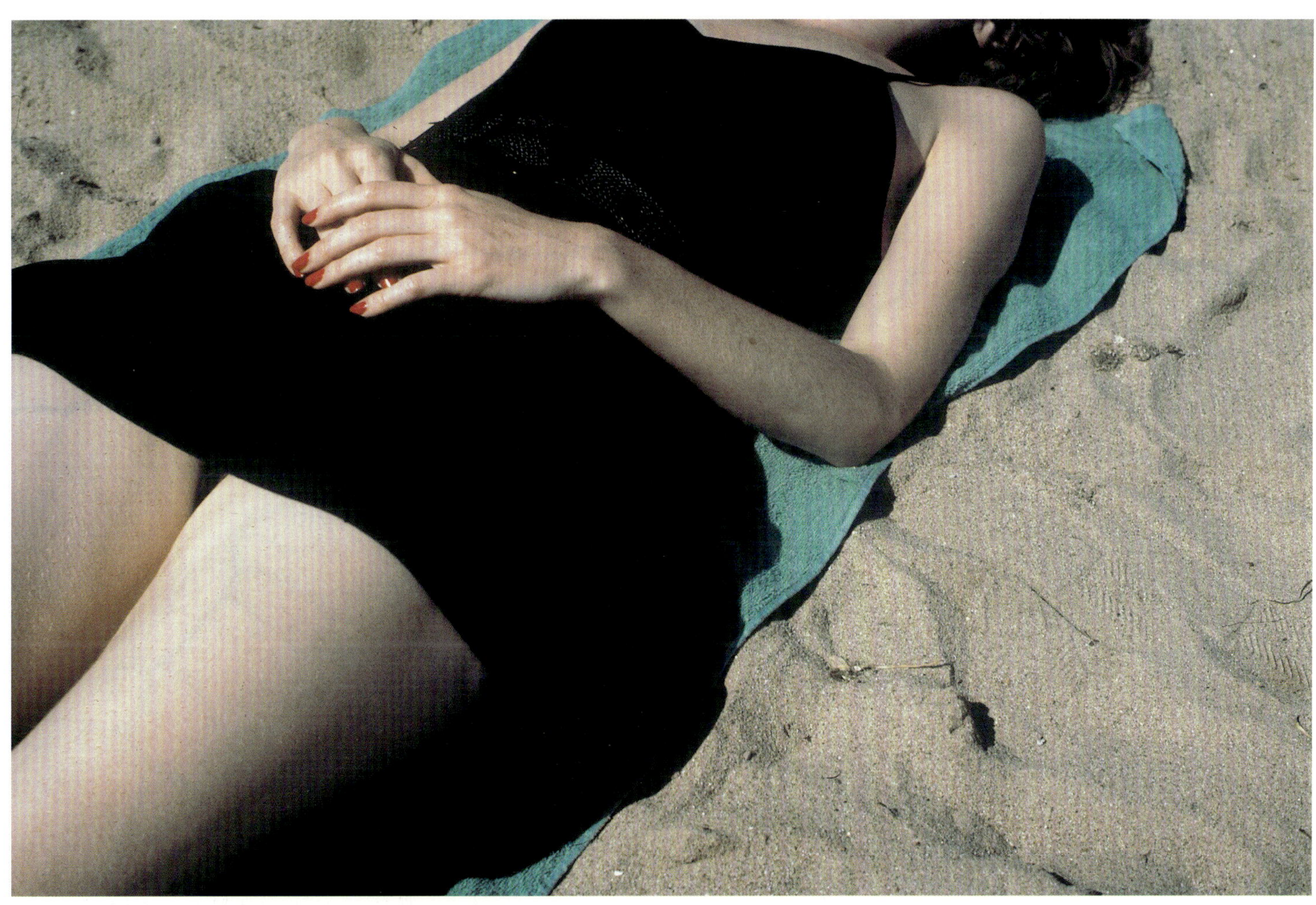

CANNES, JUNE 1979

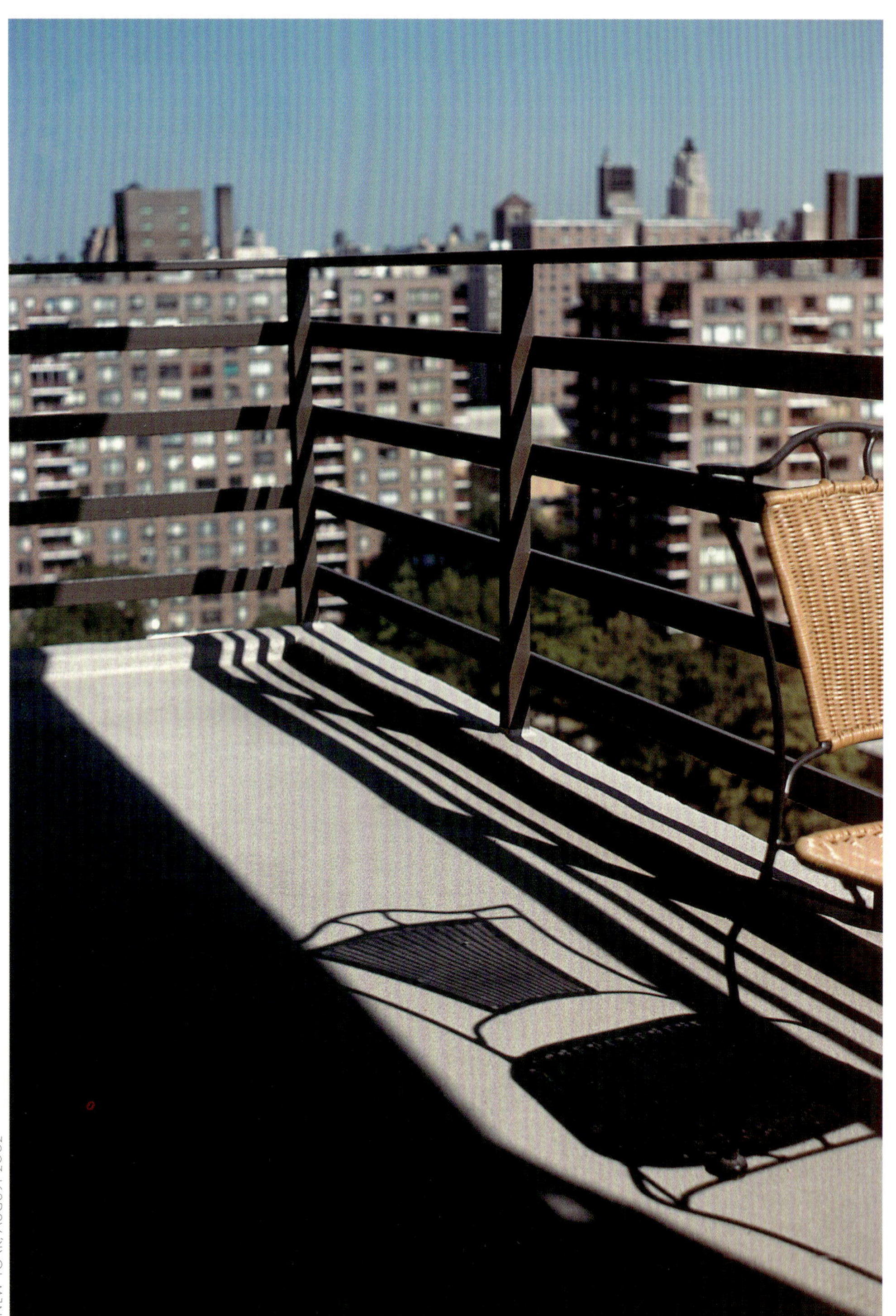

NEW YORK, AUGUST 2002

5 histories and theories

Strange, and disconcerting, that histories and theories of photography offer so little that will apply to or critically illuminate these photographs. Reichert photographs without benefit of theory and seemingly oblivious of history. Even his own history is absent except by implication: we have his word that he took these photographs and that the dates and locations are true. There is certainly a consistency – of resemblance of one image to another, of pictorial structure, of lack of affect – that makes them identifiable as the work of one photographer. So: Reichert travels; he pauses to take photographs that seem to have nothing to do with his travels (they are not snaps, they are not evidence, they are not materials for professional use, they are not documents for a travelogue or memoir, they are not commissioned for the use of others); he gathers the photographs together; he presents them in no particular order.

6 captions

These photographs have no titles. (Each might be entitled *Untitled*, or *Ohne Titel*.) A date, a place: caption information we take on trust. The place names are, as it were, generic rather than specific: Paris, Madrid, Pegwell Bay, New York, Savannah, Ramsgate, etc. Sometimes one might guess at a particular city: two photographs taken on the same visit to Paris – that most photographed of cities – in February 1977 bring Atget to mind, or have perhaps, rather, the 'voluntary banality' of Boiffard's 1928 photos of Paris frontages taken for Breton's novel *Nadja* (these early photos of Reichert have a touch of the 'atmospherics' that his later work abjures). New York – another city recreated in every mind by photography – is sometimes recognisable. But in most cases there is no information in the photograph that would enable identification, and the captions offer nothing more particular. Sometimes an aspect surprises: Ramsgate looks Mediterranean; Madrid looks merely generic modern; Savannah seems mysterious and diverse. There is no intention, one guesses, to achieve these particular effects. The captions deny topography, and repudiate the banally familiar photographic 'spirit of place' as a concern of the photographer.

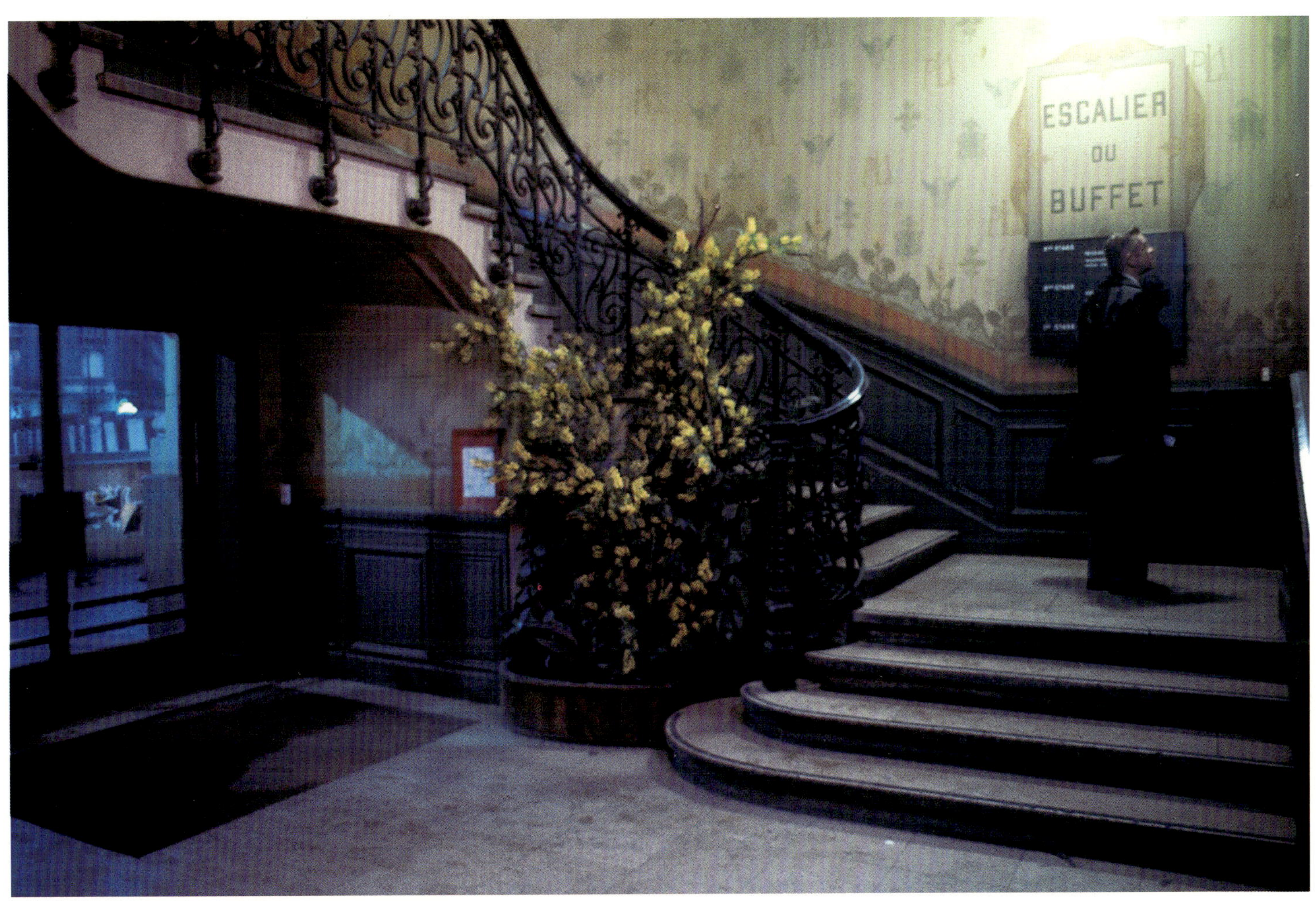

PARIS, JANUARY 1997

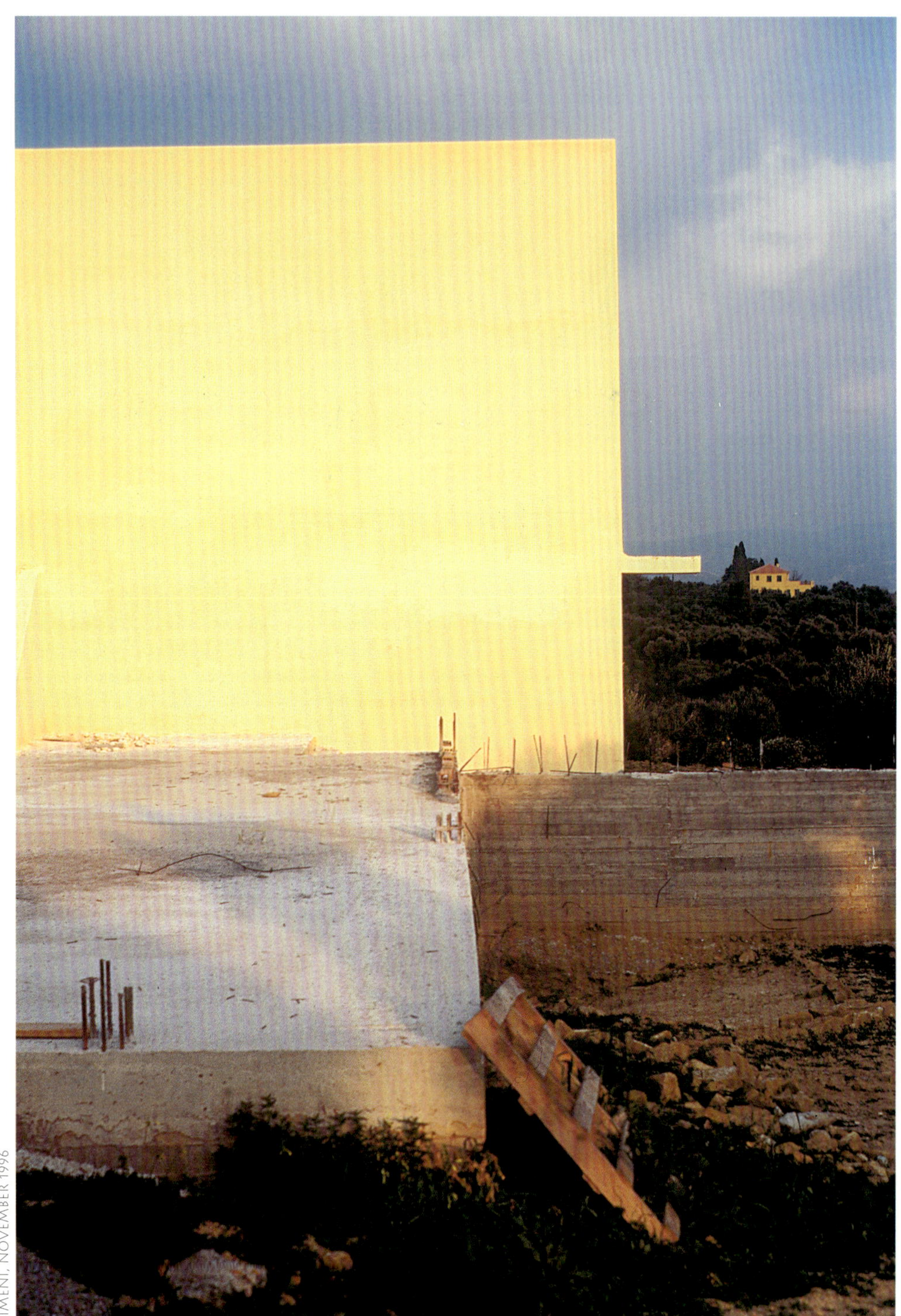

LIMENI, NOVEMBER 1996

7 image / text

Barthes described the photograph as 'a message without a code': it is the caption,
the linguistic description, the supply of external information, that brings meaning to
the image. Sometimes context supplies information that makes the image 'readable':
photographs may fall recognisably into genres, or, to borrow the term as it is used in
linguistics, into 'registers' of formality (wedding photographs, portraits) and informality
(family snaps). Even in cases of the everyday usages of circumstance, purpose and
intent (news, architectural topography, technical information, policing, etc.) their
entry into the circumambient discourse is inescapably verbal. Reichert's photographs,
however, resist words beyond the banal and obvious. The captions give no clues of
any great use to interpretation.

8 contexts

Photographic history: so many other possibilities from the beginning (from Niépce, Daguerre, Fox Talbot to Atget, Kertész, Friedlander, Stieglitz, Arbus and Mapplethorpe); possibilities avoided with a rigour absolute enough to make comparisons and parallels unhelpful. *Painting*: abstract, not topographical, not landscape, not narrative. *Philosophy*: aesthetics; the problem of meaning. We shall not get far with these, however. Best, probably, not to pursue the matter: an inappropriate and undeserved pretentiousness lies in wait. Reichert is himself happy to let well alone. Allowing for his images a refreshing banality, a beautiful dumbness, he admits to an egocentric aesthetic. (*Take it or leave it*.)

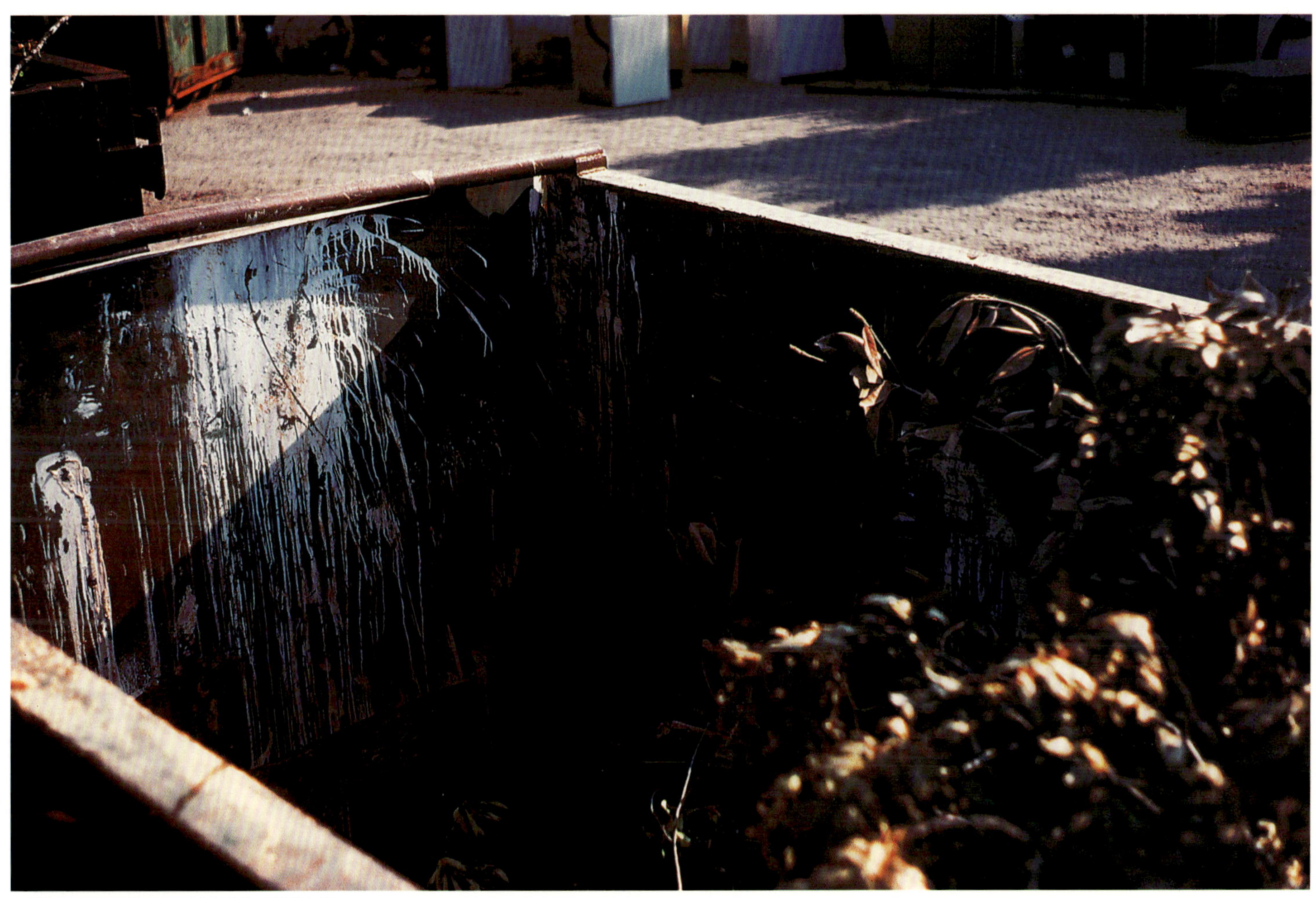

WASHINGTON, NORTH CAROLINA, JULY 2002

23

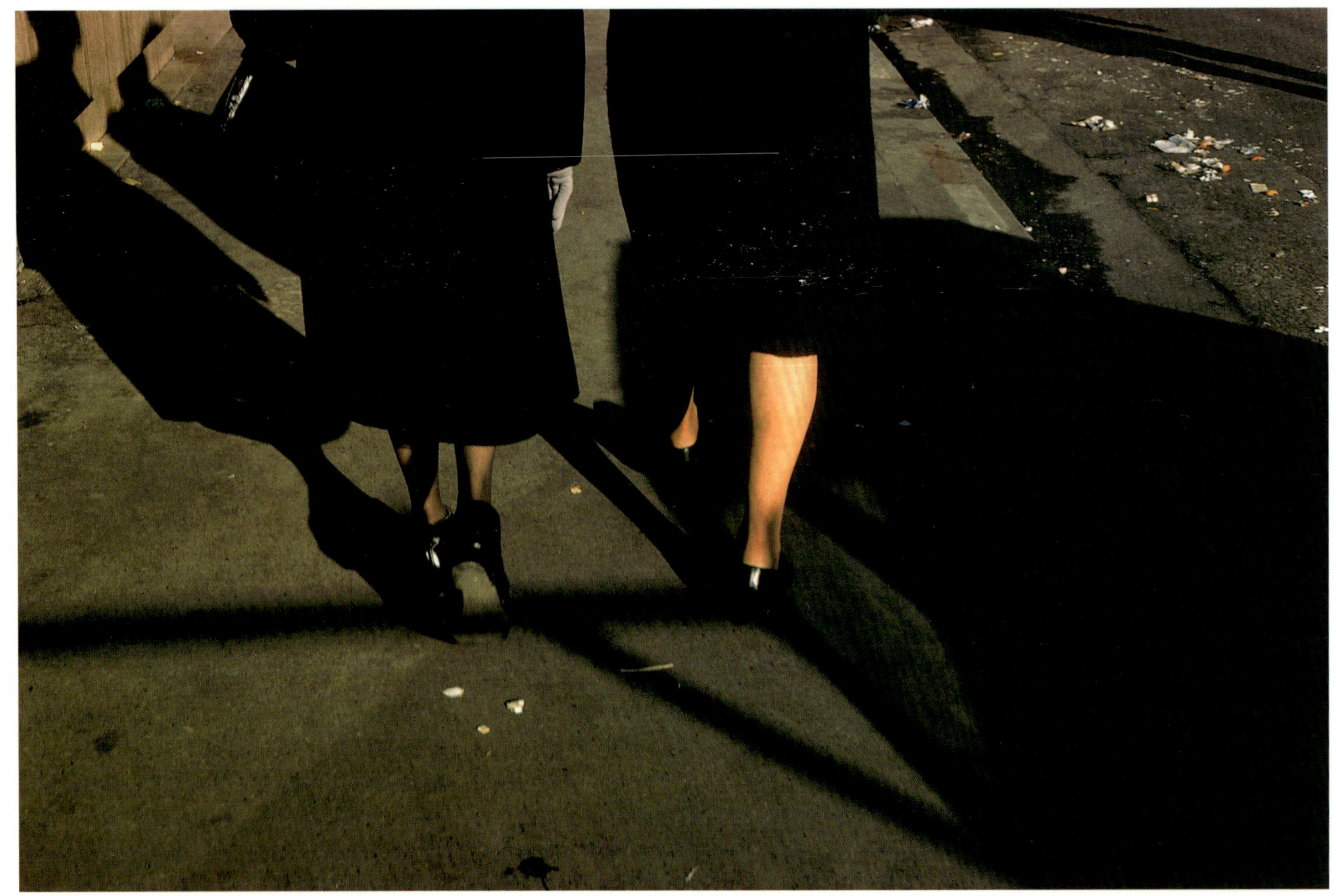

PARIS, FEBRUARY 1977

9 documents and presence

Atget: 'They are simply documents I make.' The remark was made hastily and in agitation, at the moment when Atget refused to be credited for a photograph of his to be used by the Surrealists for their own purposes. He was making clear his own purposes. It is Atget I have thought of often as I have looked at these photographs of buildings and interiors. Atget's documentation was at once systematic and arbitrary, but its very clarity in execution, its concentration on its subject, gave his photographs the uncanny quality that appealed to the Surrealists with whom he had so little sympathy. It is a quality at a pole from that of Reichert's strangeness, his absence. For Atget, whose photographs were aptly described as like those of a scene of a crime, is present even in the most deserted of his imaged places: his eye is at the service of a mind obsessed with a mission of documentary record. His photographs whisper, like a witness to a crime: 'I was here to see this courtyard, to look at this shopfront, this alleyway, this scrapyard, this tree. This is what I saw.' Reichert's photographs say nothing of the sort; rather, simply: 'look at this photograph'. No reasons are advanced to justify this injunction. It is the photograph that is the thing, not the thing – the person, the corner, the stairway – that has been photographed.

10 nudes and other people

No stories. Look at this shoulder of a naked figure in a bath, at this face dragging on a cigarette, at this figure on a sandy beach (Ramsgate? No, Cannes), this reclining figure at a New York bus stop: the image begins and ends in the photograph. No narrative, no record of a relationship, no exposure but that of light on the plate. A man in Ramsgate looks up at the sky: no why and wherefore, no clue to relations, no indication of what he is looking at. He is not 'interesting', this man in the photograph, he is simply there. A man sits on a fire hydrant in New York: no comment, no information, no record beyond that of a moment's beauty. Not that of the event: if it is anywhere, the beauty is in the photograph. Look, here is another nude, another face, a naked swimmer, a woman's paddling feet: Milan, New York, Vermont. These are not documents, diary entries; the question of love does not arise; the question of the woman's beauty does not arise; the question of circumstance does not arise. No drama: no clue to what has gone before, no expectation of action, no suggestion of *dénouement*. These are photographs, not acts of homage or of love. Or if they were, they do not say. It is none of our business. Look. What do you see? It is a secret: your secret.

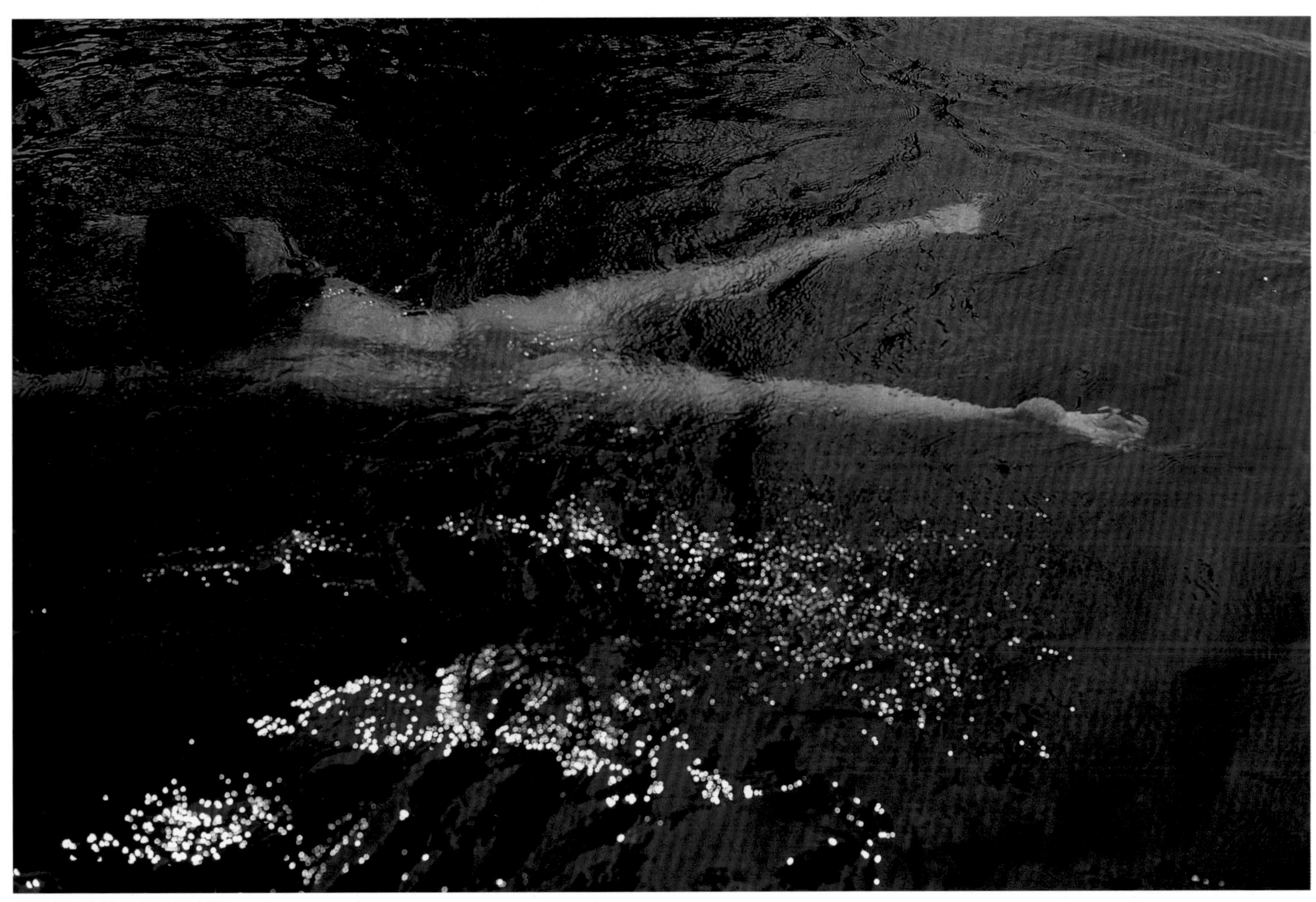

BENSON, VERMONT, JULY 1981

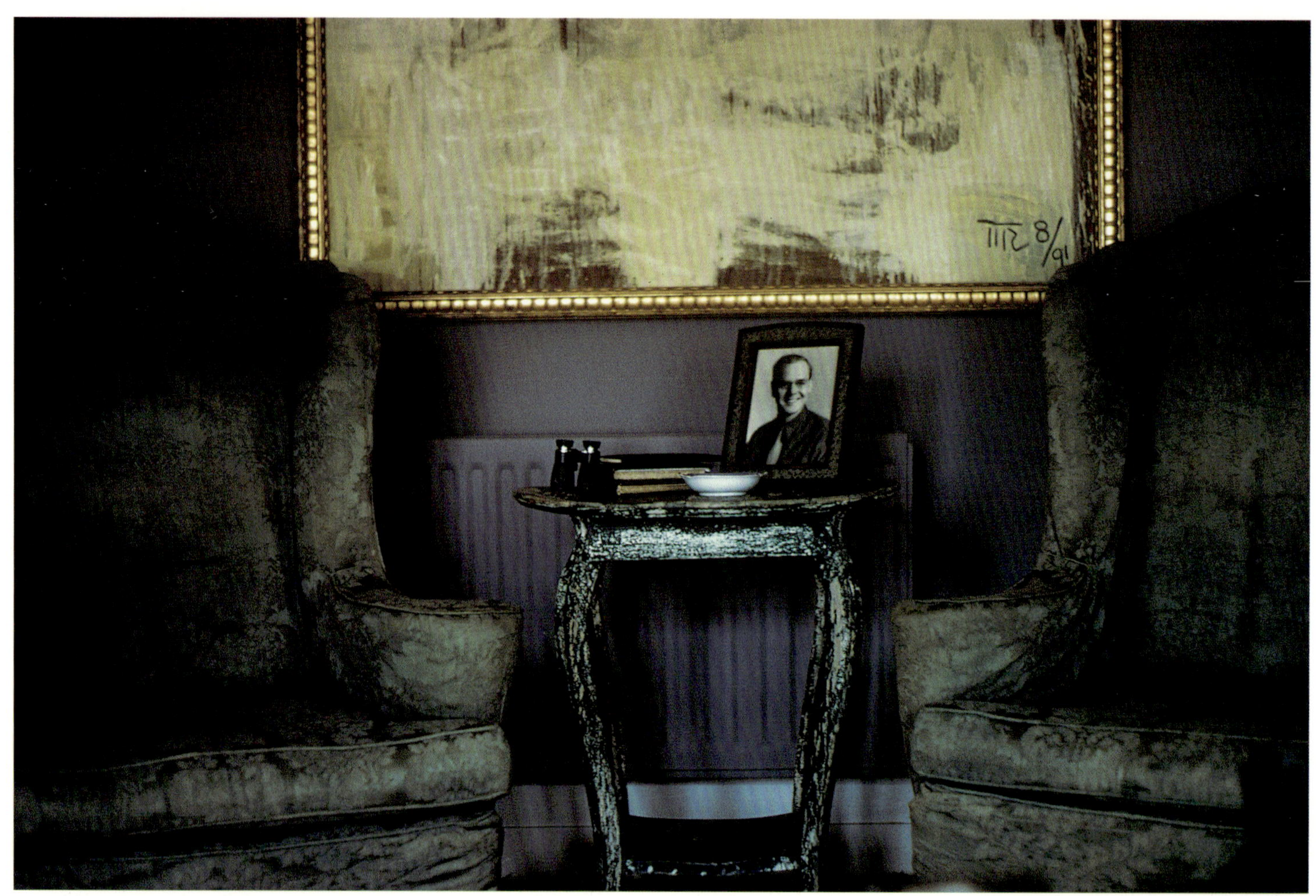

28

RAMSGATE, MAY 2002

11 interiors

Every interior suggests a set: a setting for action. Entries and exits; props; a *mis-en-scène*. Every photograph of a room, however empty, suggests the drama of presence. Someone was here; someone will enter this space, sometime. Things have happened here; things will happen here. And every interior suggests the presence of the photographer. It is odd that even more than in the photographs of figures this *authorial* presence is manifest in Reichert's interiors. These are the only photographs in the book in which the subject matter asserts its *interest*, implies narrative, is fraught. Looking at these pictures it is impossible to empty the mind of association and implication, to let the eye and mind simply seize the abstract from the circumstantial. These photographs of interiors tell me too much. Others may enjoy their plenitude.

12 beauty

The world is not beautiful. It is what we make of it. Coming upon things we may find them beautiful, and present them to others as if they were so, seeking assent. The eye sees, the mind composes into beauty what is seen. The camera can seize this: it 'takes', as we say, the photograph.

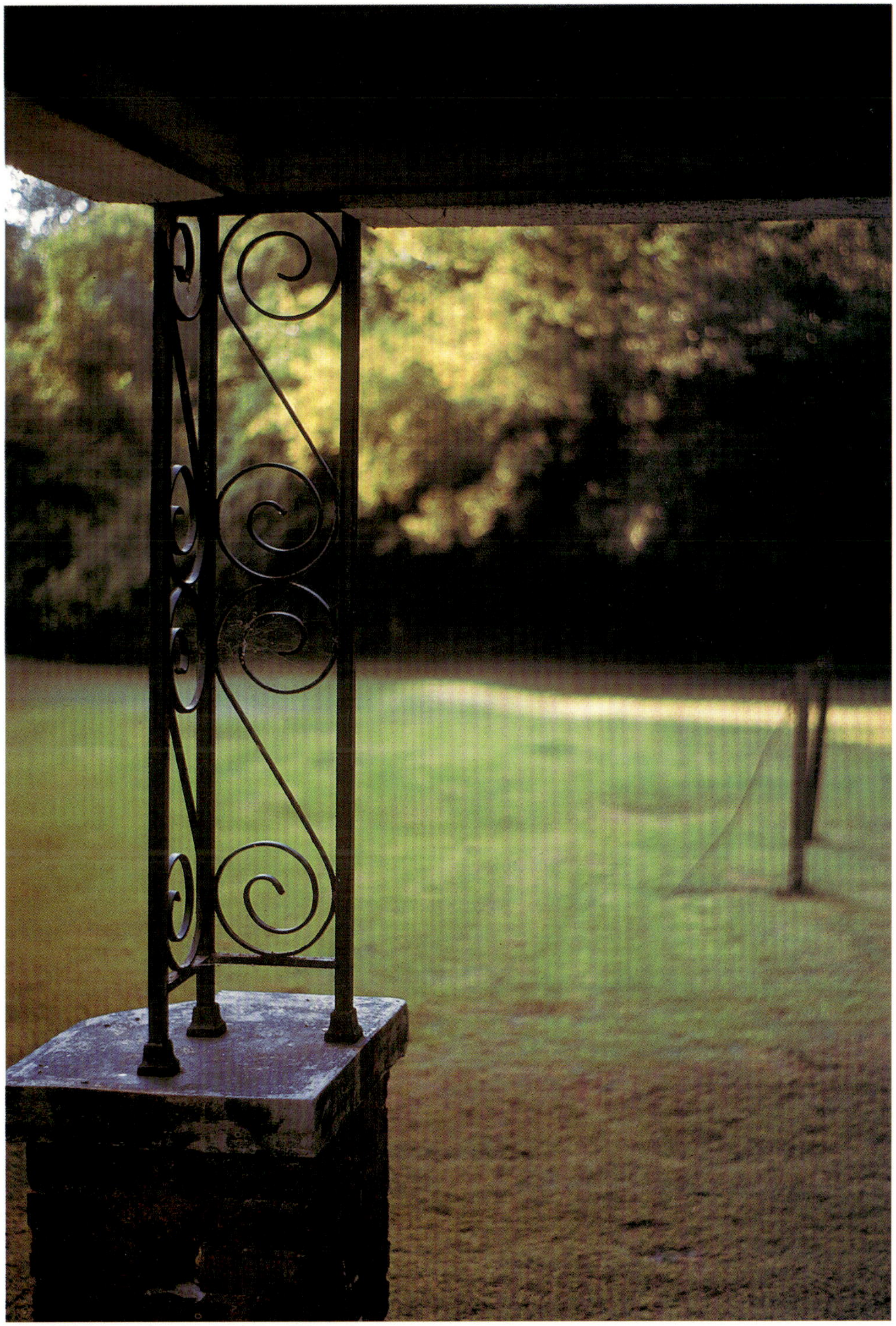

WASHINGTON, NORTH CAROLINA, JULY 2002

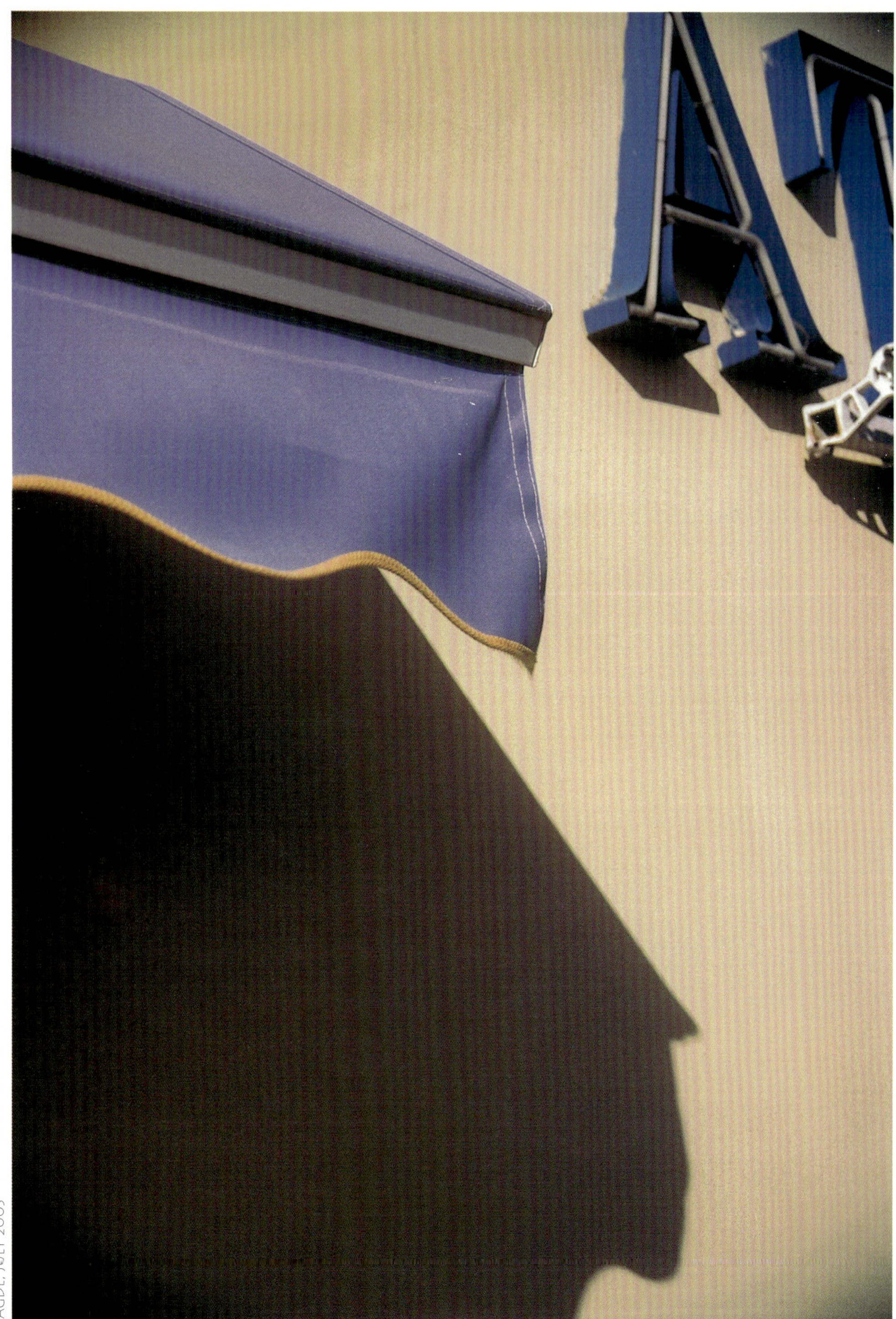

AGDE, JULY 2003

13 less is more

'When we come upon beautiful things . . . they act upon us like small tears in the surface of the world that pull us through to some vaster space.' (Elaine Scarry)

The less they tell me the more I grow to admire and enjoy these photographs by Reichert. Corners, windows, pools, the sea, the sky, a face, a room: it is not the circumstantial, it is not the substantial, it is not evocation, or remembrance, or implication, or information about the world outside the photograph. What is out there in the world enters into the rectangular visual universe of the photograph, becomes what it is in that order, and not something else, not what it was, but what it is there. It is this visual fact that pierces – the photographic fact, the photograph itself. Each is indeed like one of Scarry's 'small tears . . . that pull us through to another space'. Or as if each were an example of Barthes's punctum (but without, as it were, the studium): the 'sting, speck, cut, little hole'. I mean the visual facts of the photographs as photographs, photographs that may be arranged in any order, that carry no narrative and are components of no meta-narrative. These are what pierce, these visual facts: traces of the actual that compose themselves into the dignity and beauty of the abstract, are propositions of a new reality.

A note on sources

Elaine Scarry is quoted from *On Beauty and Being Just* (Princeton, 1999). Marcus Reichert's words are from an unpublished statement. Roland Barthes discusses the 'photographic paradox', that it is 'a message without a code', and the problems of 'denotation' and 'connotation' in 'The Photographic Message' (in *Message-Music-Text*, ed. and trans. Stephen Heath, London 1977); his distinction between the 'studium' and the 'punctum' as elements in the photograph is developed in *Camera Lucida* (London 1982). Michel Beaujour considered what he described as 'the voluntary banality' of Jacques-André Boiffard's photographs for *Nadja* as intended to avoid the convulsive effect of the surrealist 'marvellous'. Had he wanted such an effect, he suggests, Breton would have gone to Man Ray. To this eye Boiffard's photographs for *Nadja* have a distinctive if low-key poetry, not unlike that of some of Reichert's earlier work. ('Photography and the Surrealist Text' in *L'Amour Fou: photography and surrealism*, catalogue to an exhibition at the Hayward Gallery, London 1966.) Eugène Atget's avowal – 'These are simply documents I make' – was made to Man Ray in anticipation of the publication, on the cover of *La Révolution Surréaliste*, of his photograph of Parisians observing the eclipse of April, 1912. The incident and its implications are described in the prologue to Molly Nesbit's *Atget's Seven Albums* (Yale, 1992).

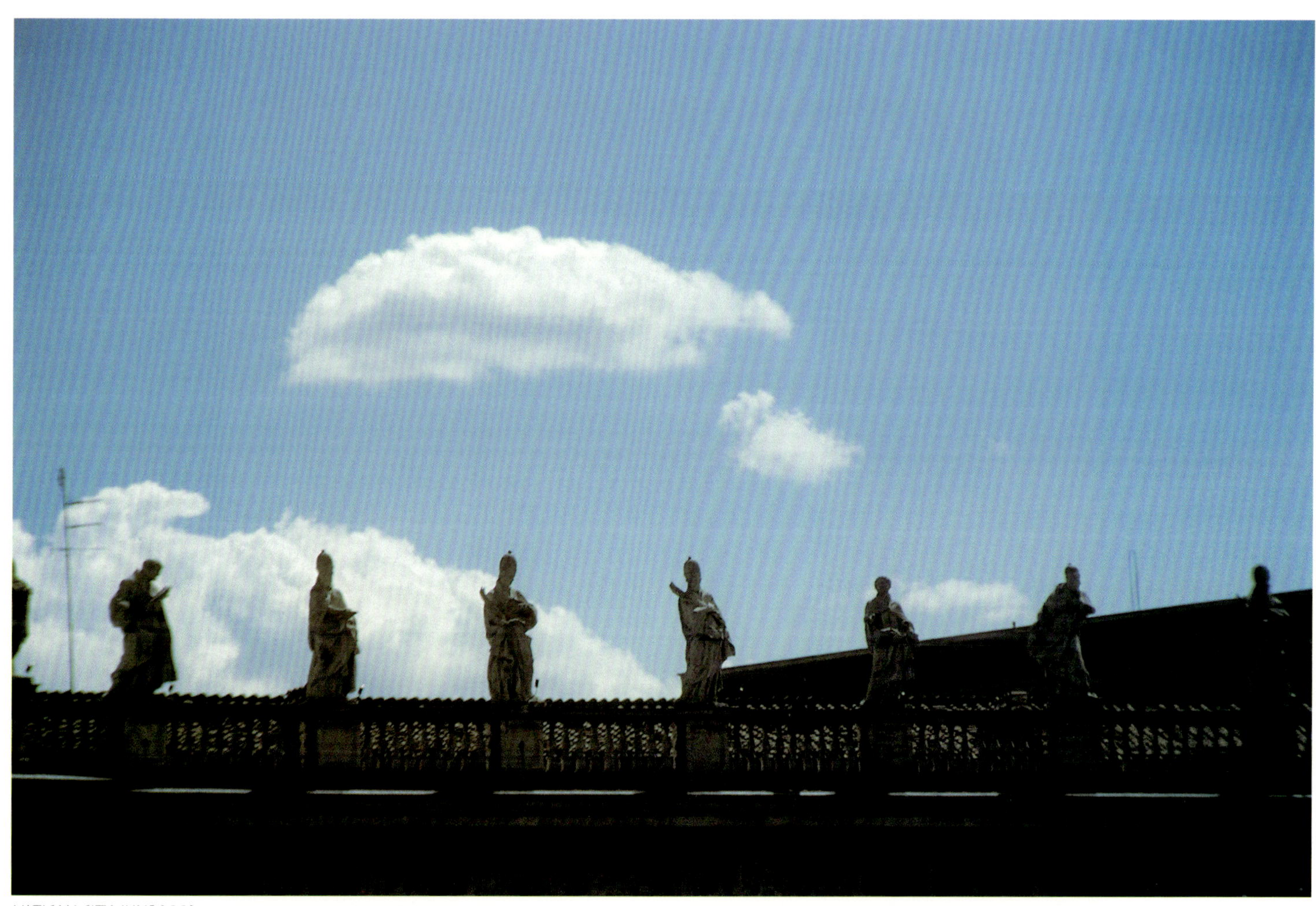

VATICAN CITY, JUNE 2003

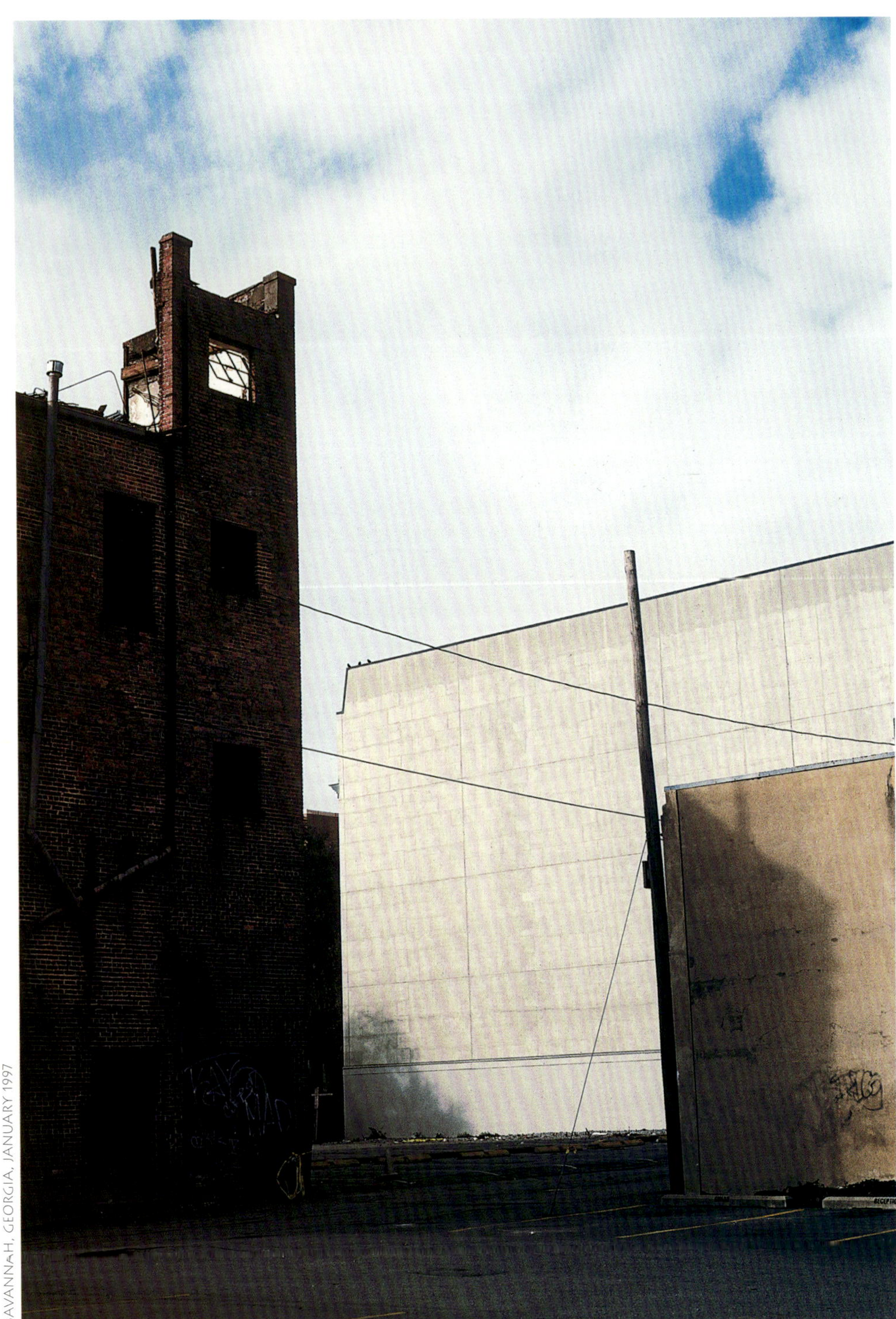

36

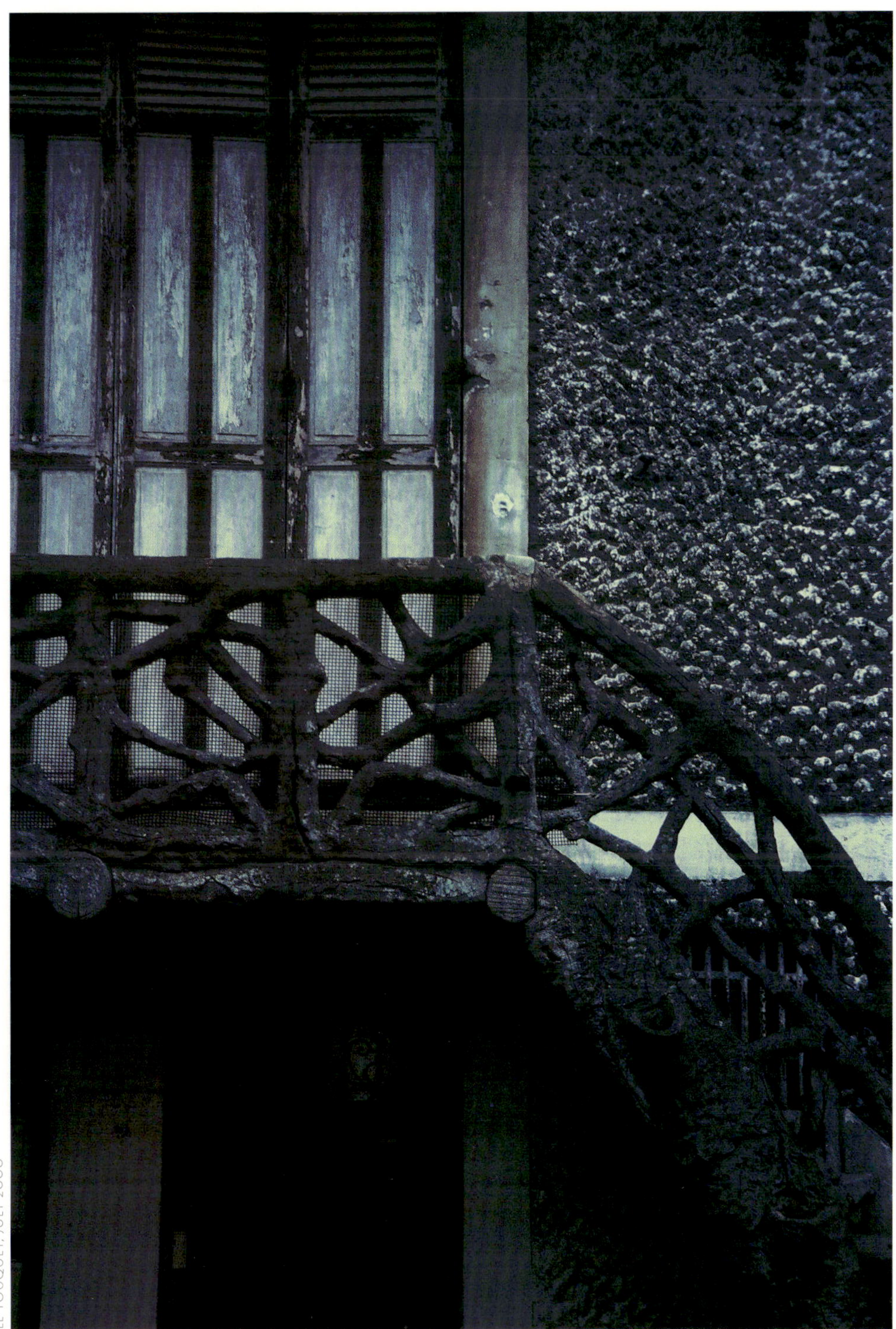

LE TOUQUET, JULY 2000

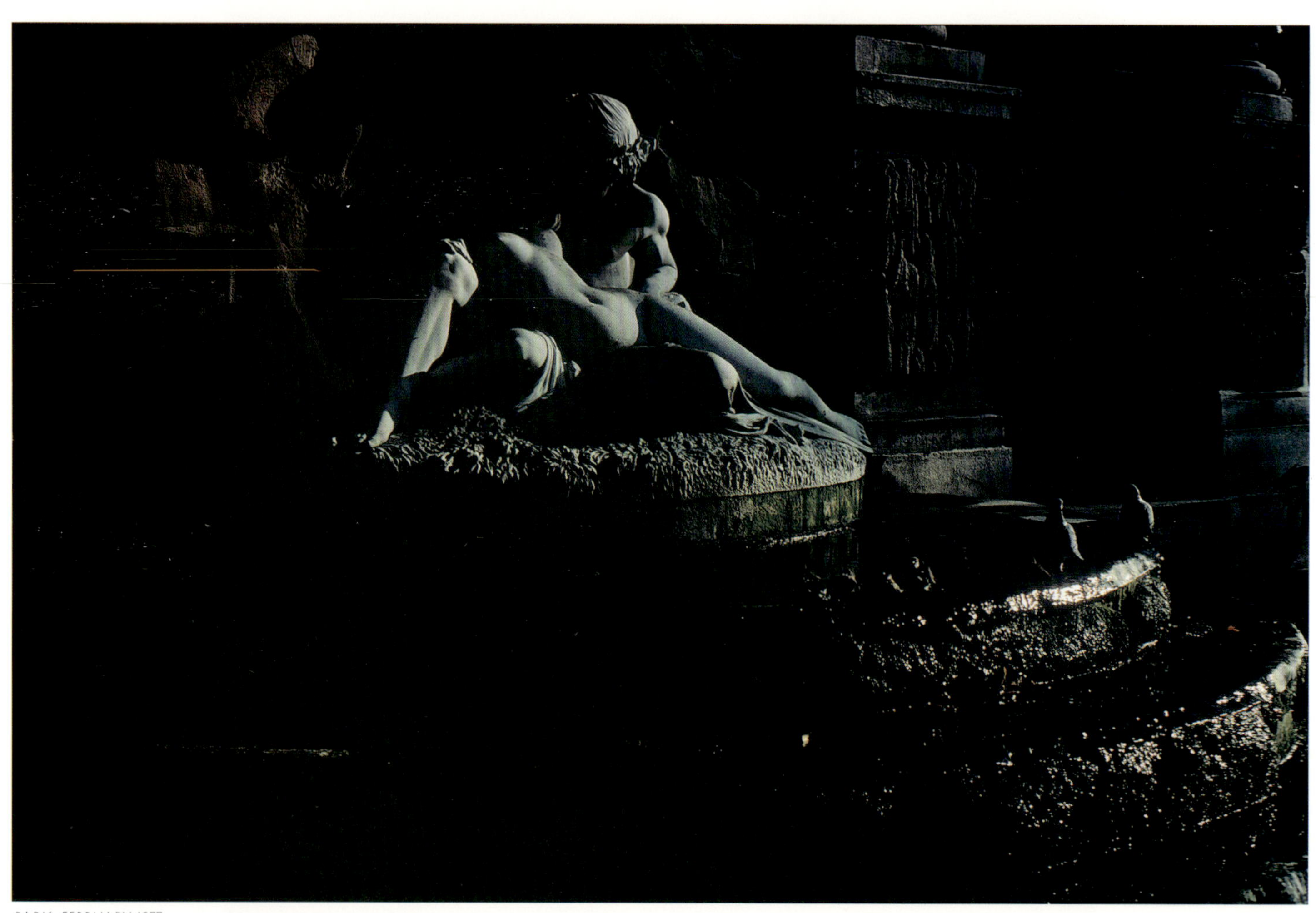

38

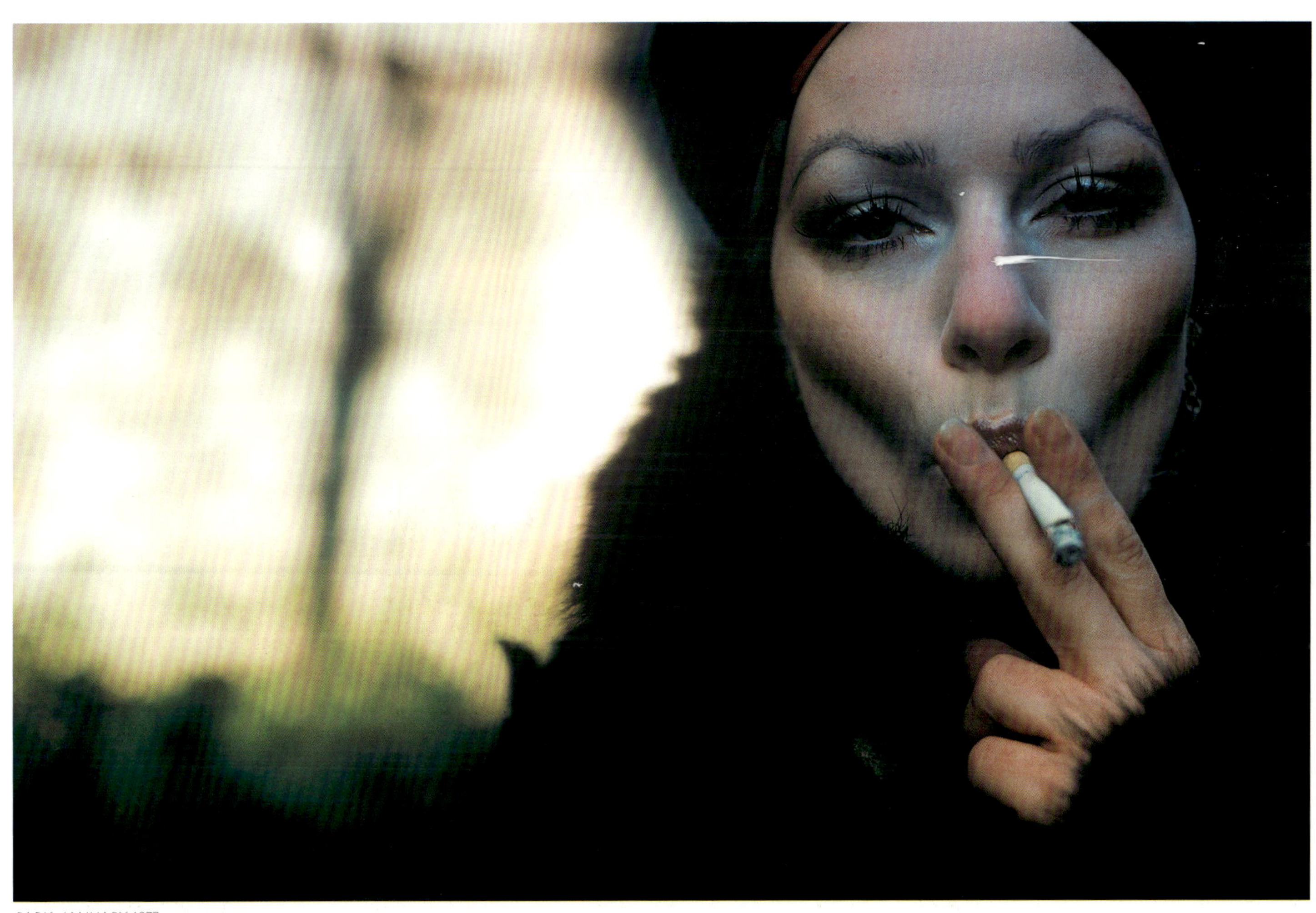

PARIS, JANUARY 1977

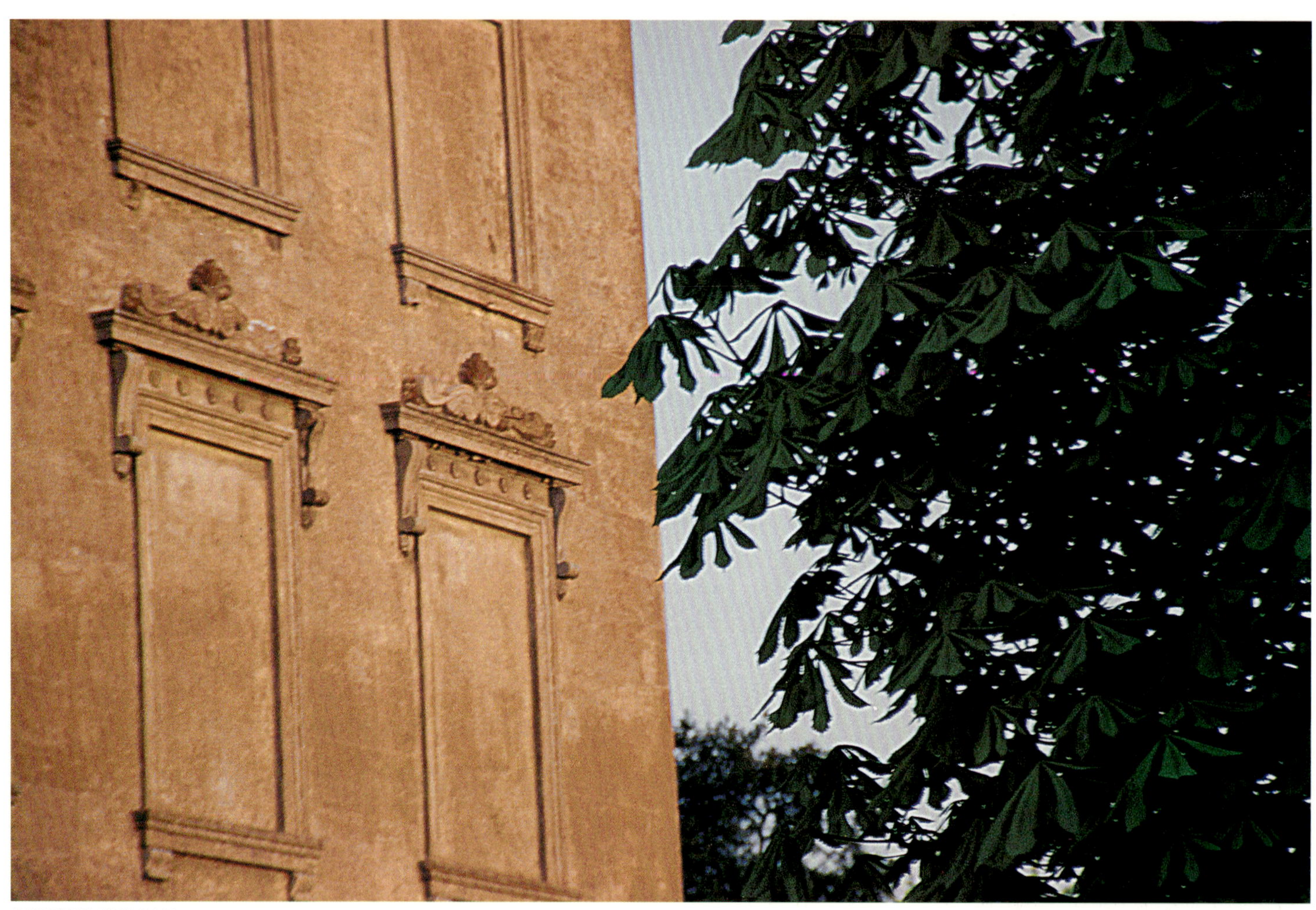

RAMSGATE, APRIL 2002

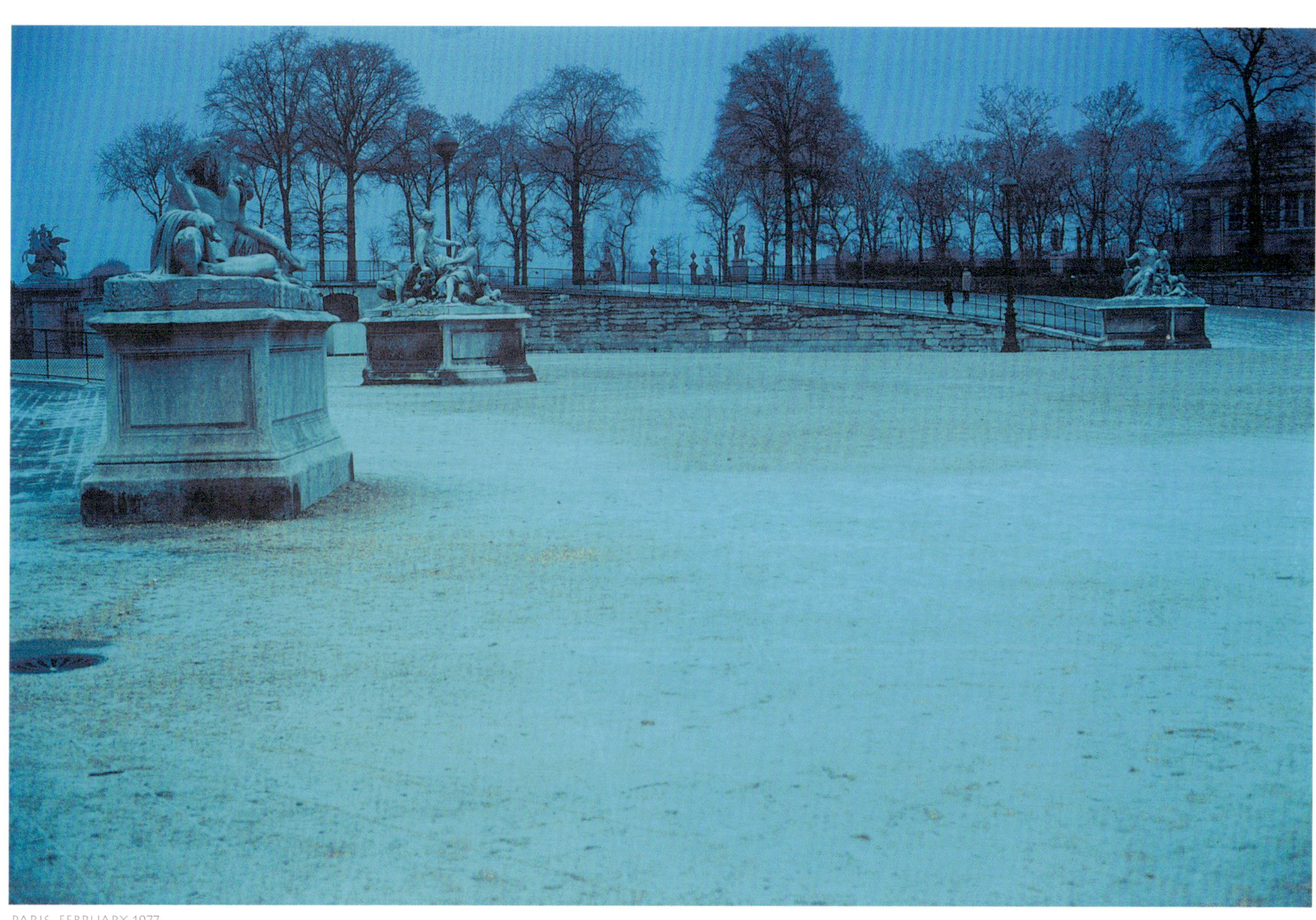

41

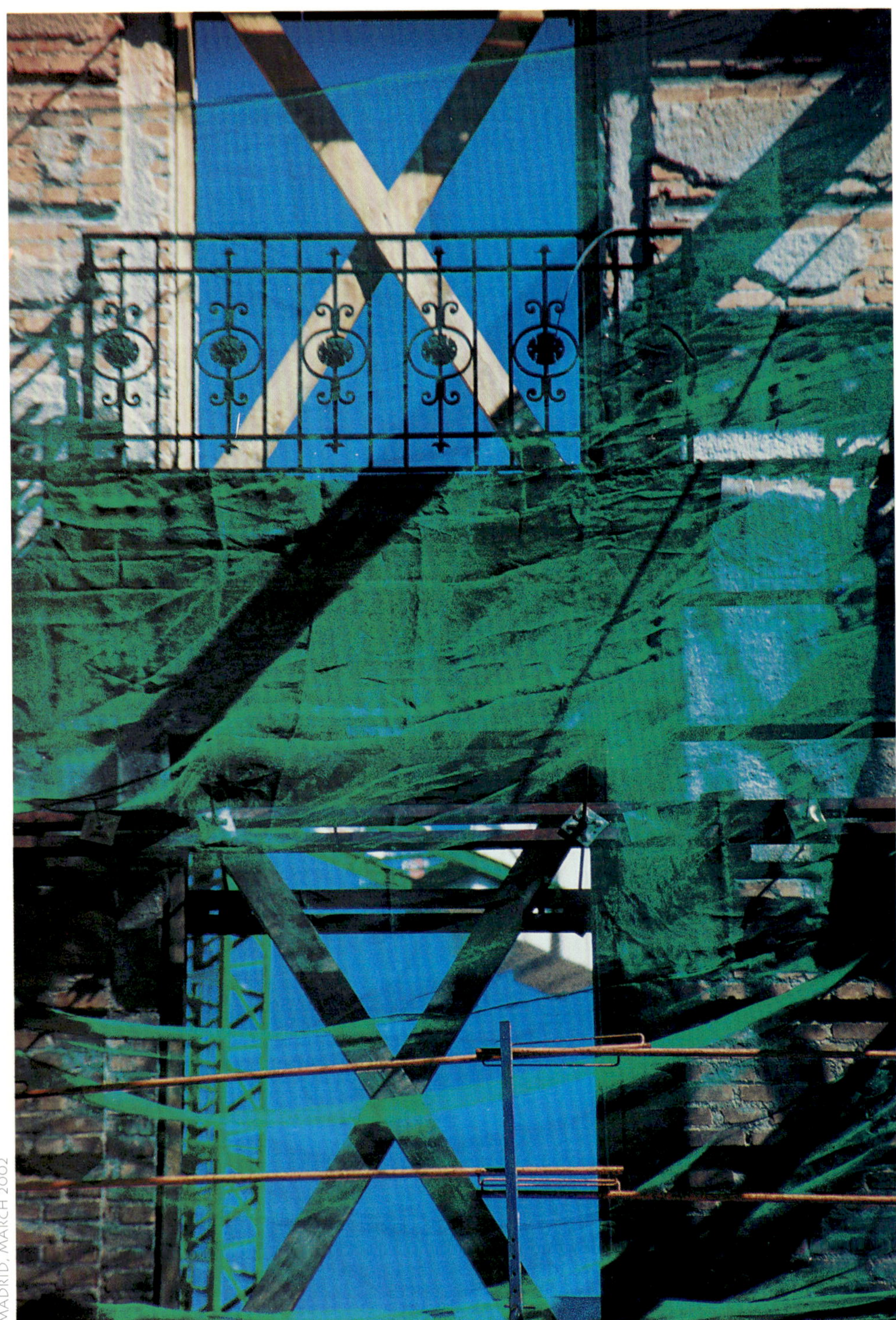

42

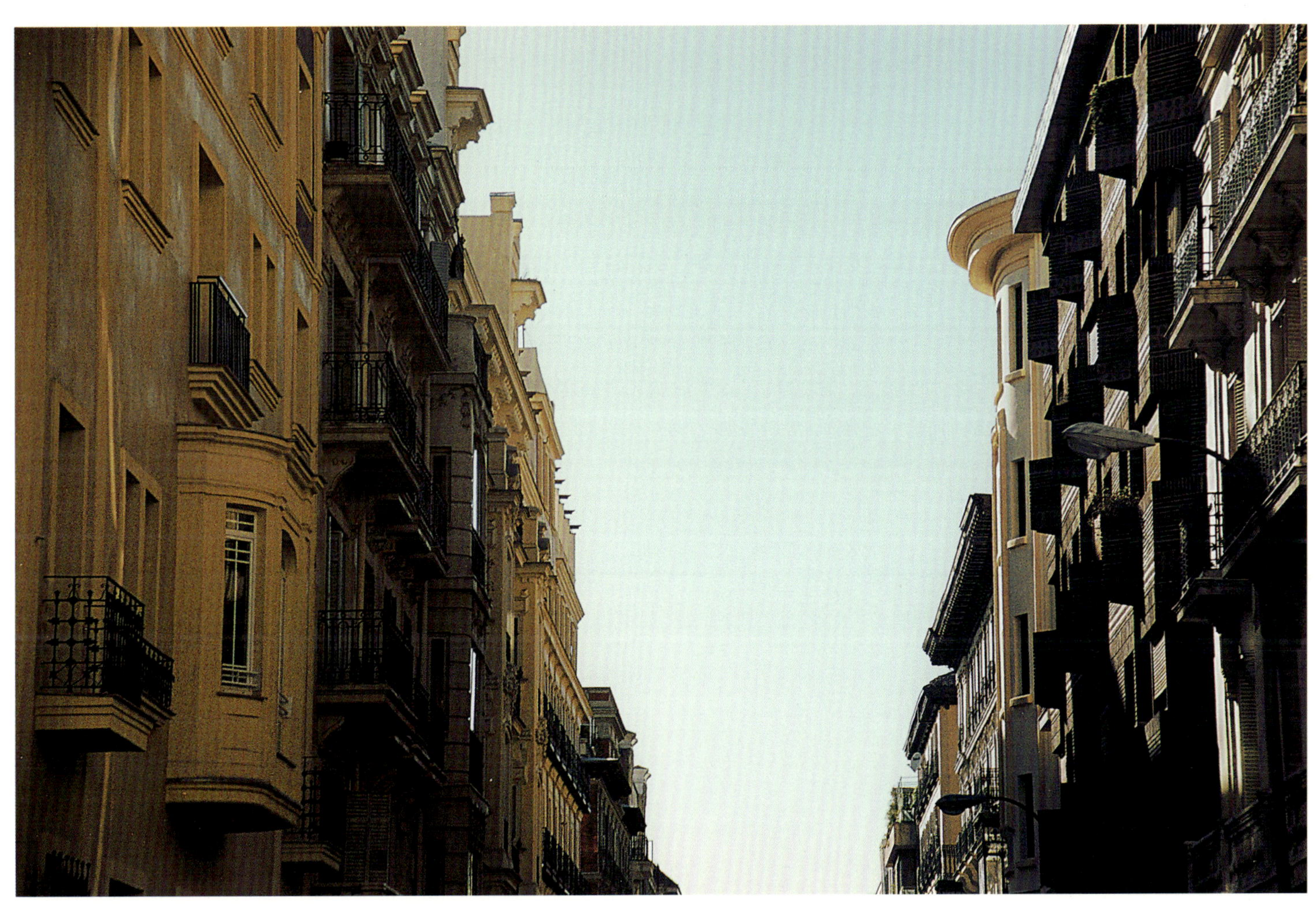

MADRID, MARCH 2002

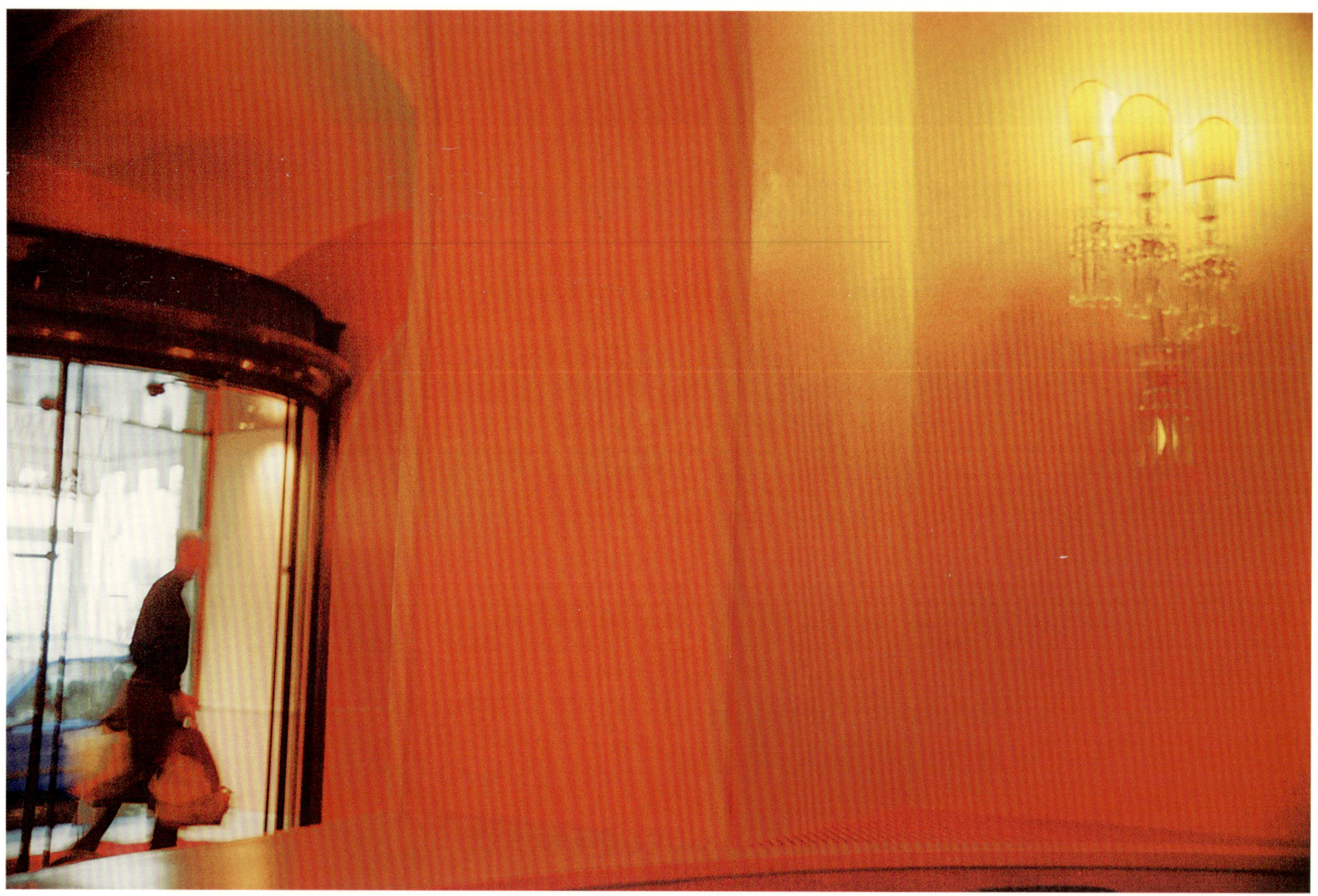

44

ROME, JUNE 2003

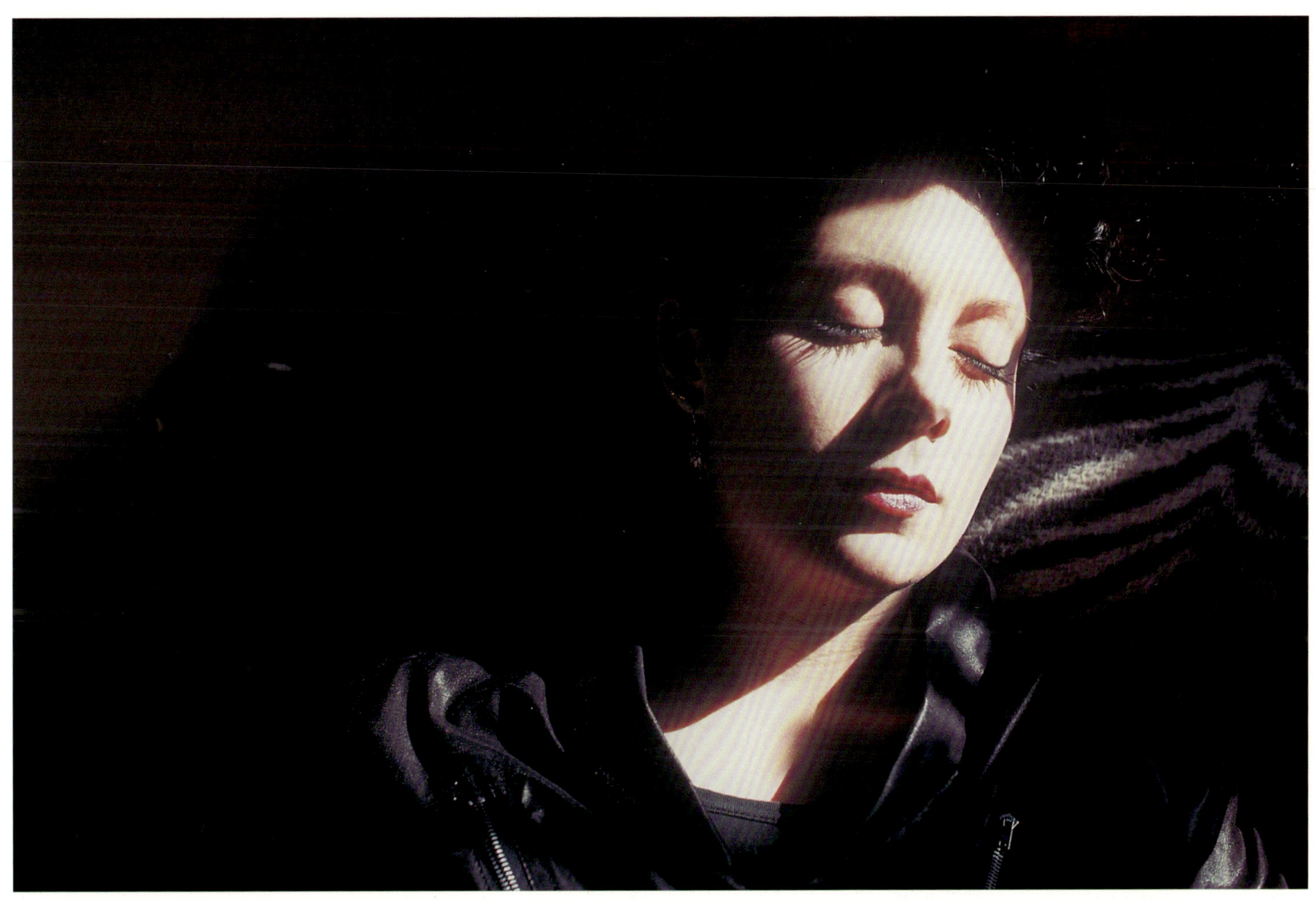

NEW YORK, OCTOBER 1980

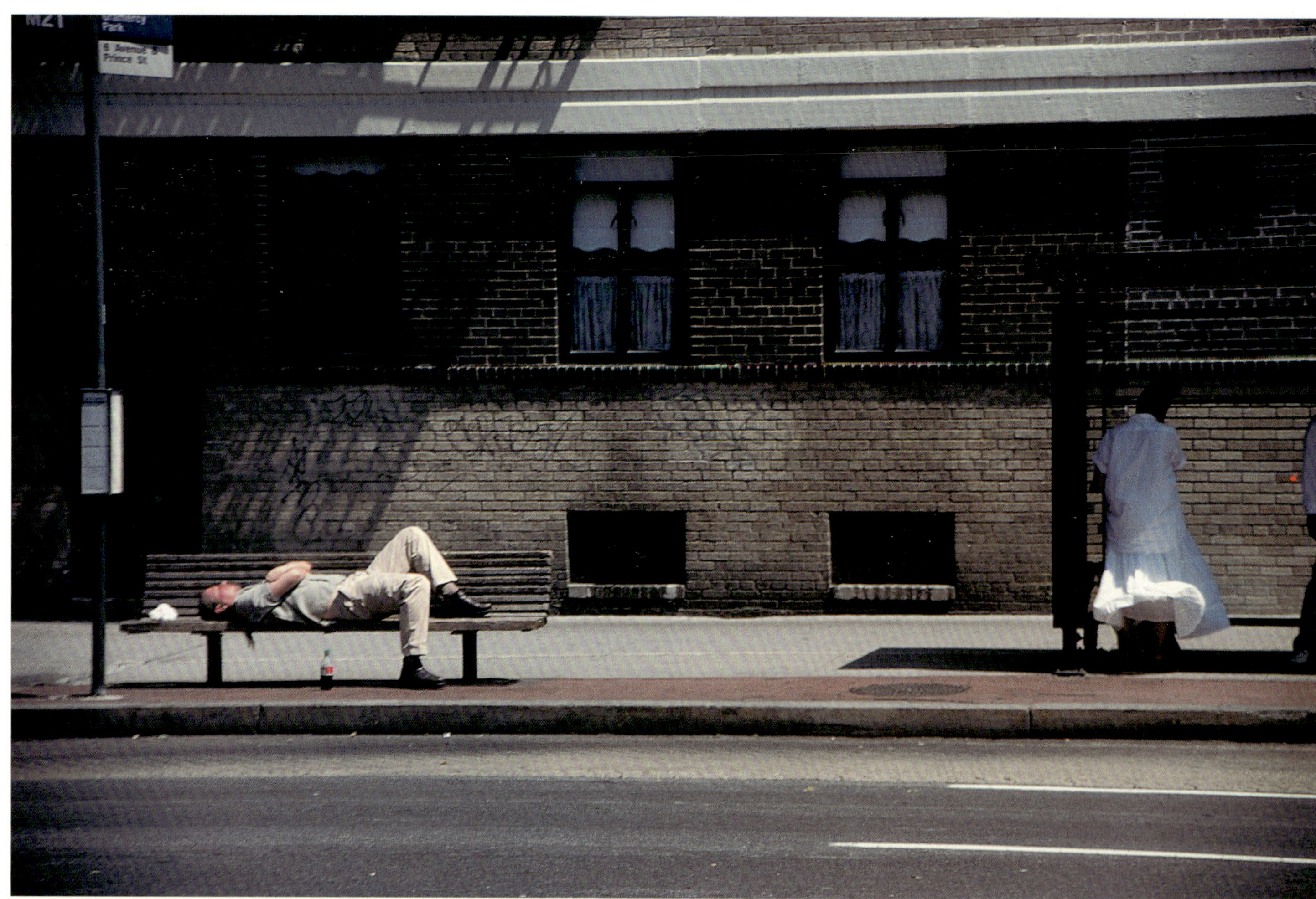

NEW YORK, AUGUST 2002

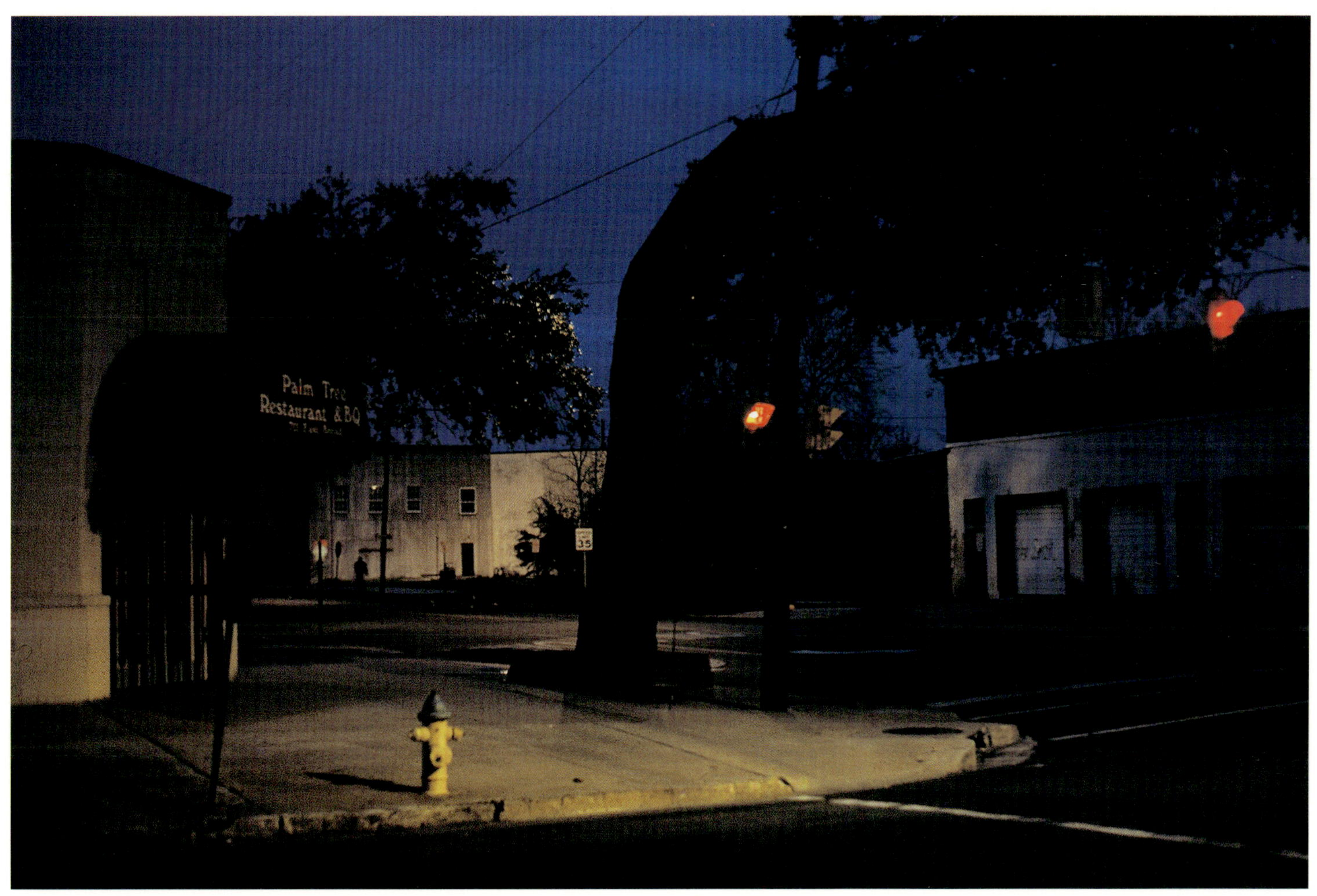

SAVANNAH, GEORGIA, JANUARY 1997

48

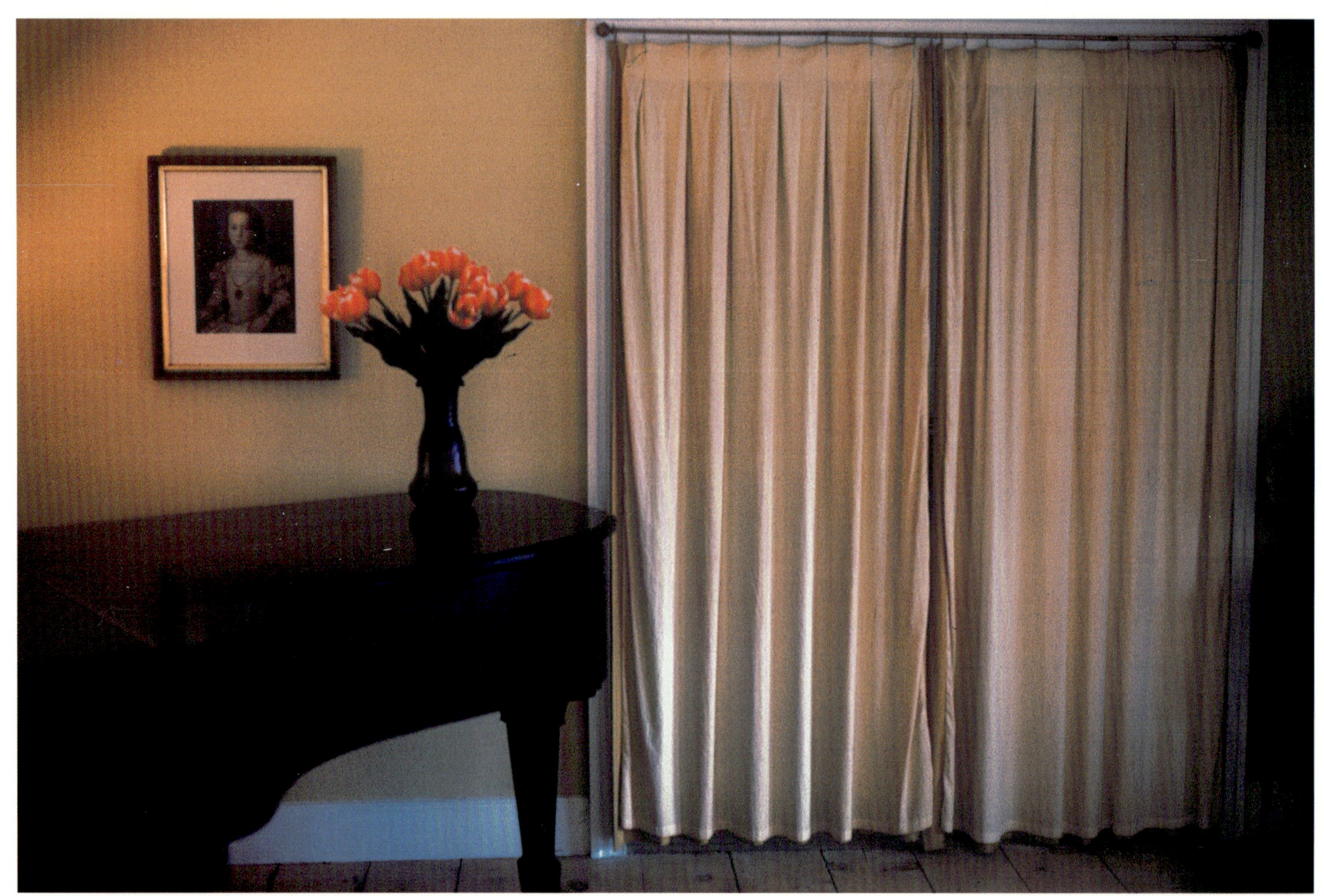

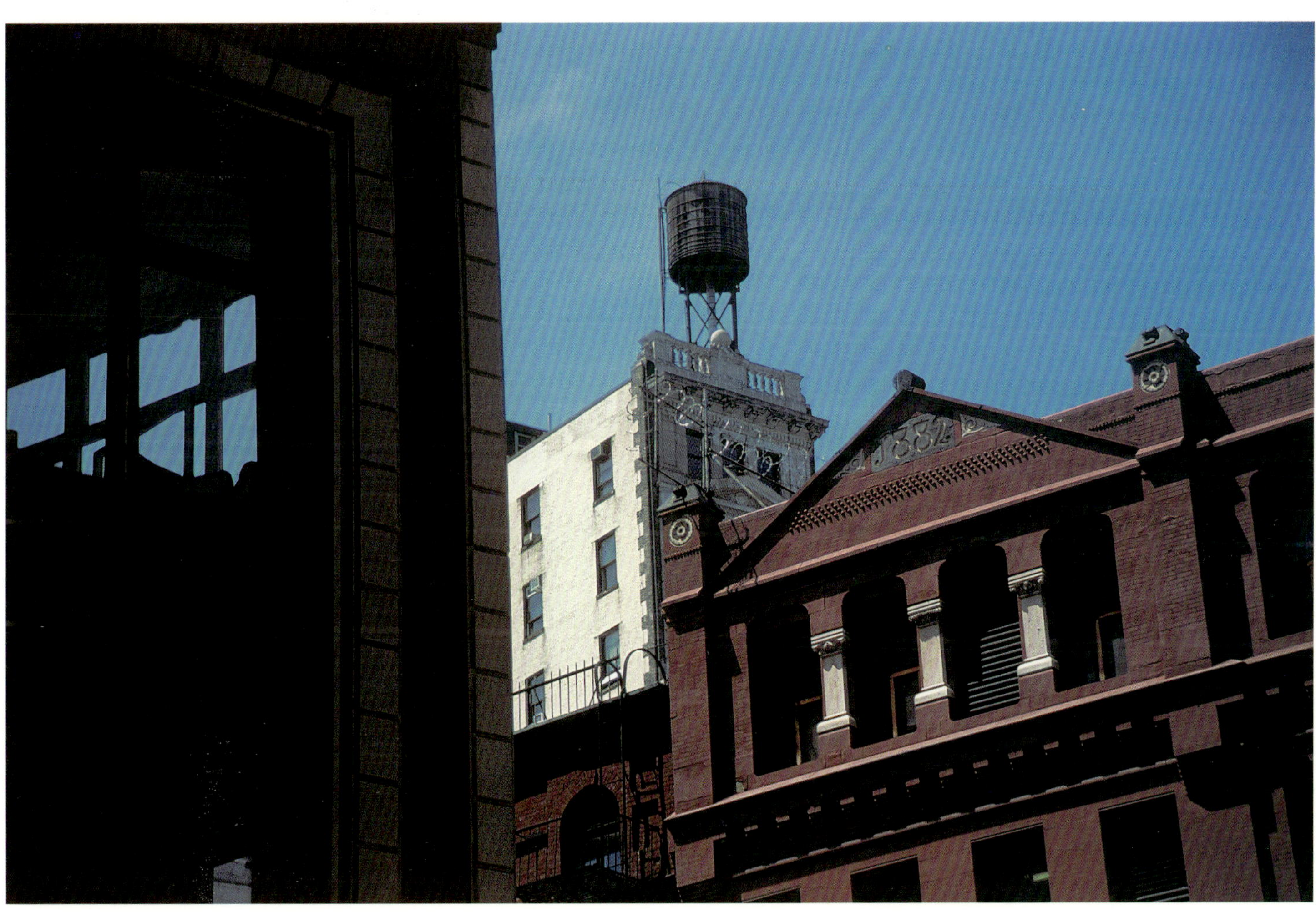

NEW YORK, AUGUST 2002

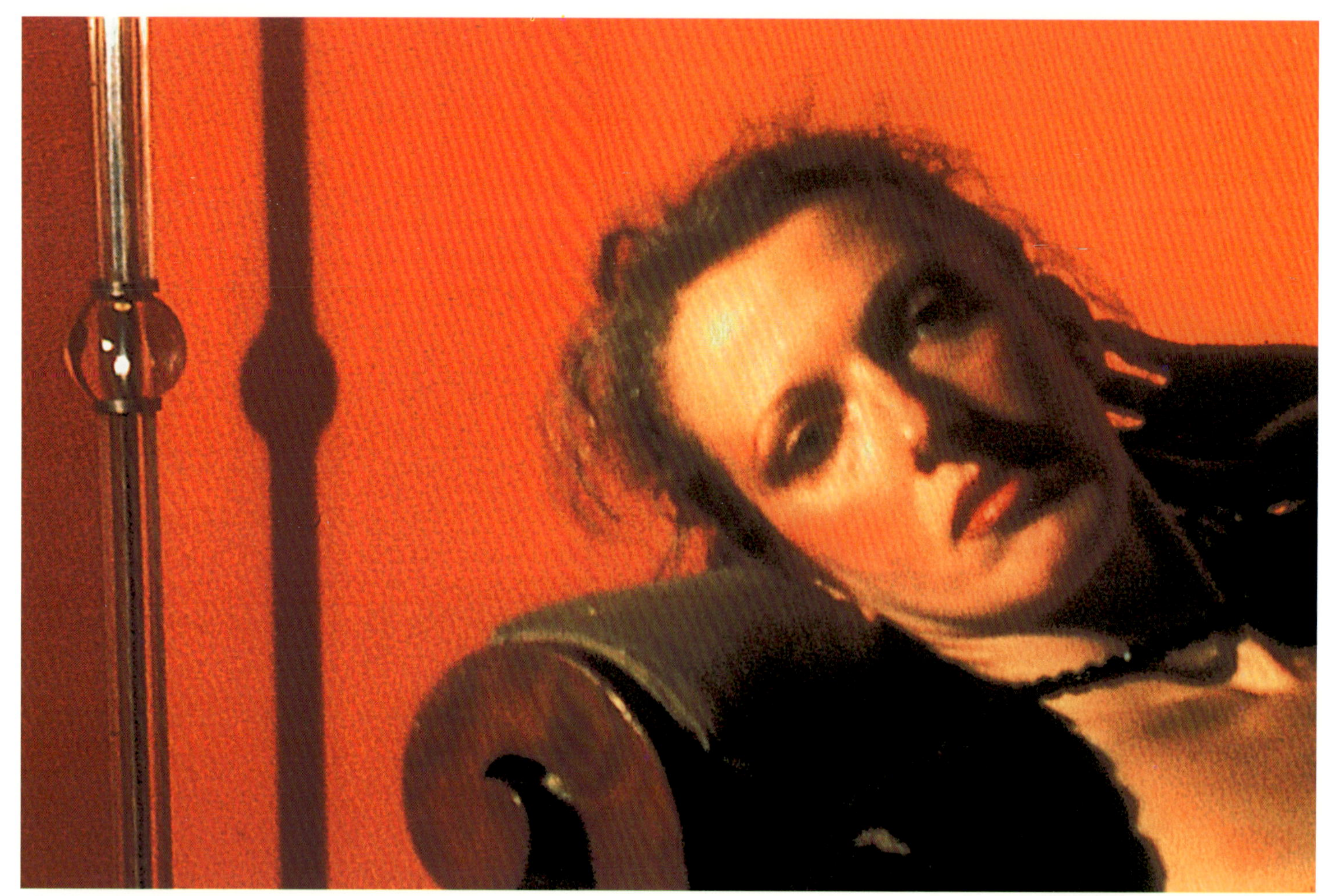

NEW YORK, JANUARY 1980

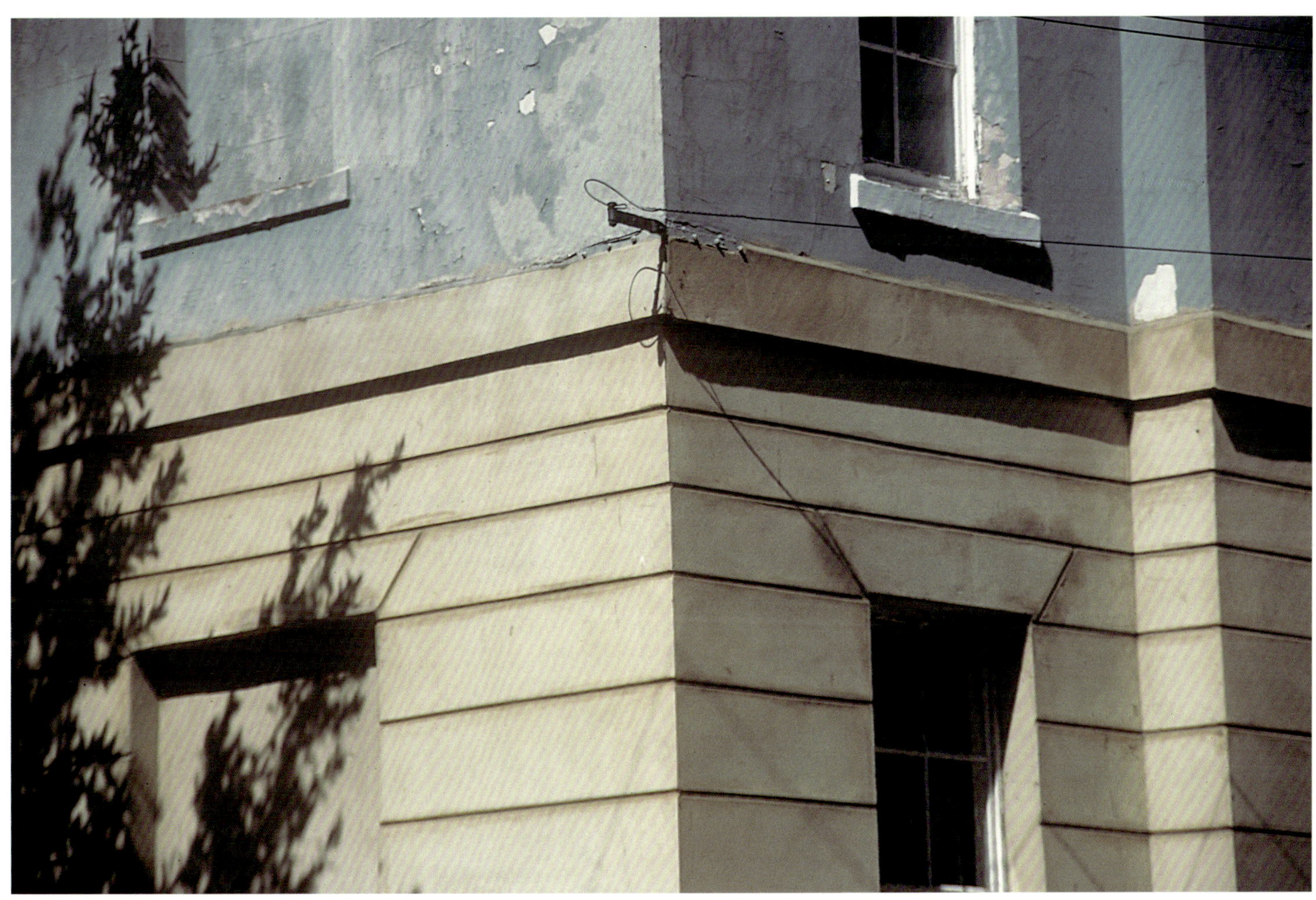

RAMSGATE, MAY 2002

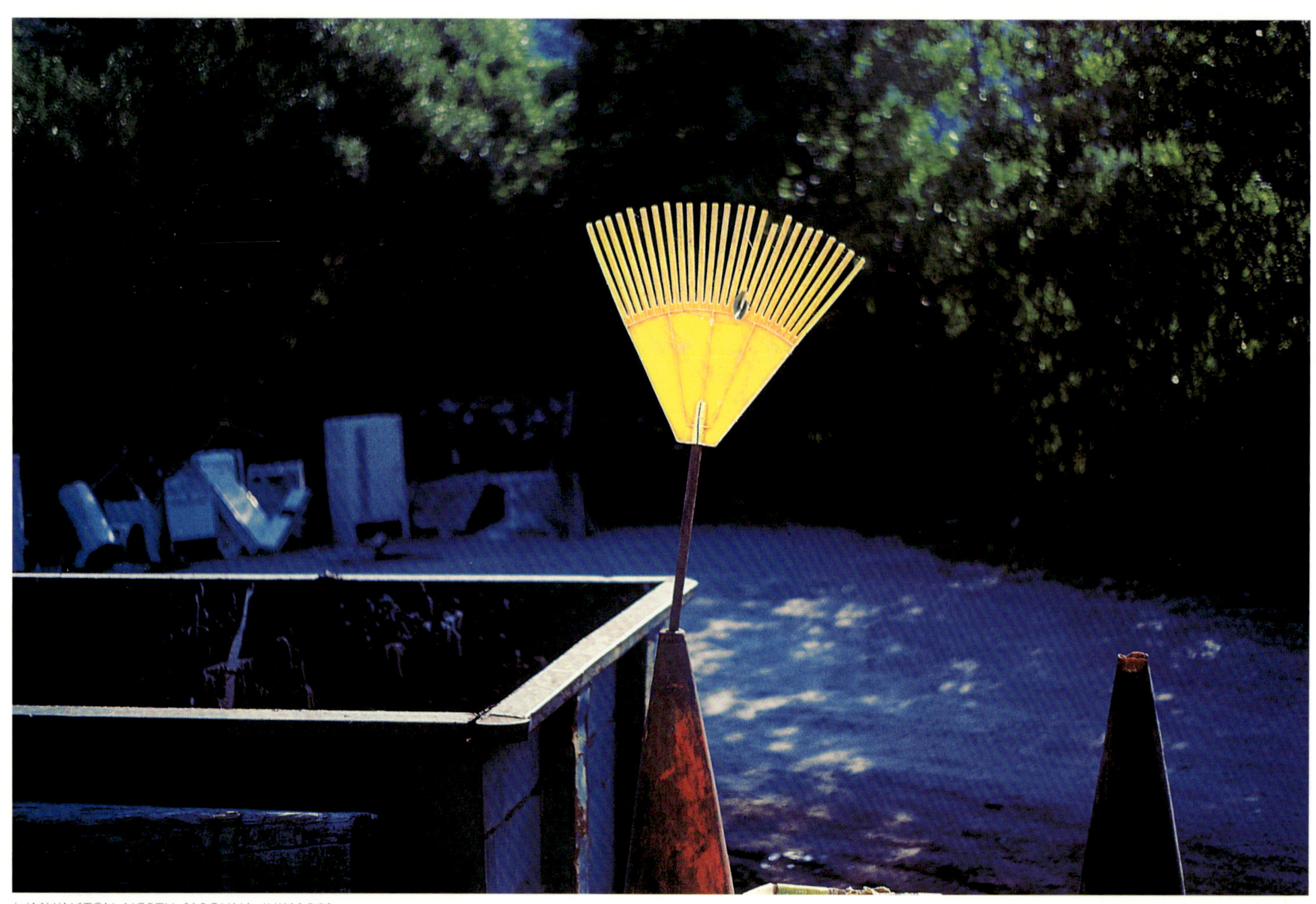

WASHINGTON, NORTH CAROLINA, JULY 2002

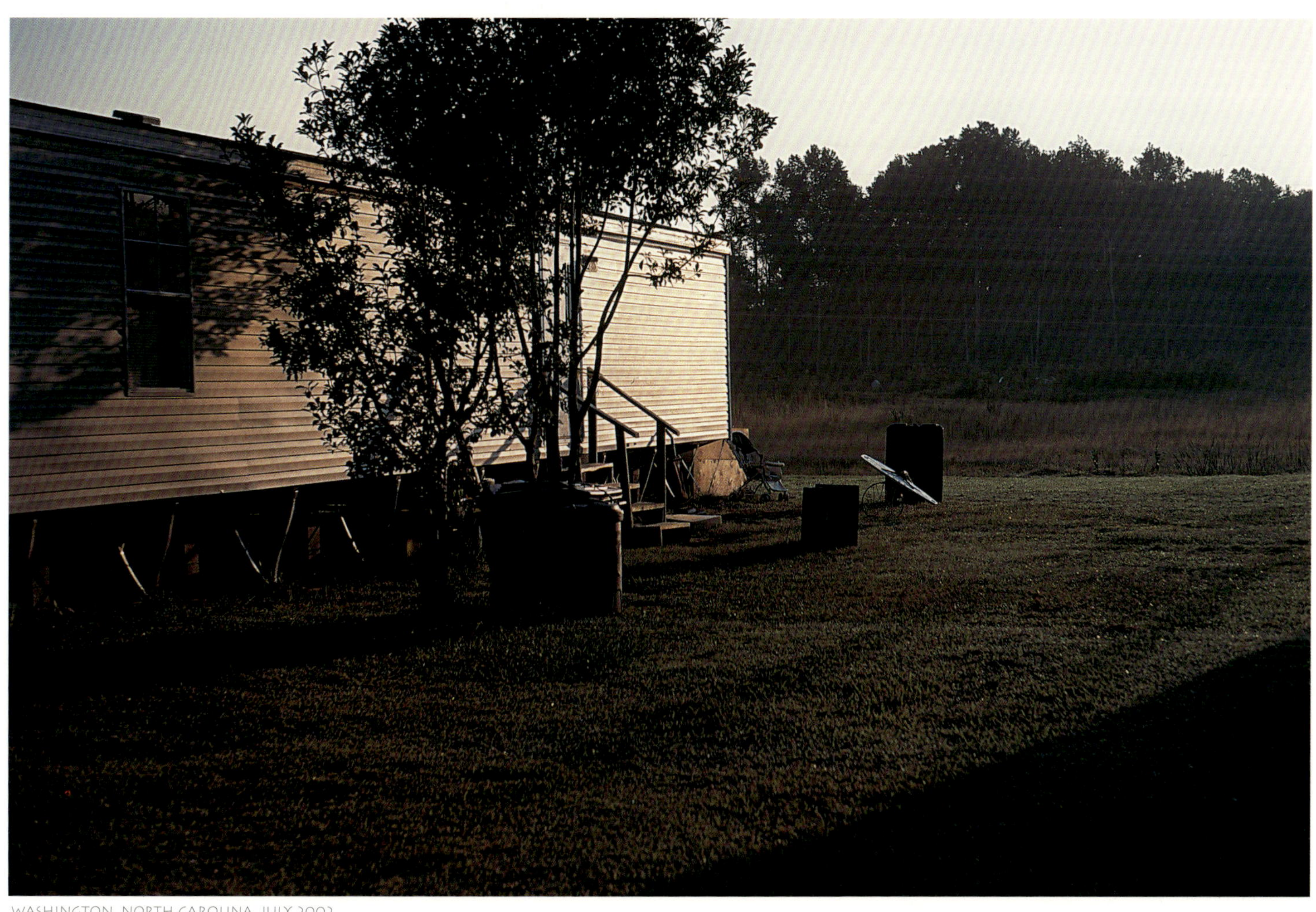

WASHINGTON, NORTH CAROLINA, JULY 2002

53

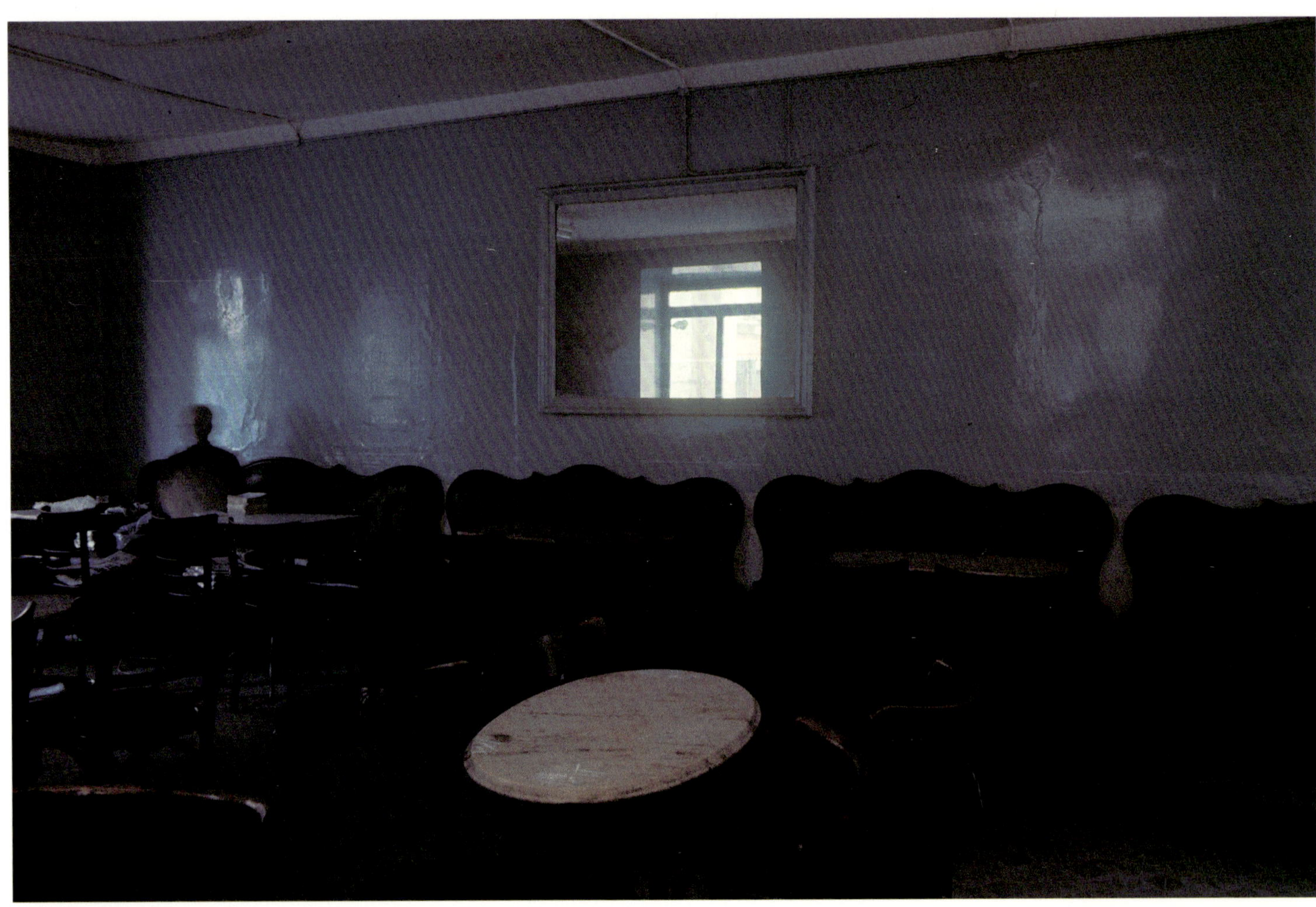

54

SYROS, JUNE 1976

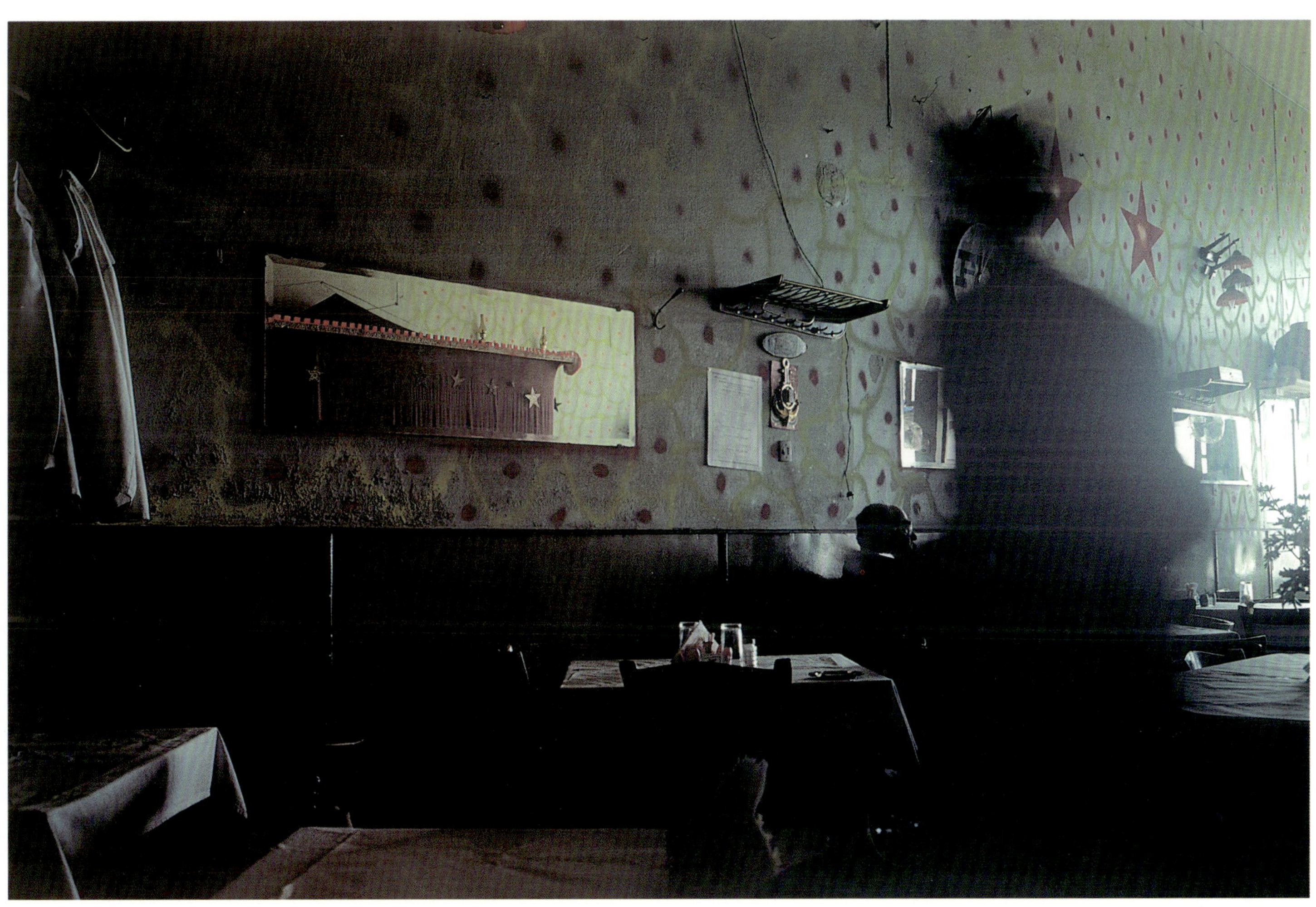

SYROS, JUNE 1976

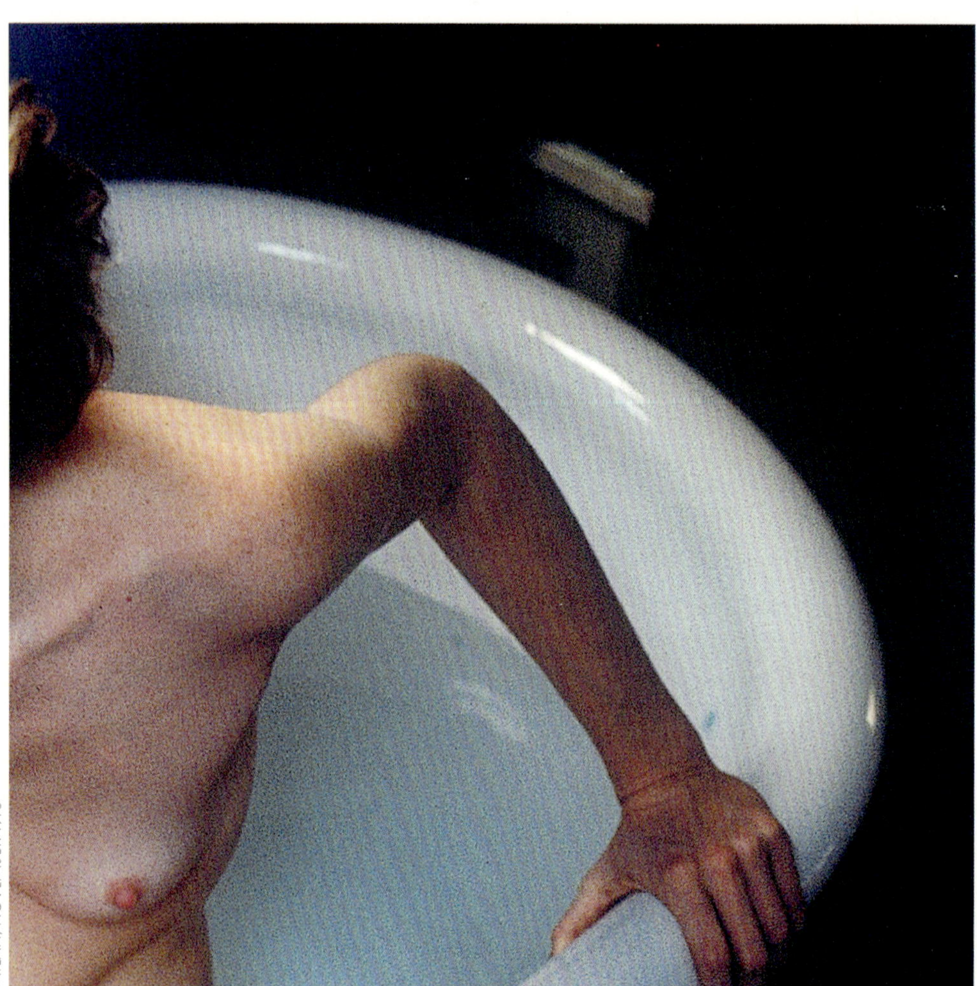

MILAN, NOVEMBER 1978

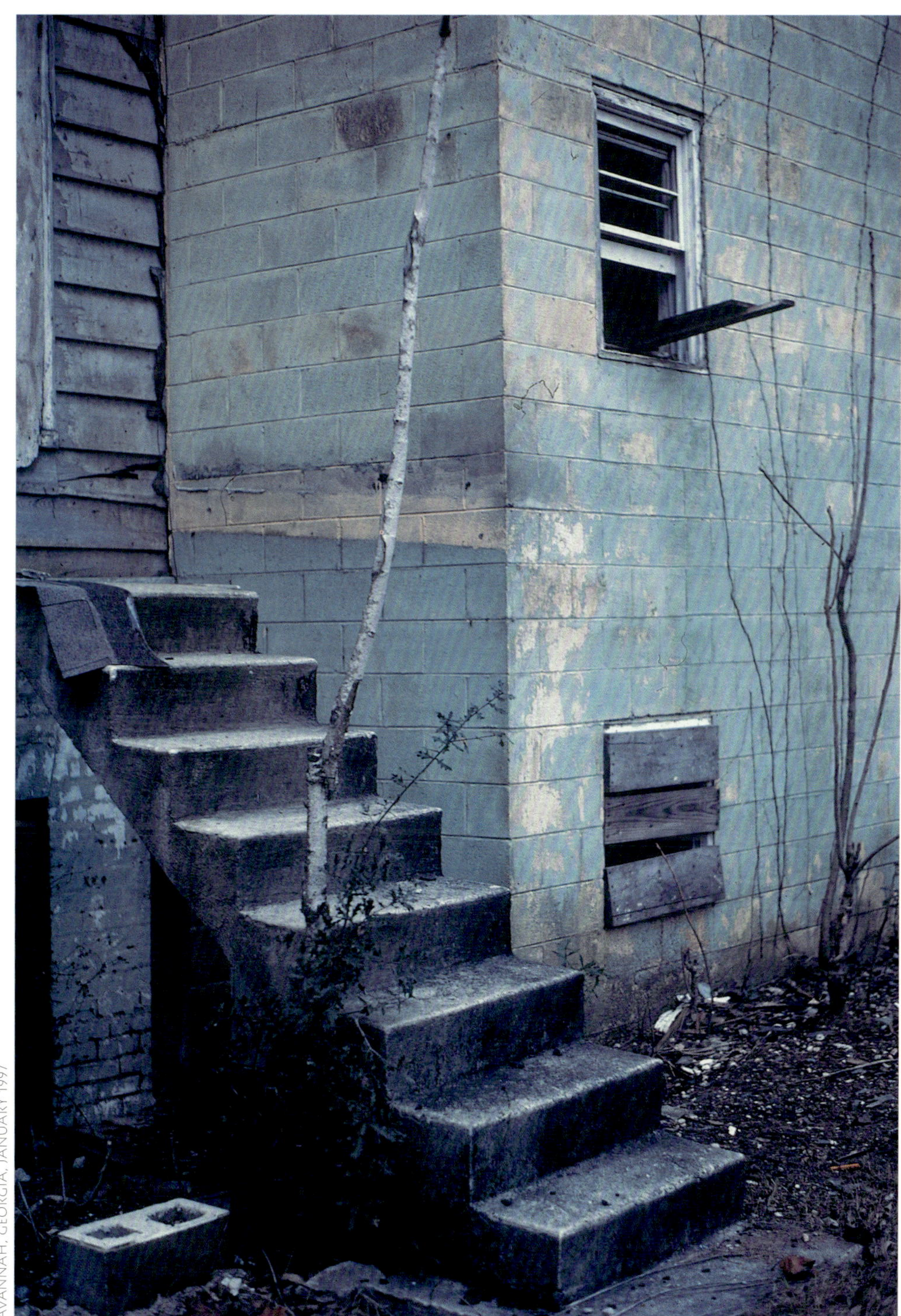

SAVANNAH, GEORGIA, JANUARY 1997

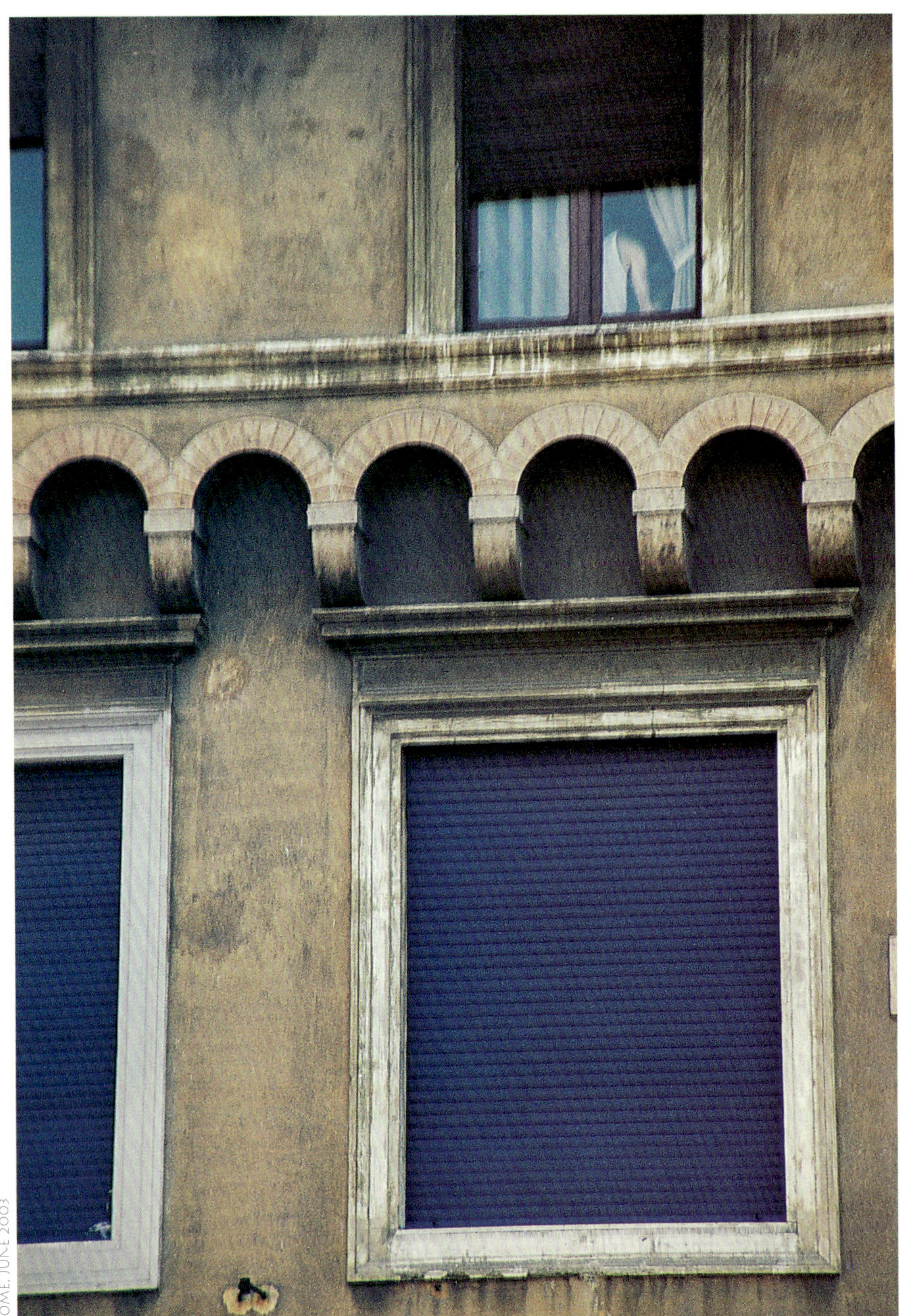

ROME, JUNE 2003

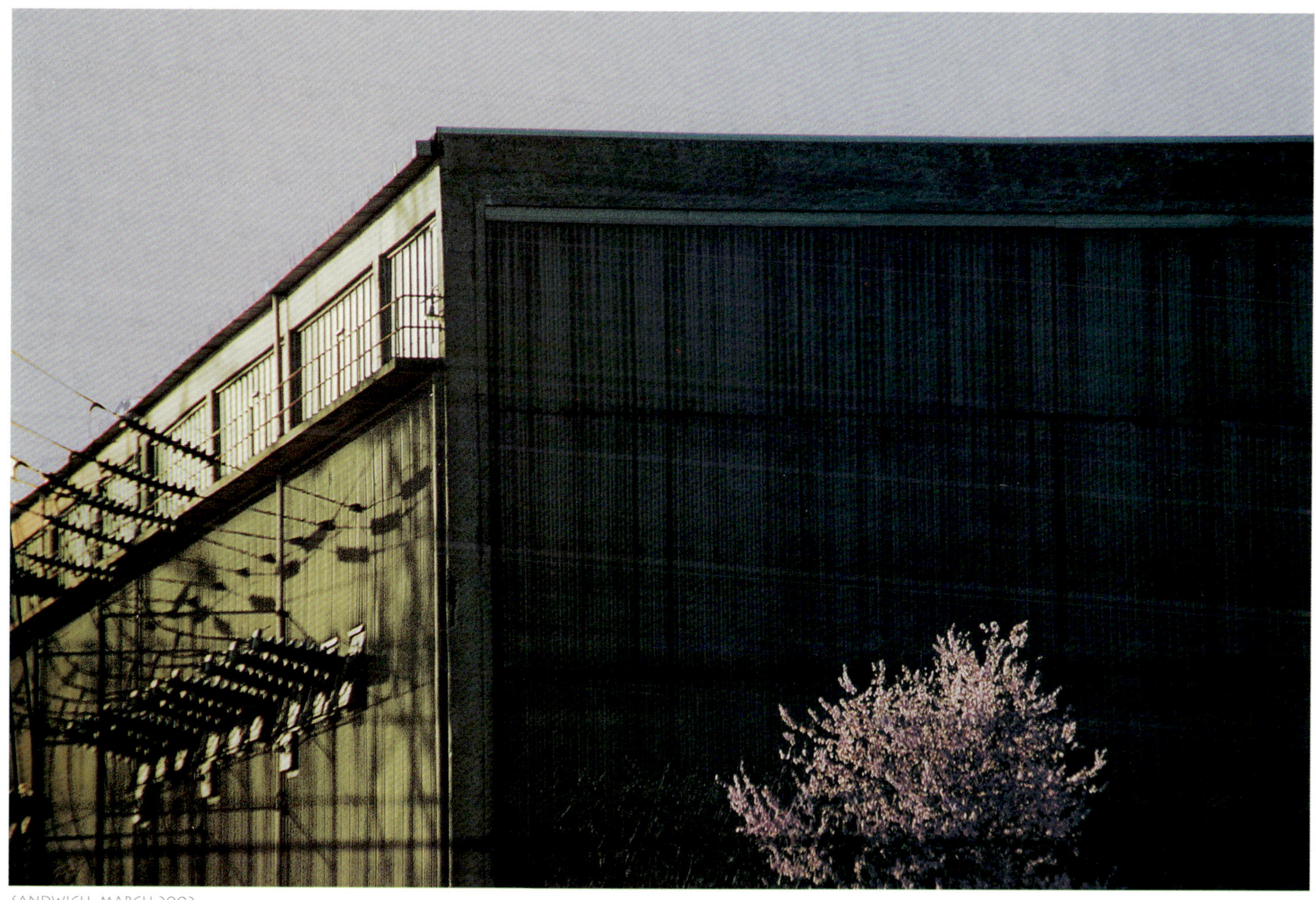

SANDWICH, MARCH 2002

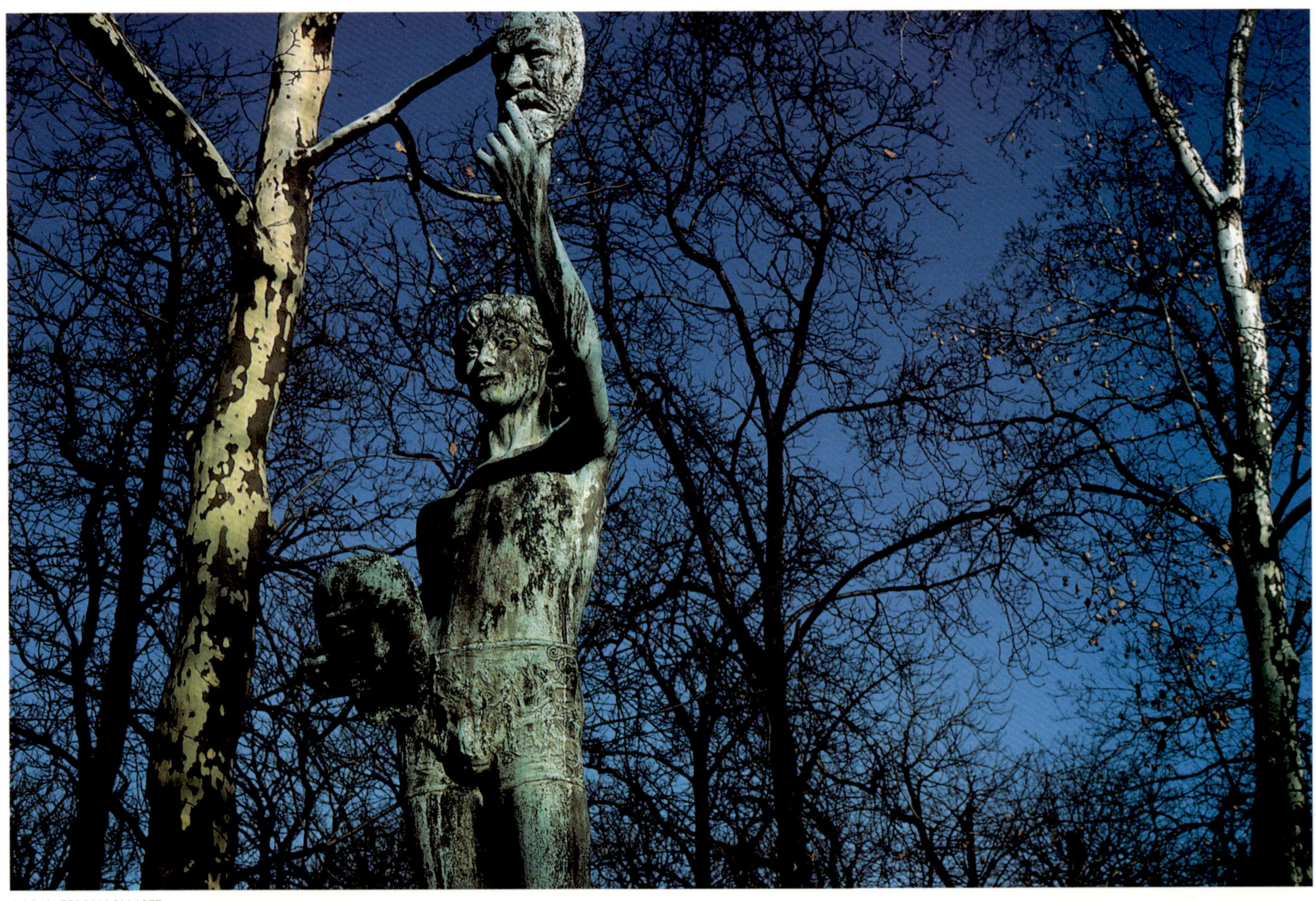

PARIS, FEBRUARY 1977

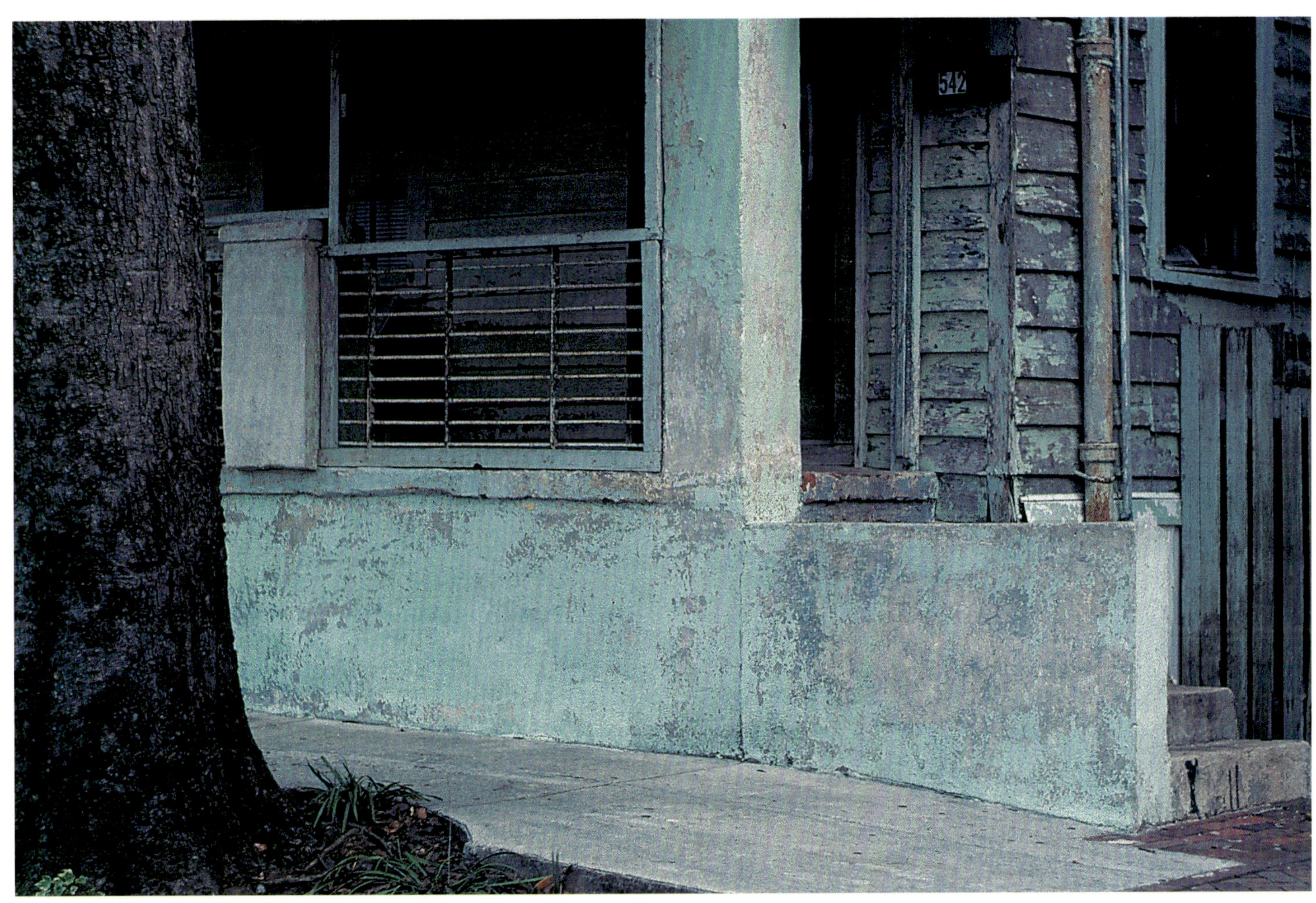

SAVANNAH, GEORGIA, JANUARY 1997

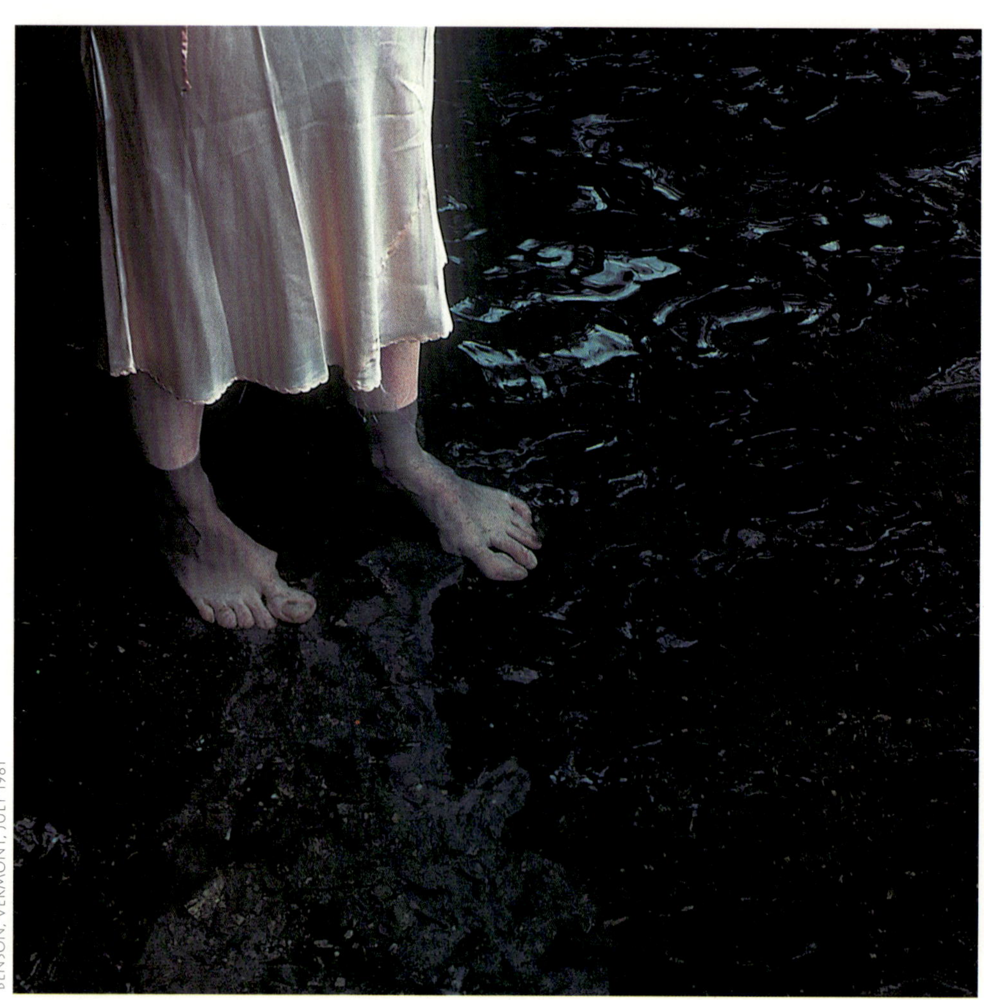

BENSON, VERMONT, JULY 1981

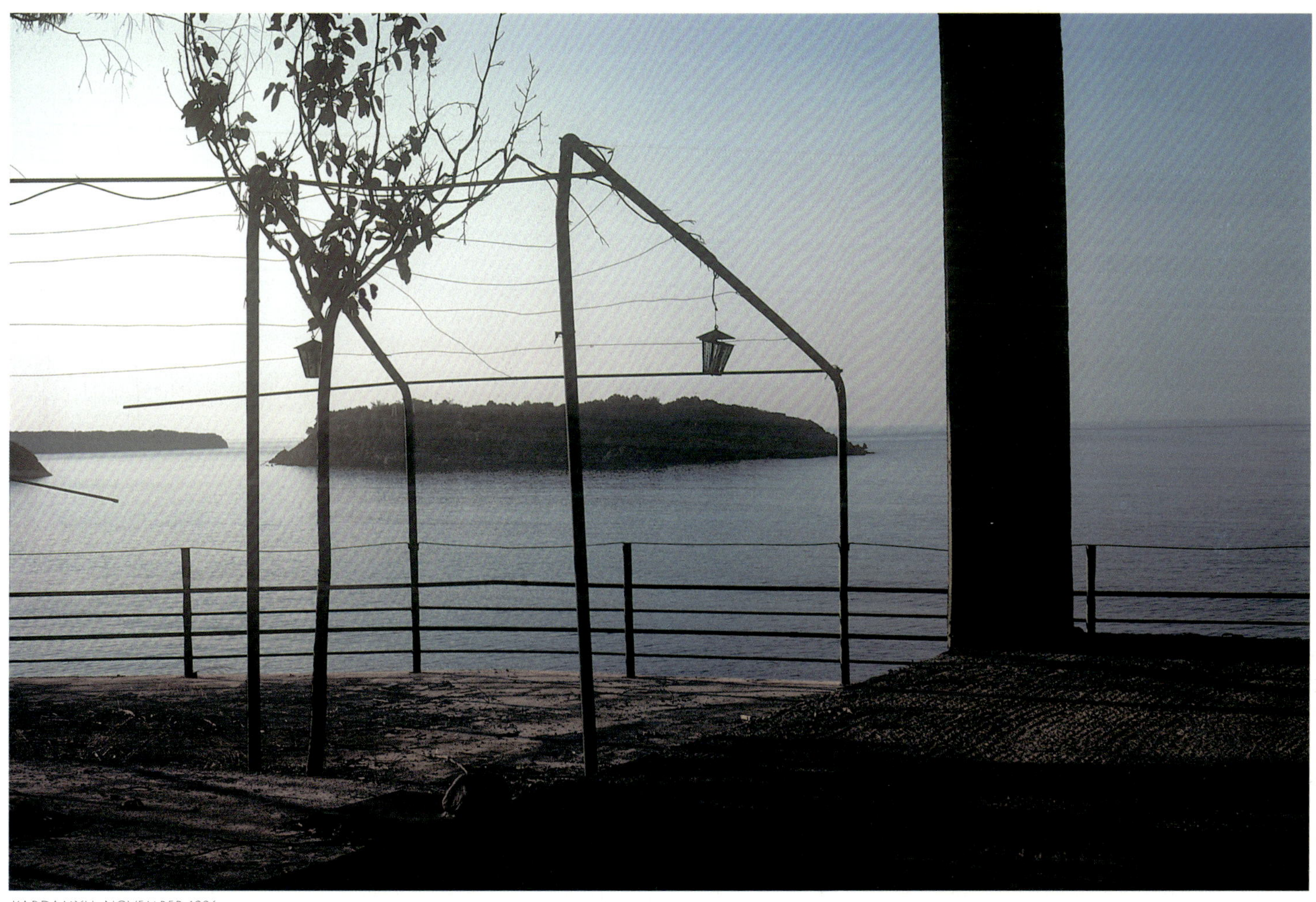

KARDAMYLI, NOVEMBER 1996

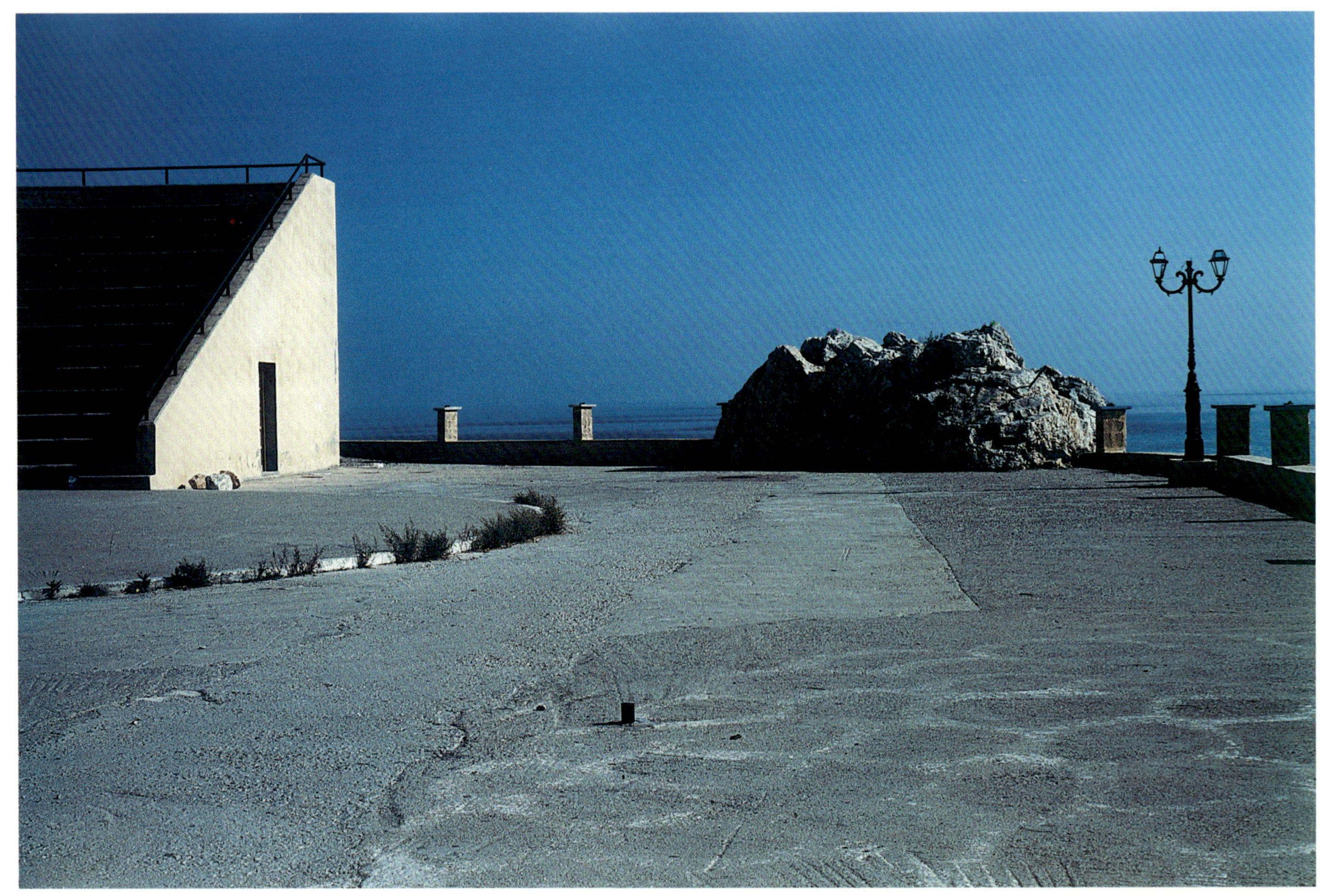

64

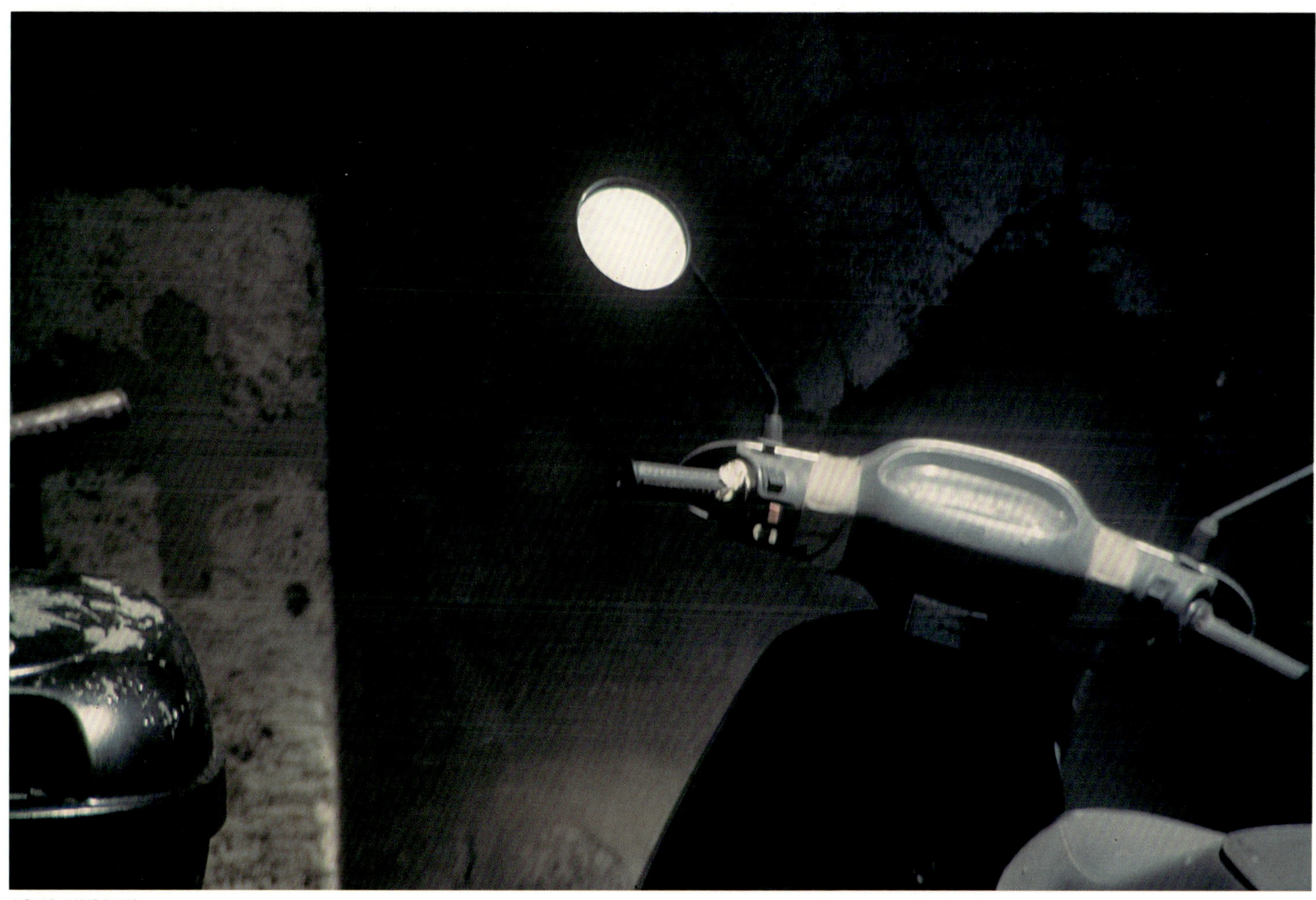

ROME, JUNE 2003

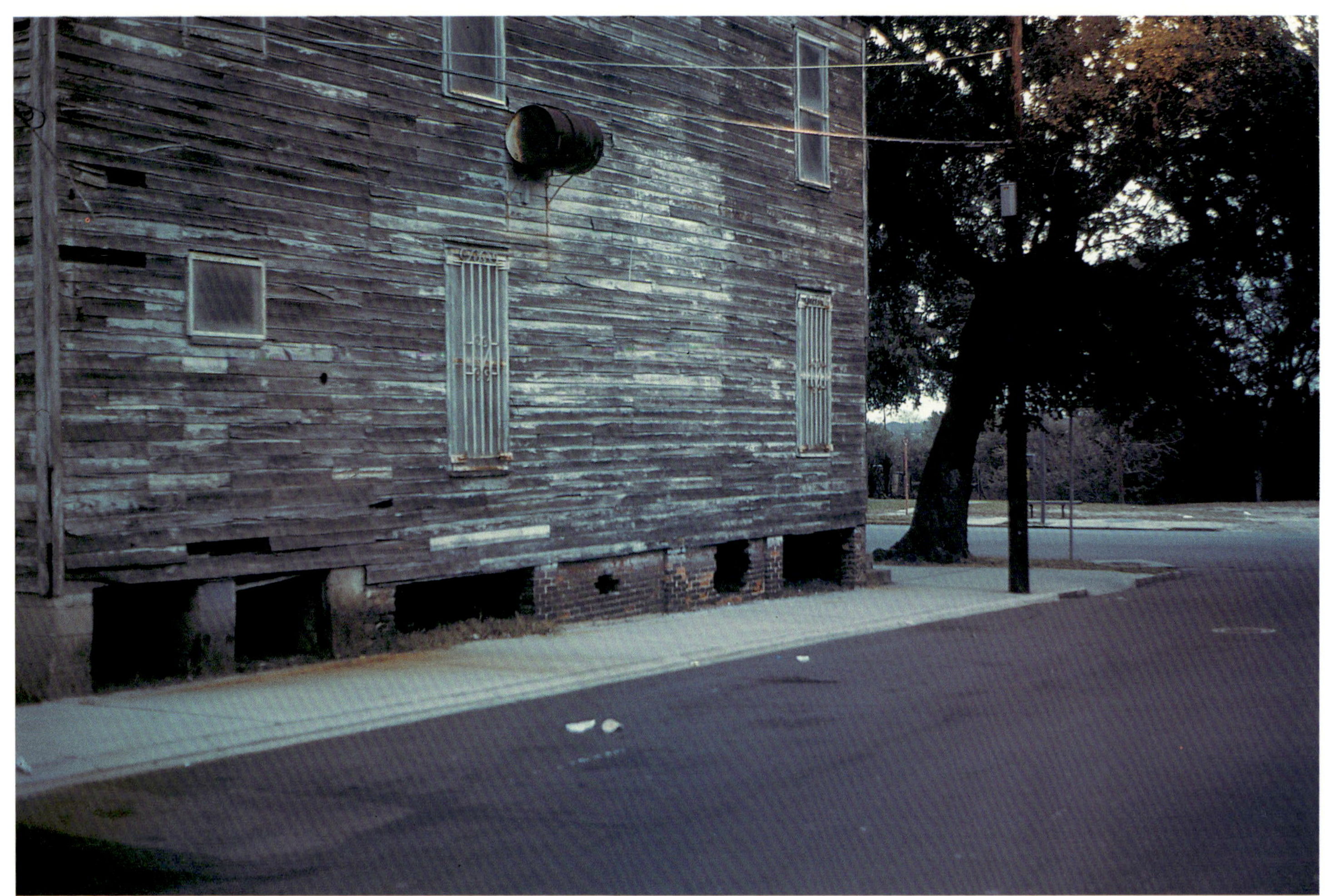

SAVANNAH, GEORGIA, JANUARY 1997

66

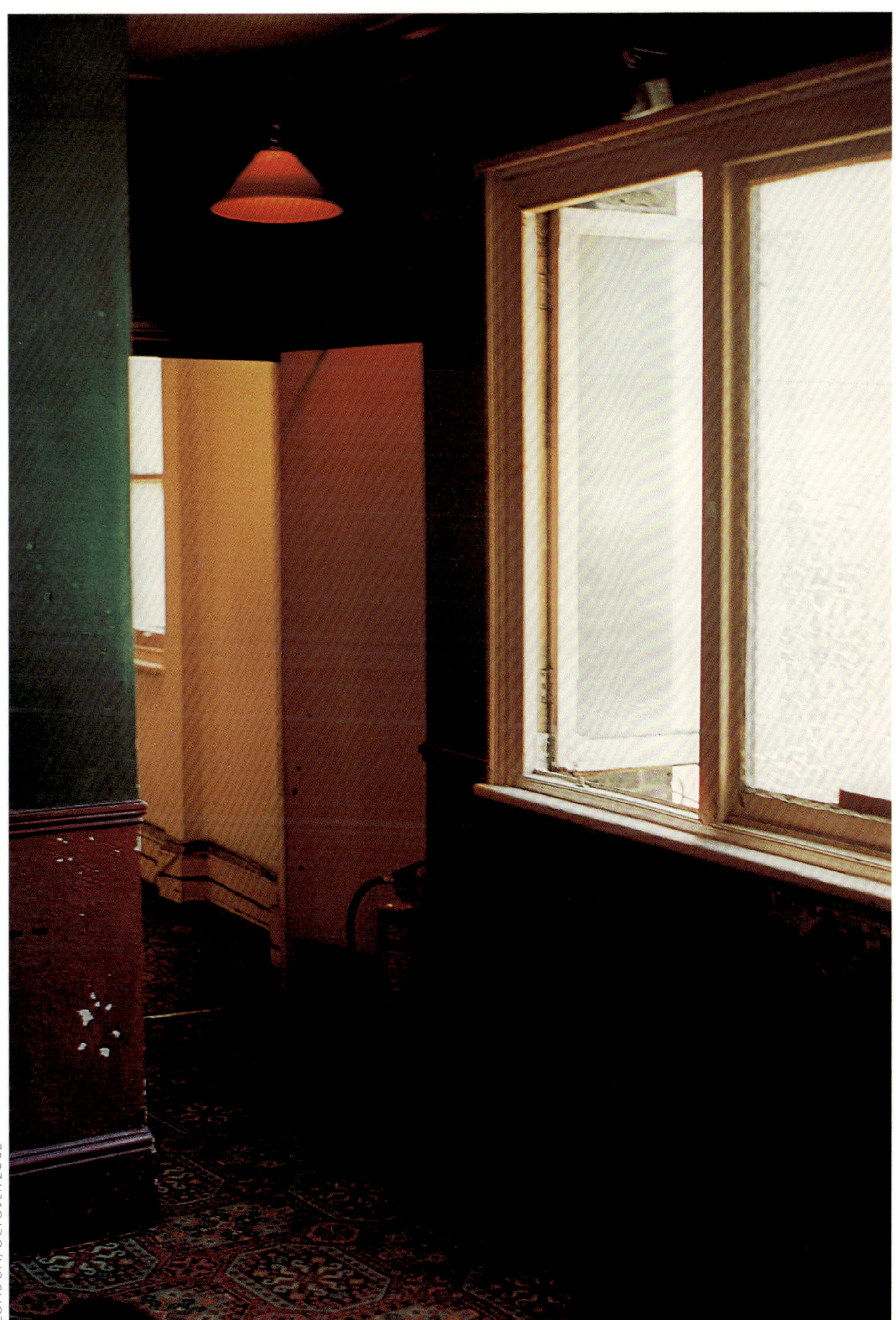

LONDON, OCTOBER 2002

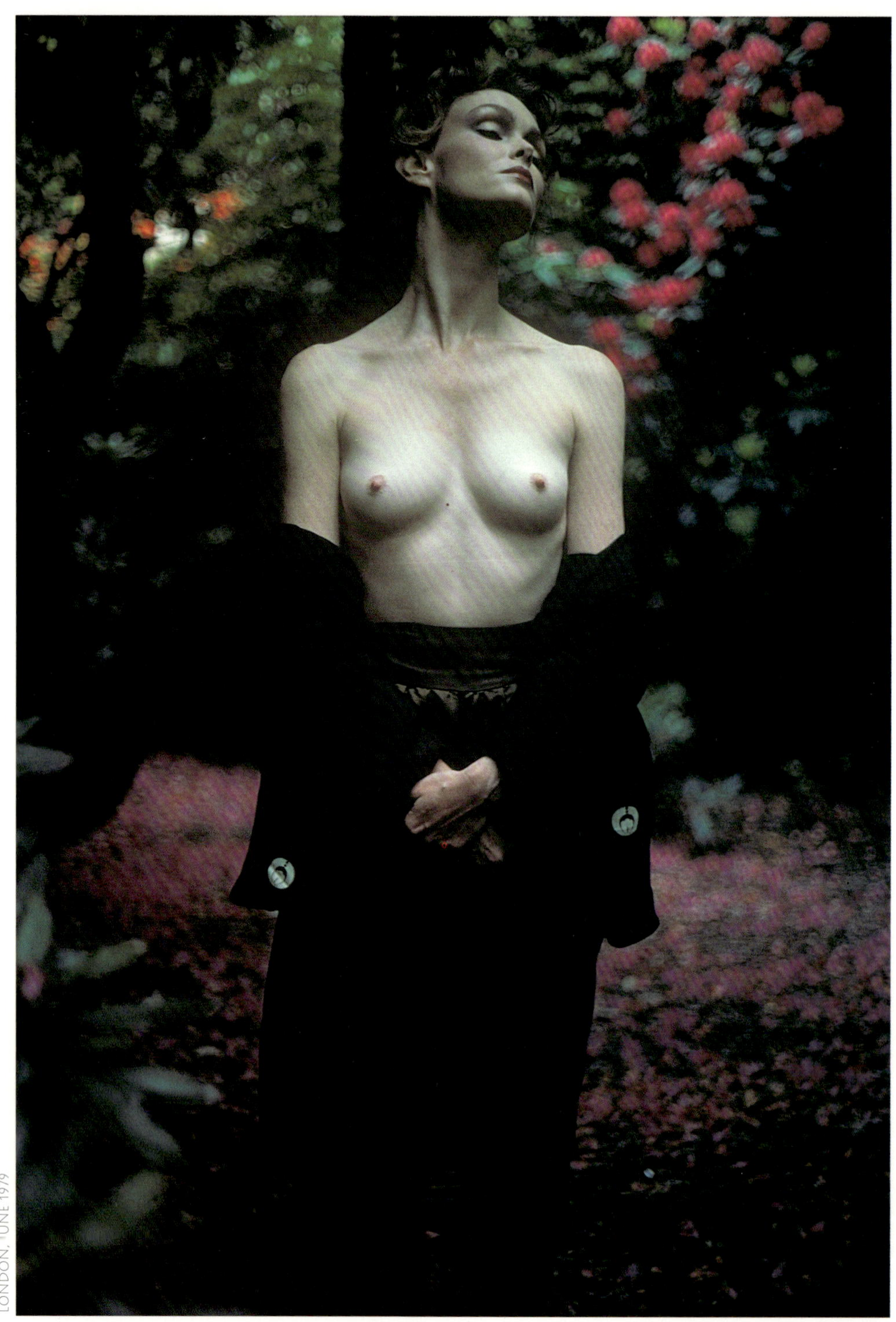

LONDON, JUNE 1979

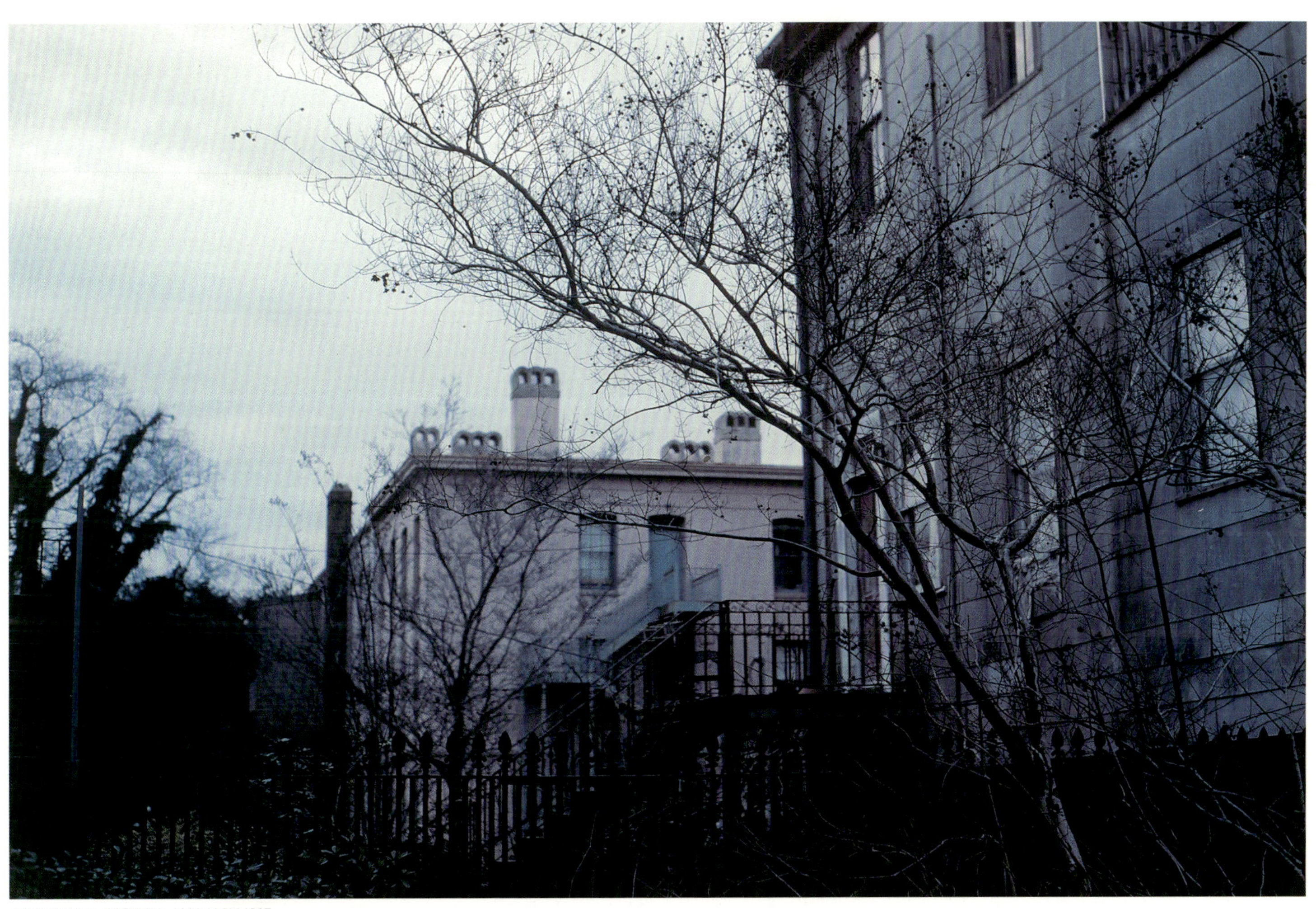

SAVANNAH, GEORGIA, JANUARY 1997

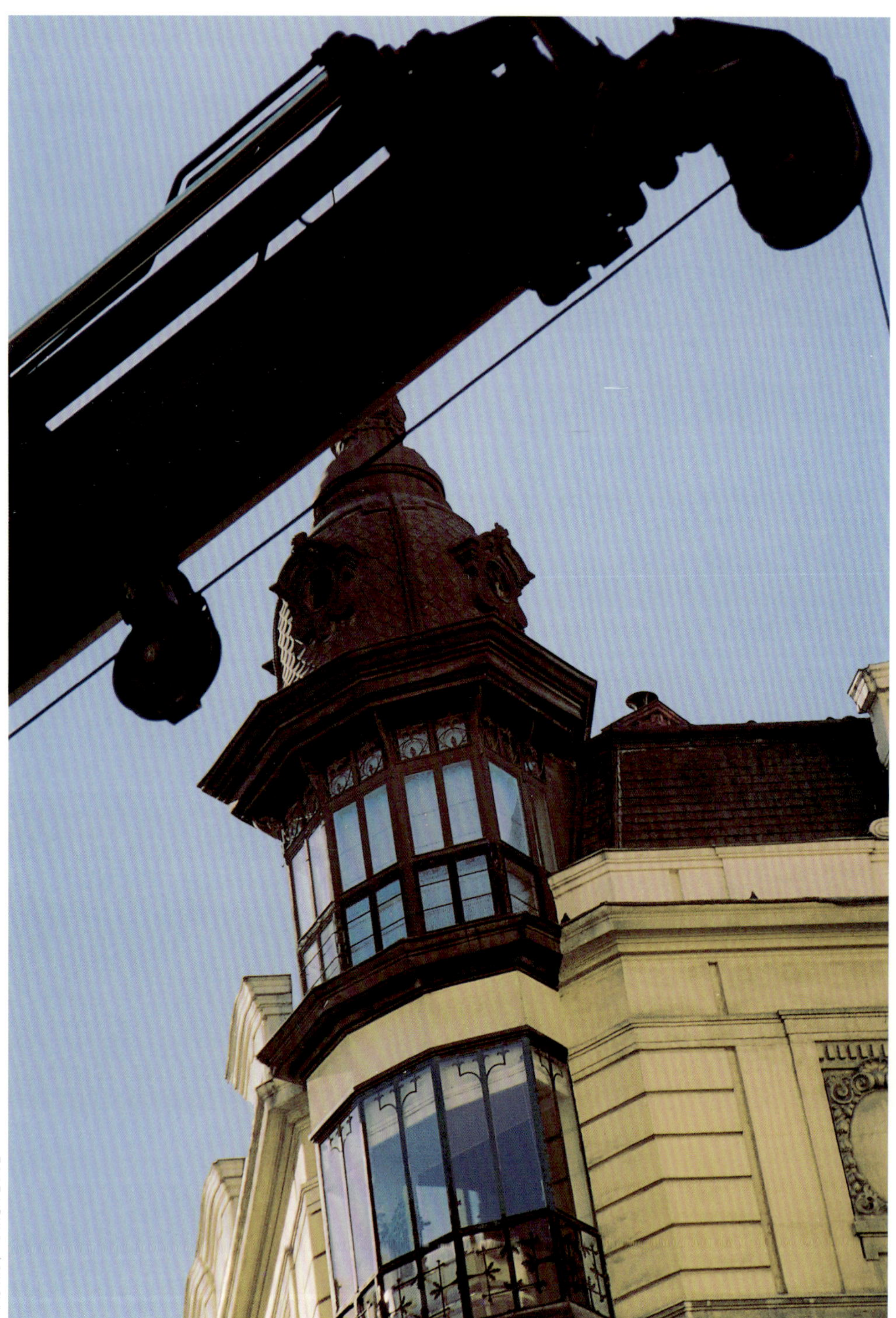

MADRID, MARCH 2002

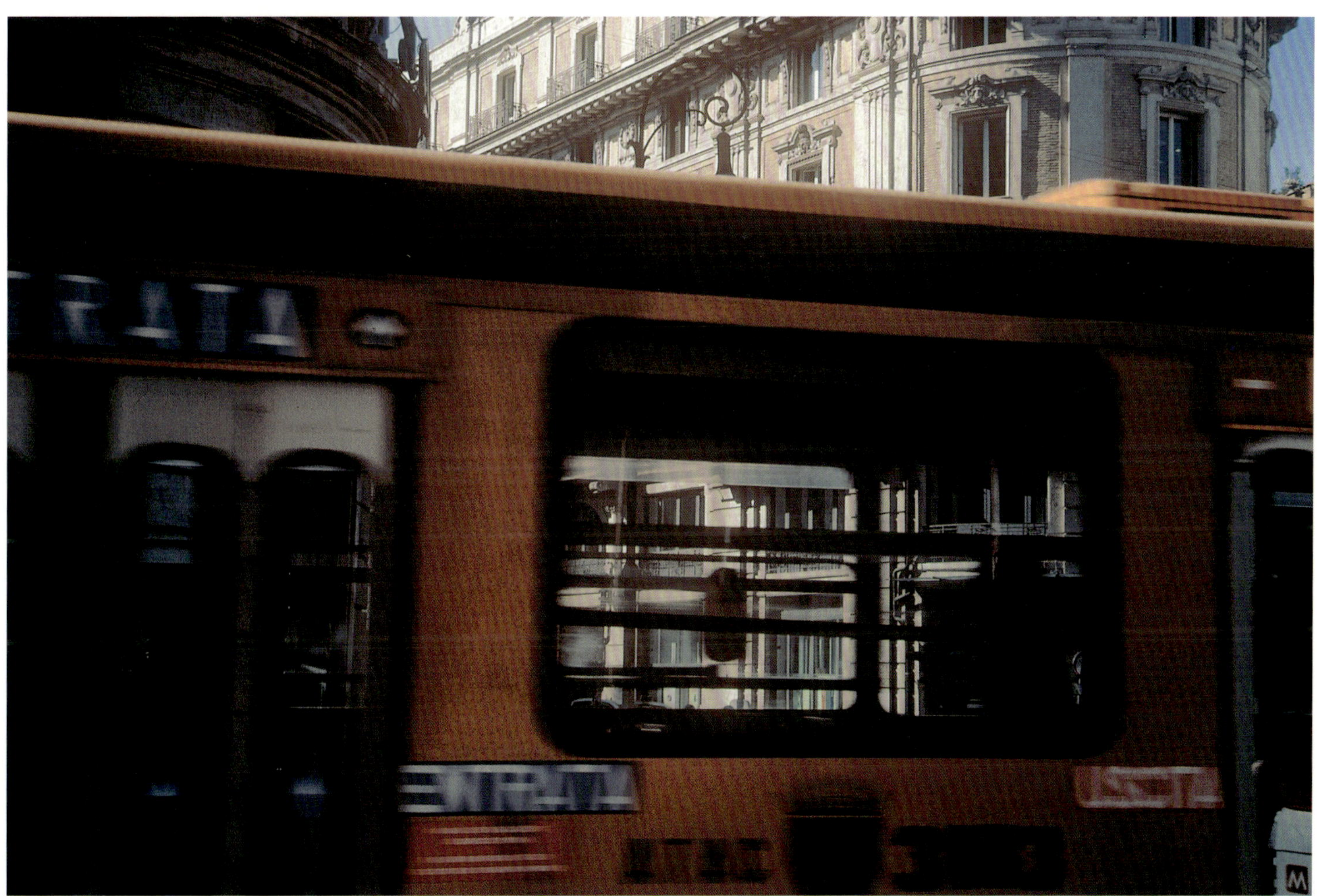

ROME, JUNE 2003

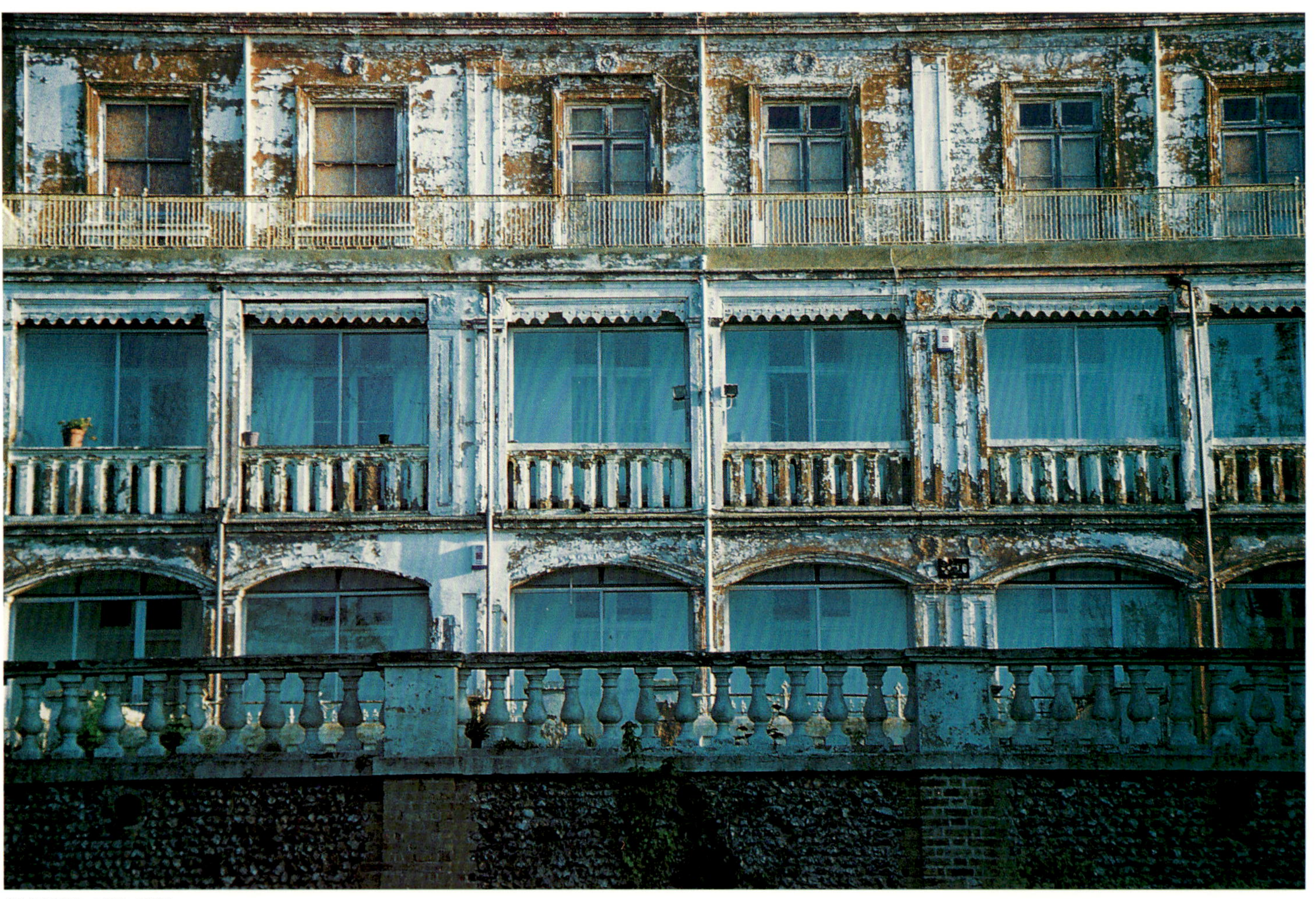

72

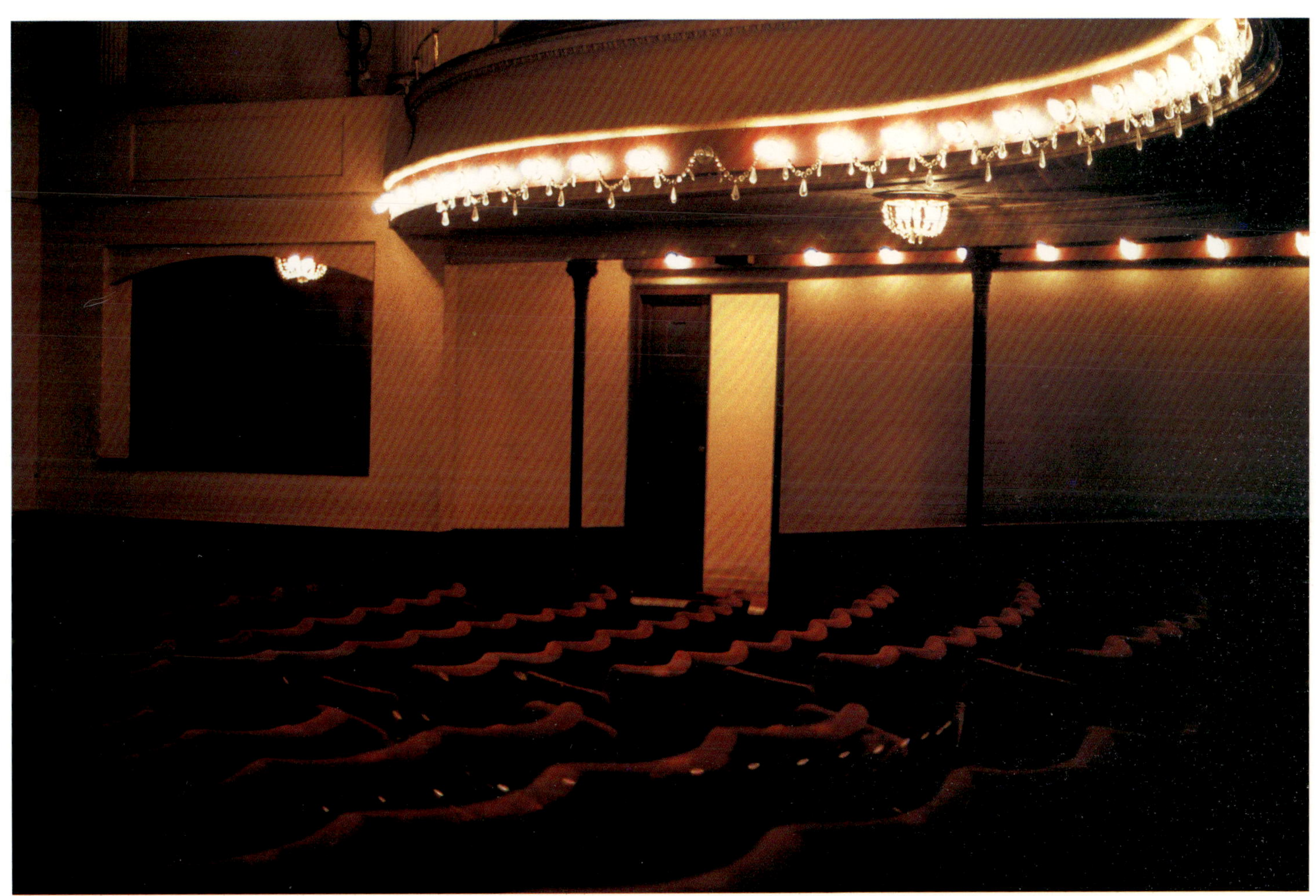

PARIS, FEBRUARY 1977

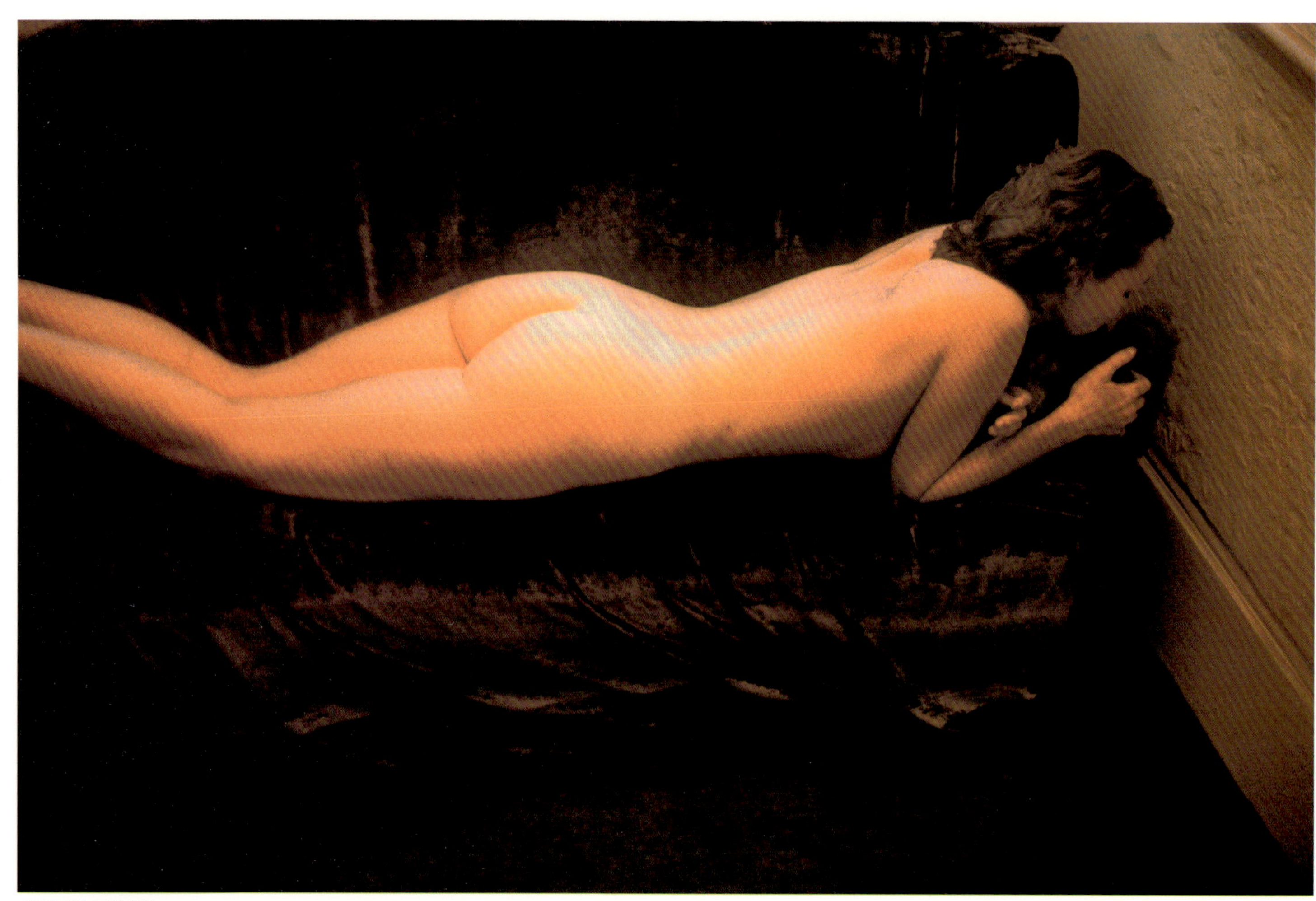

74

LONDON, JULY 1983

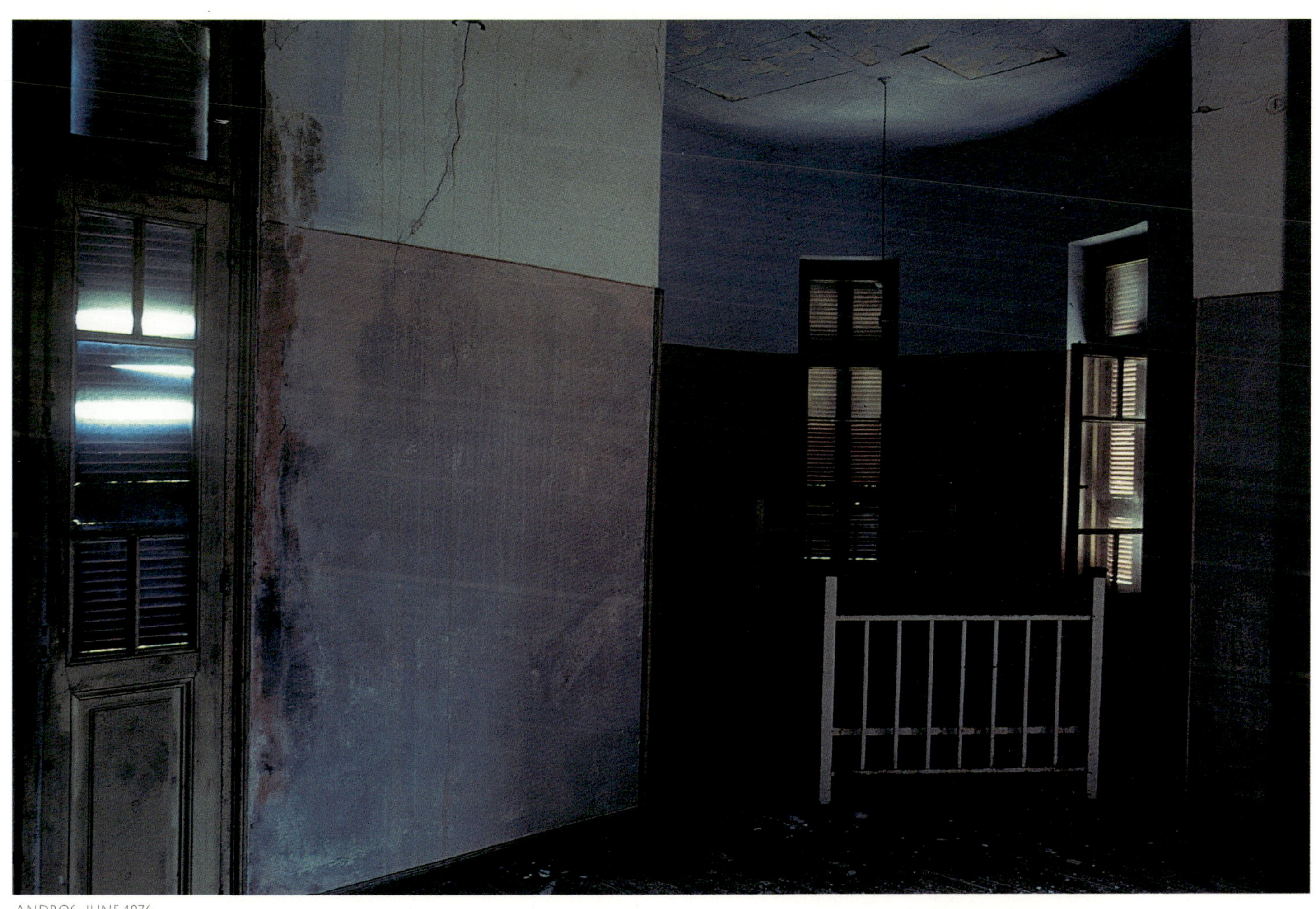

ANDROS, JUNE 1976

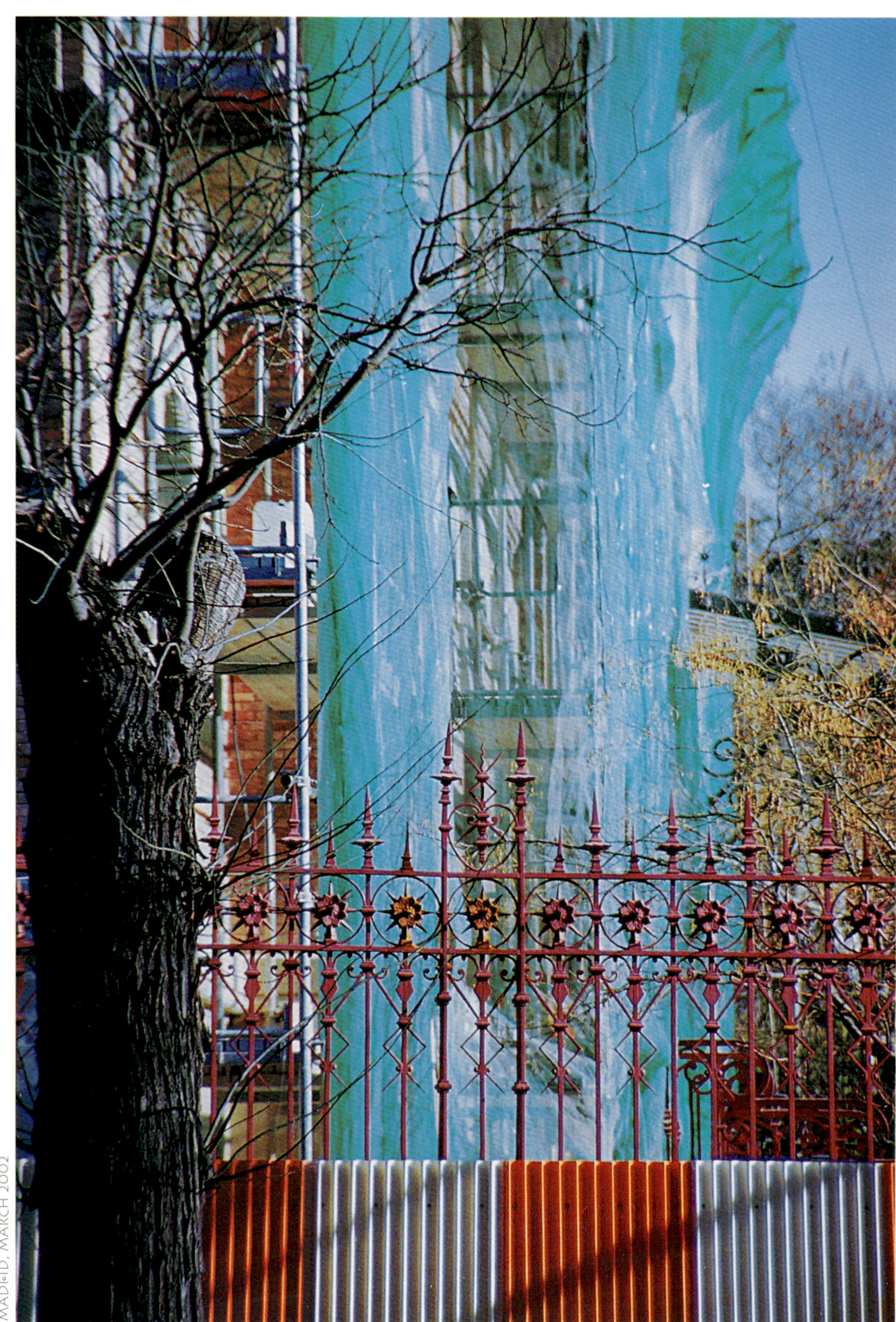

MADRID, MARCH 2002

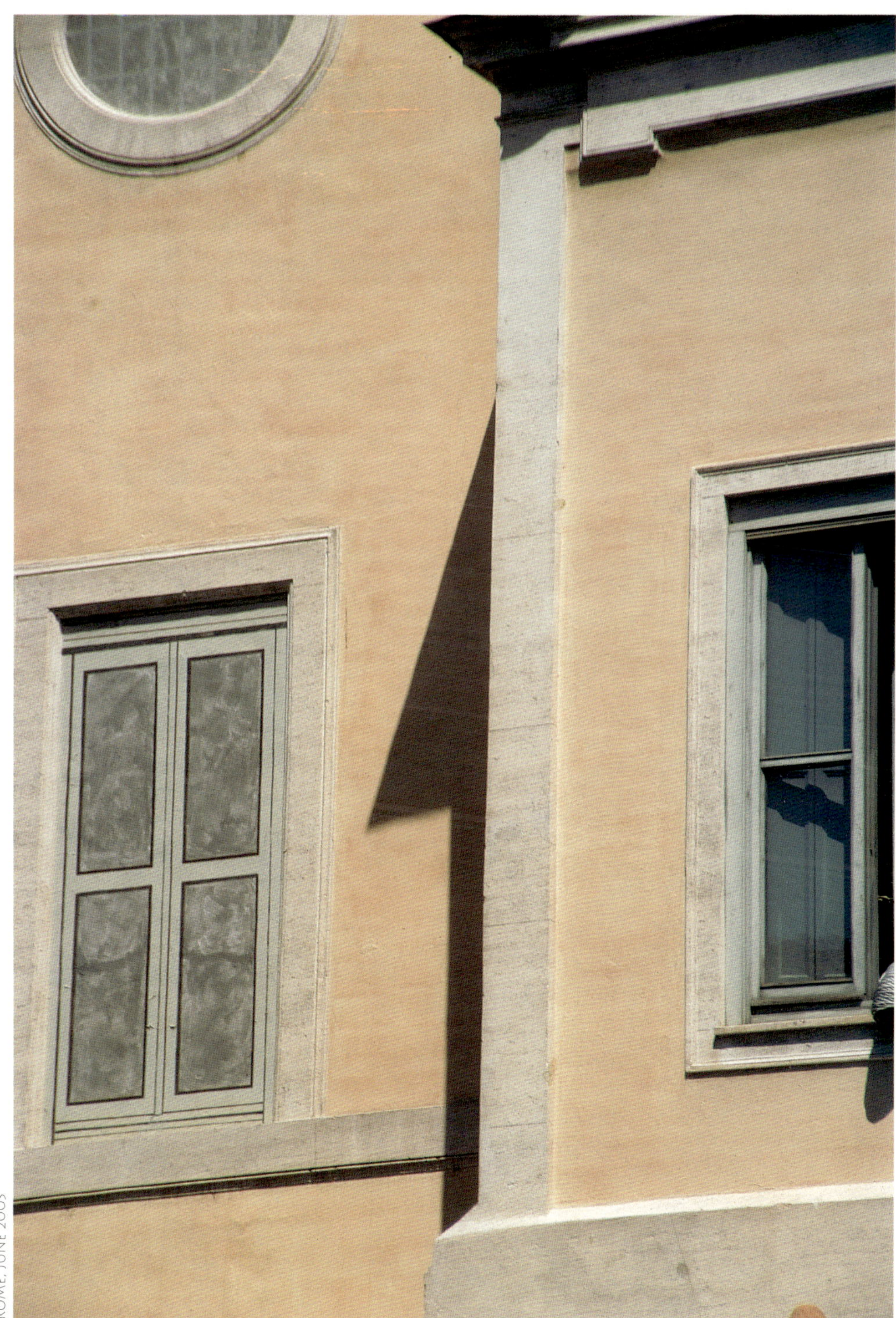

ROME, JUNE 2003

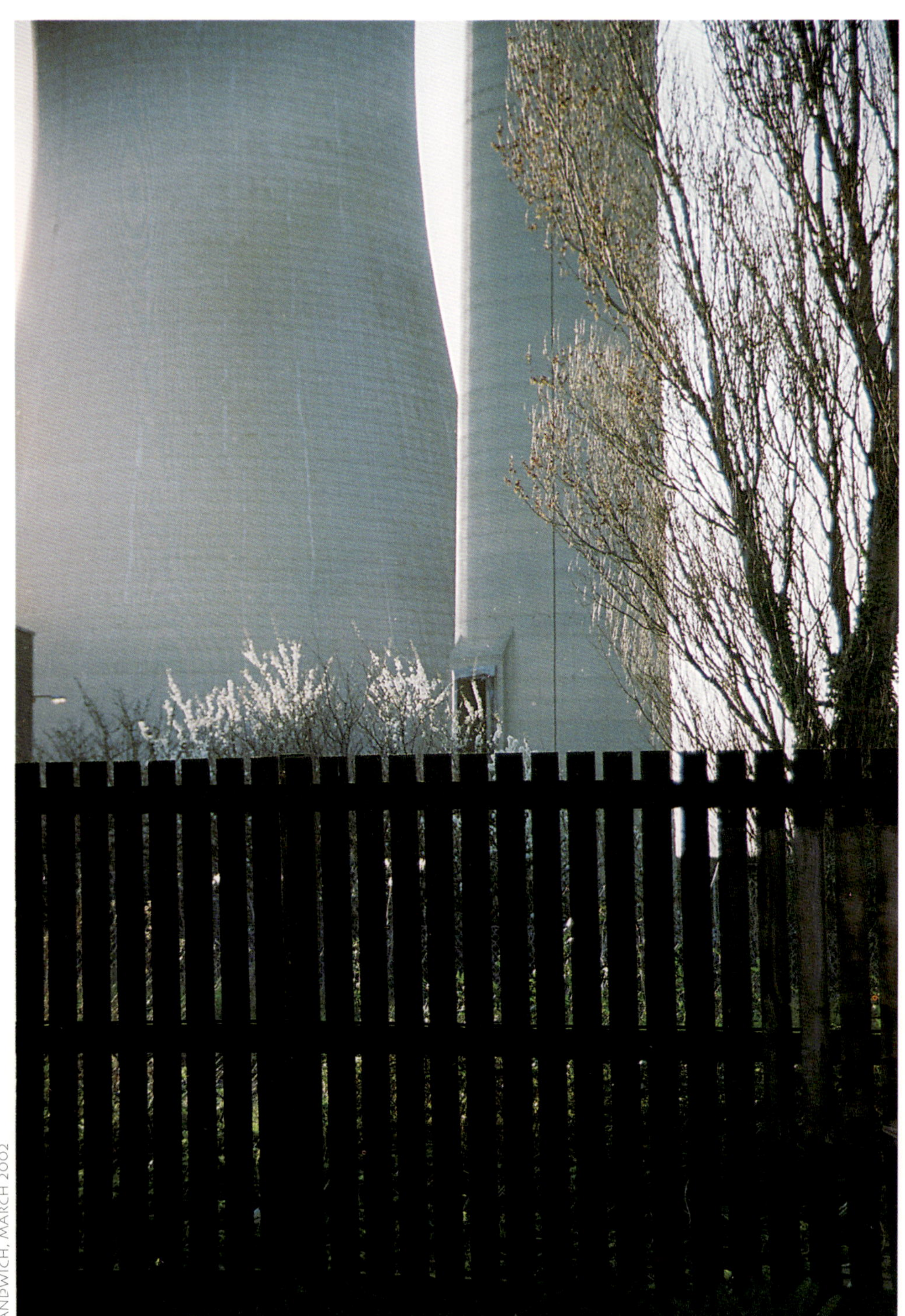

SANDWICH, MARCH 2002

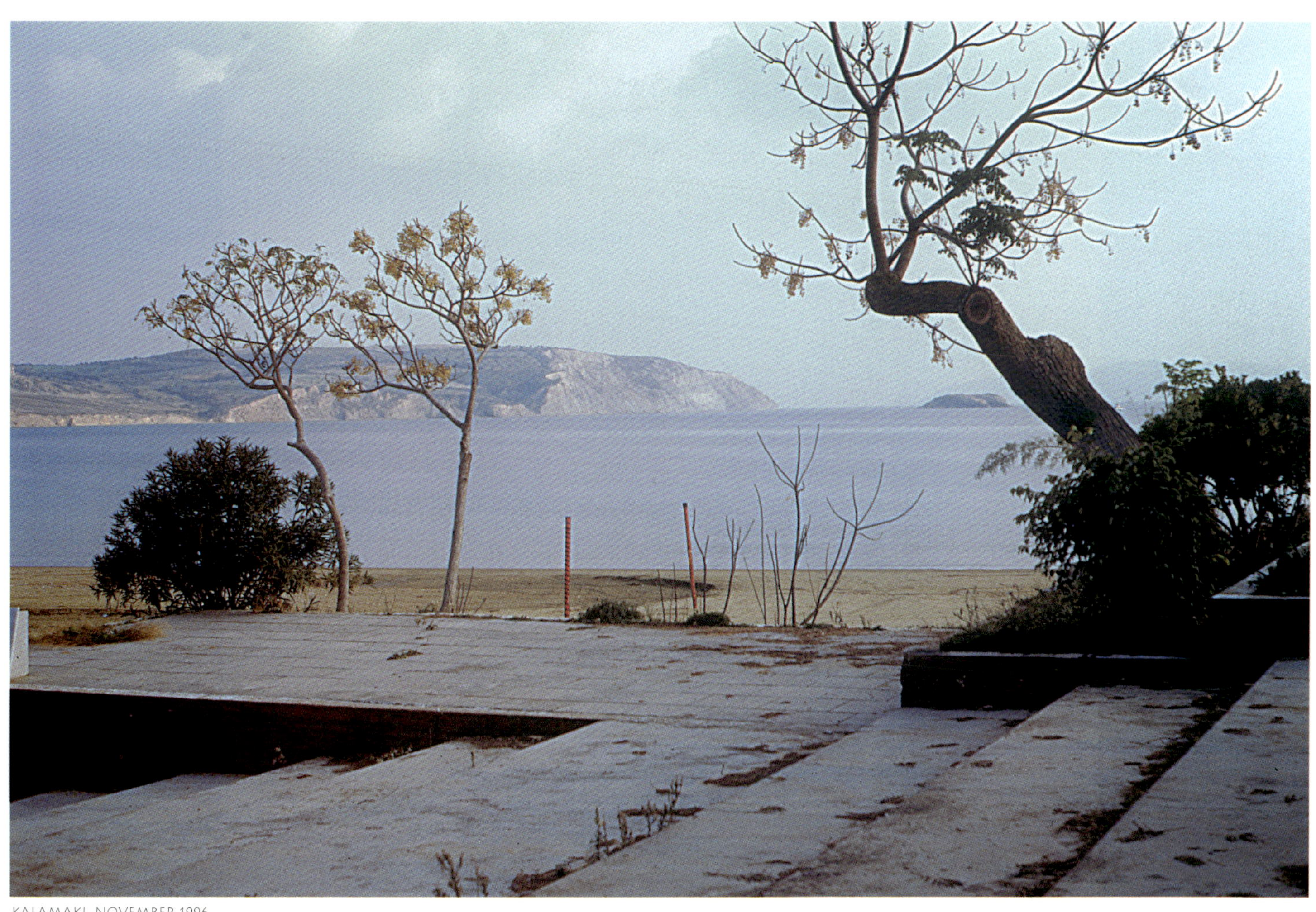

KALAMAKI, NOVEMBER 1996

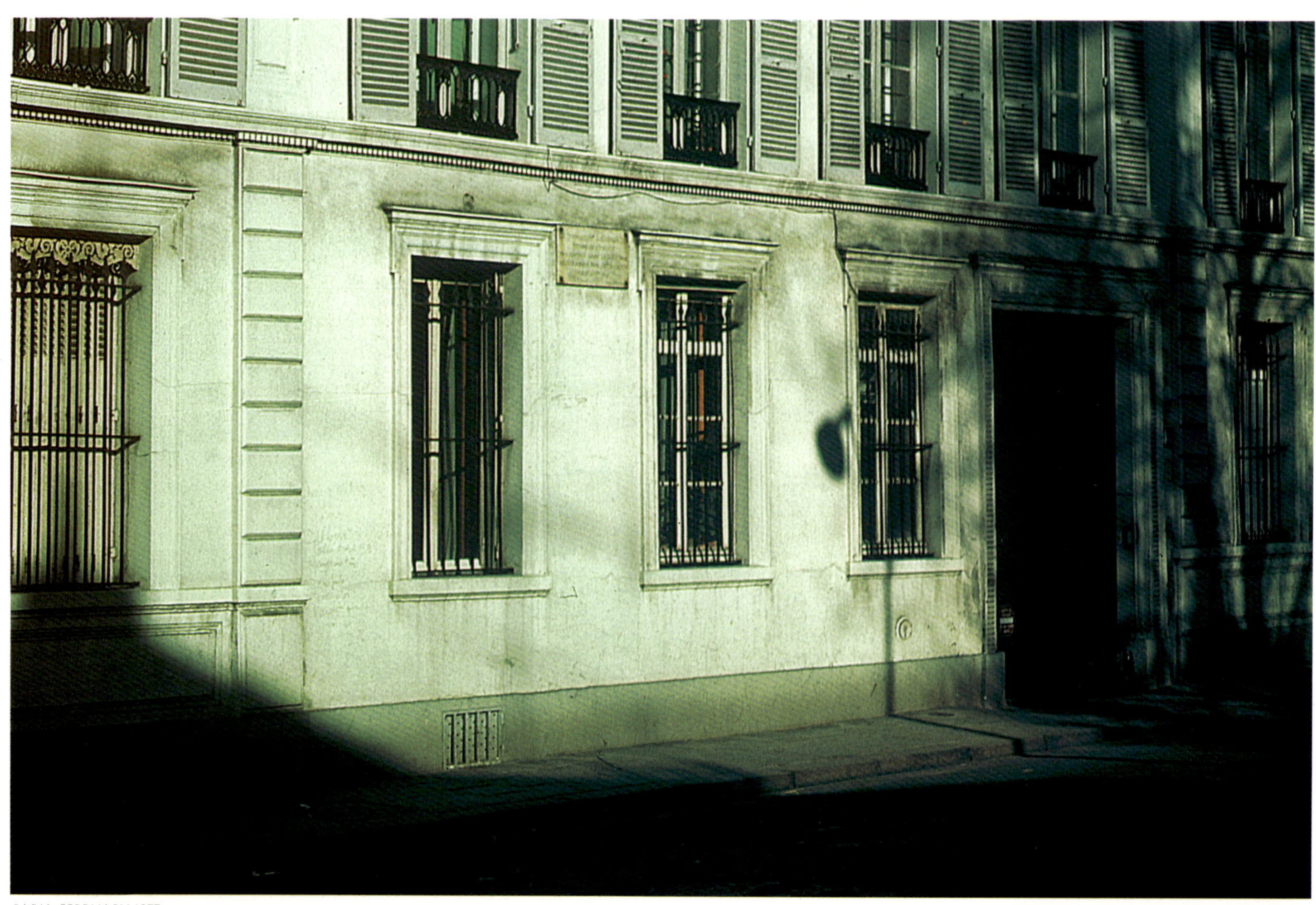

PARIS, FEBRUARY 1977

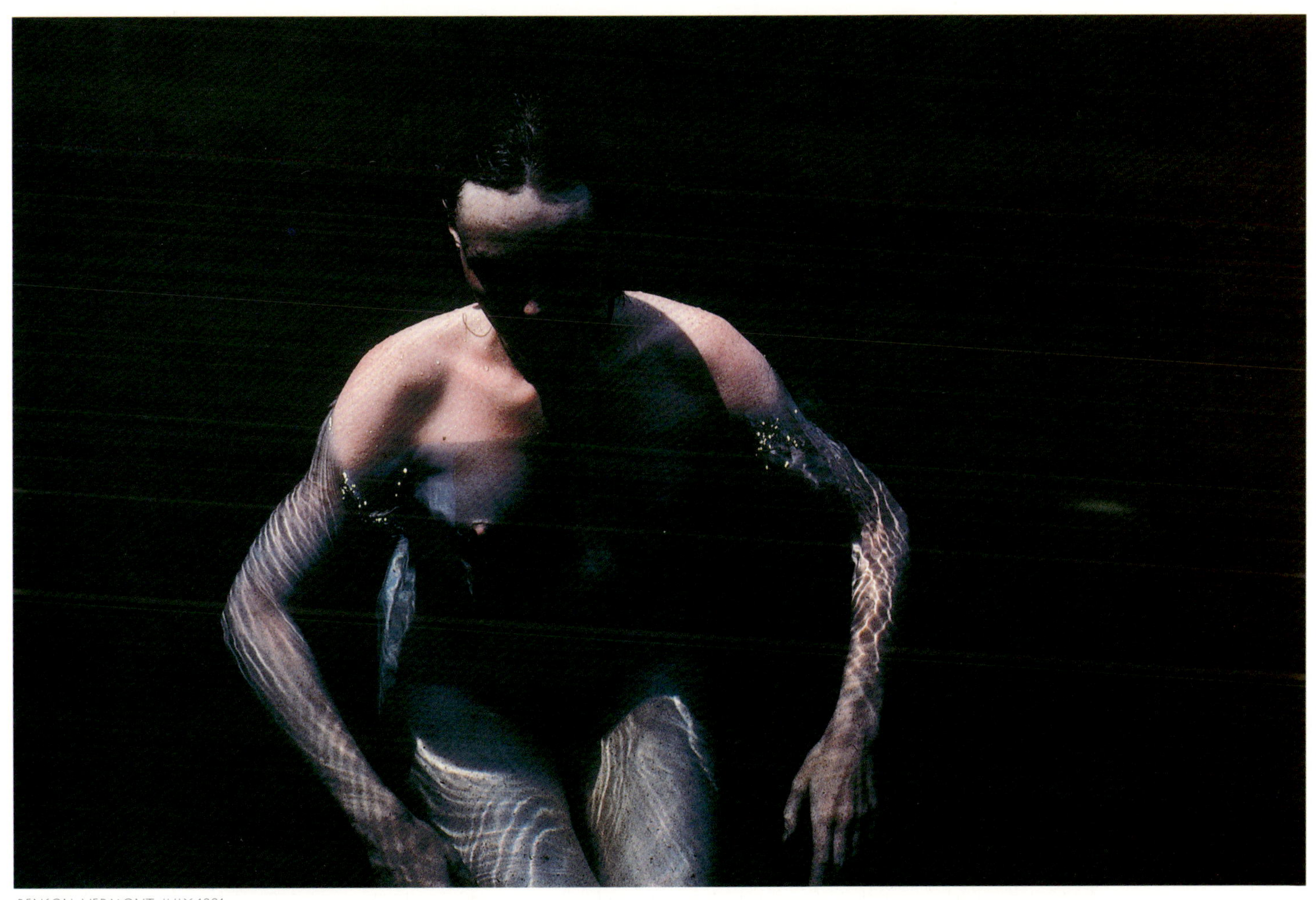

BENSON, VERMONT, JULY 1981

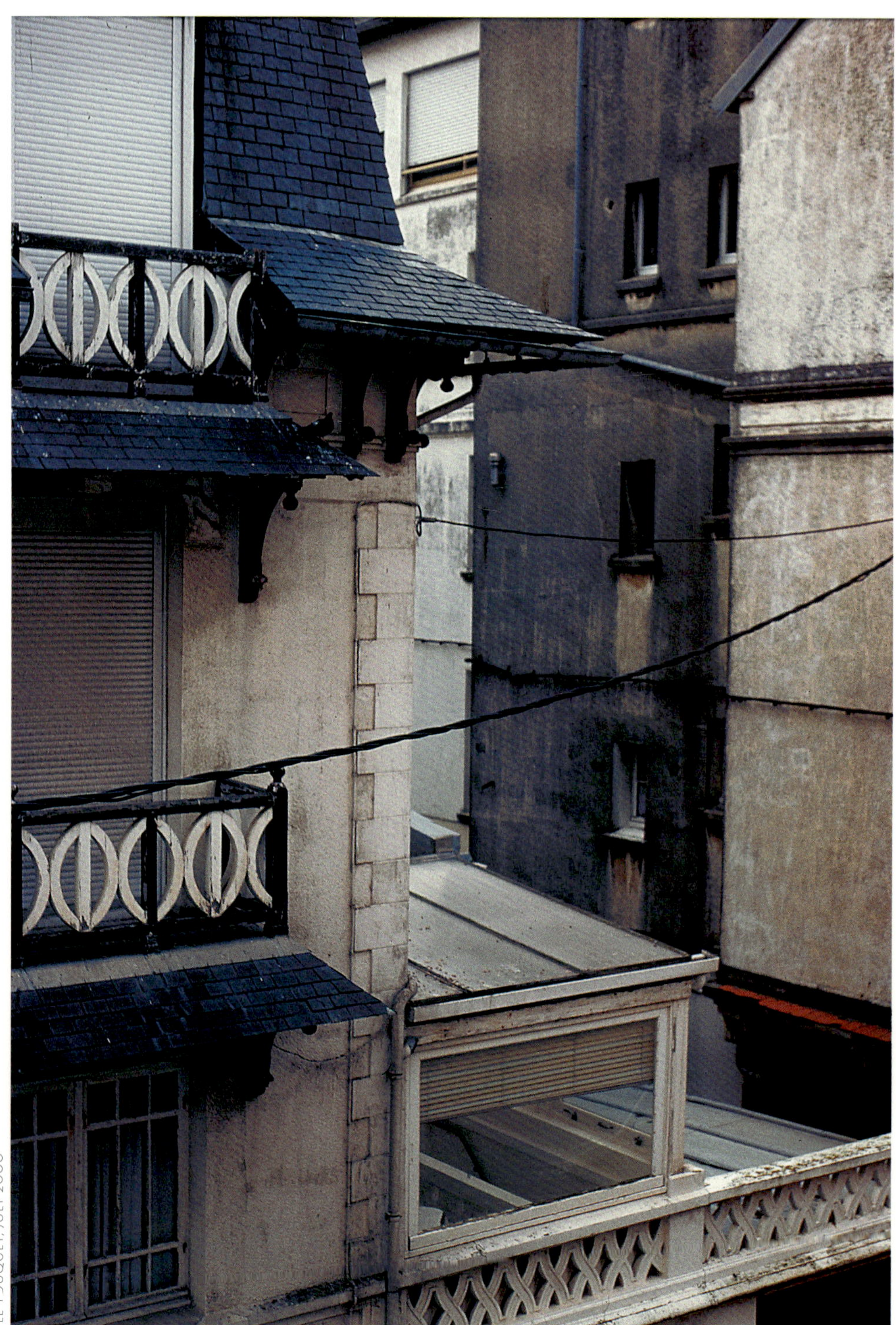

LE TOUQUET, JULY 2000

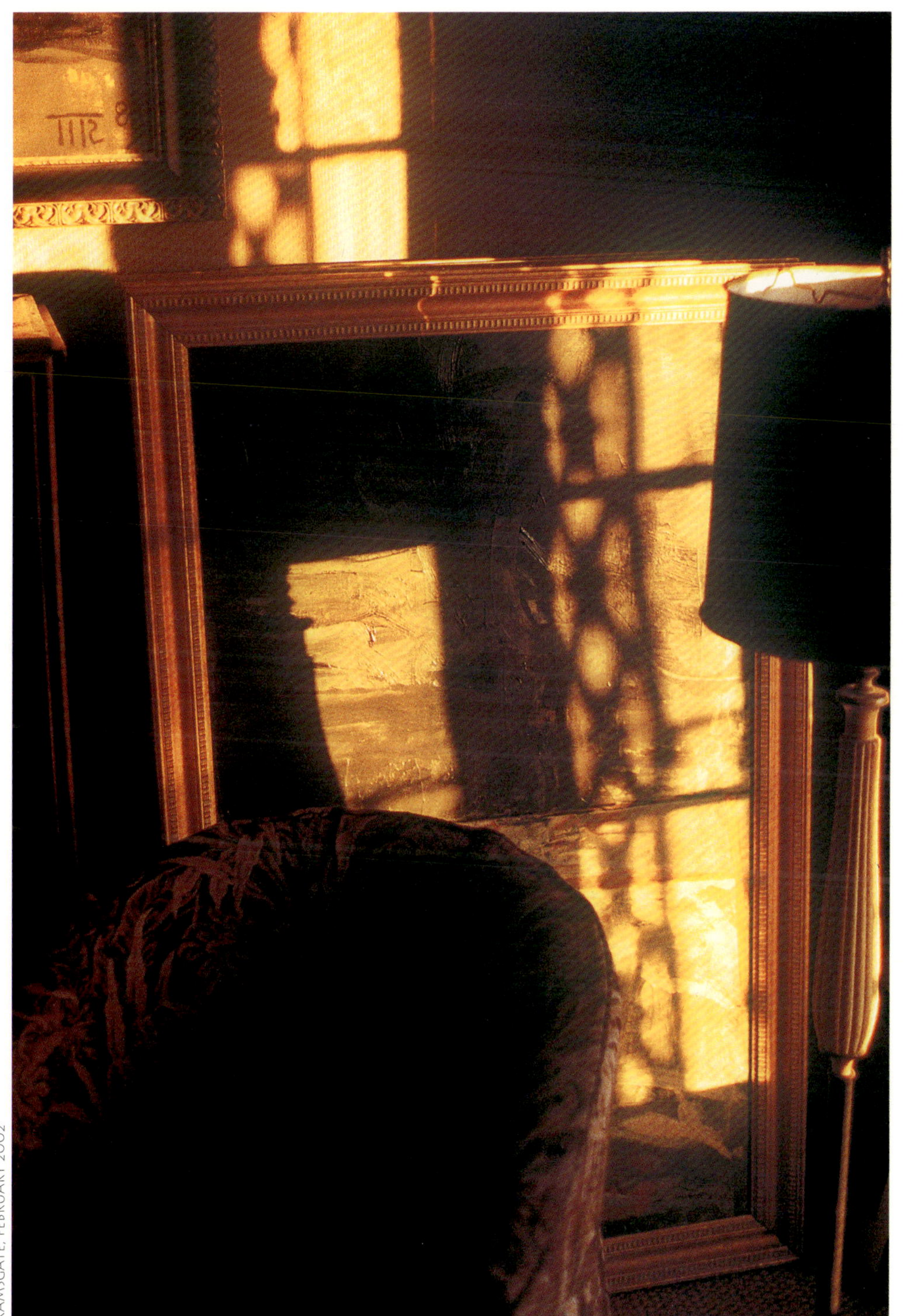

RAMSGATE, FEBRUARY 2002

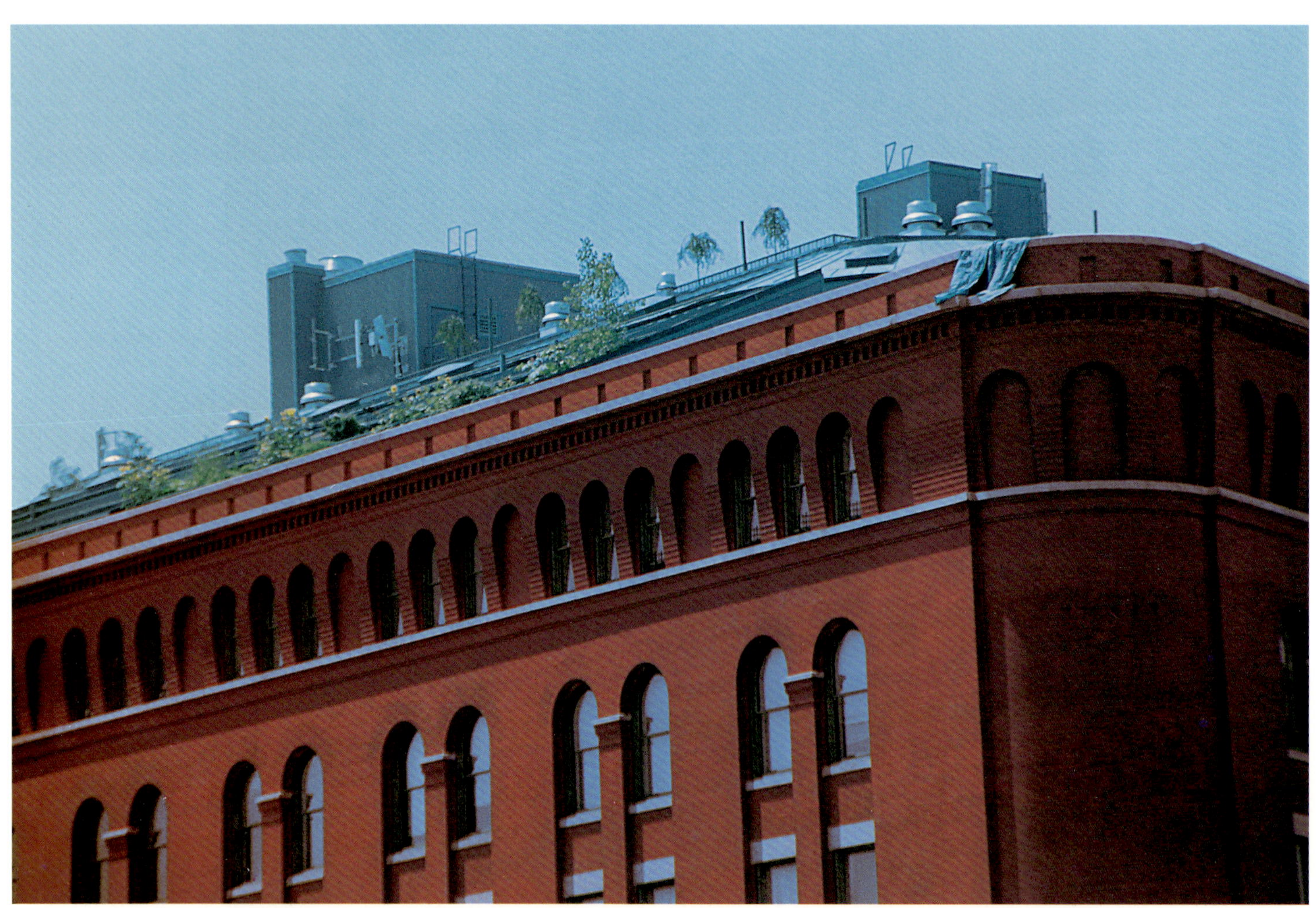

NEW YORK, AUGUST 2002

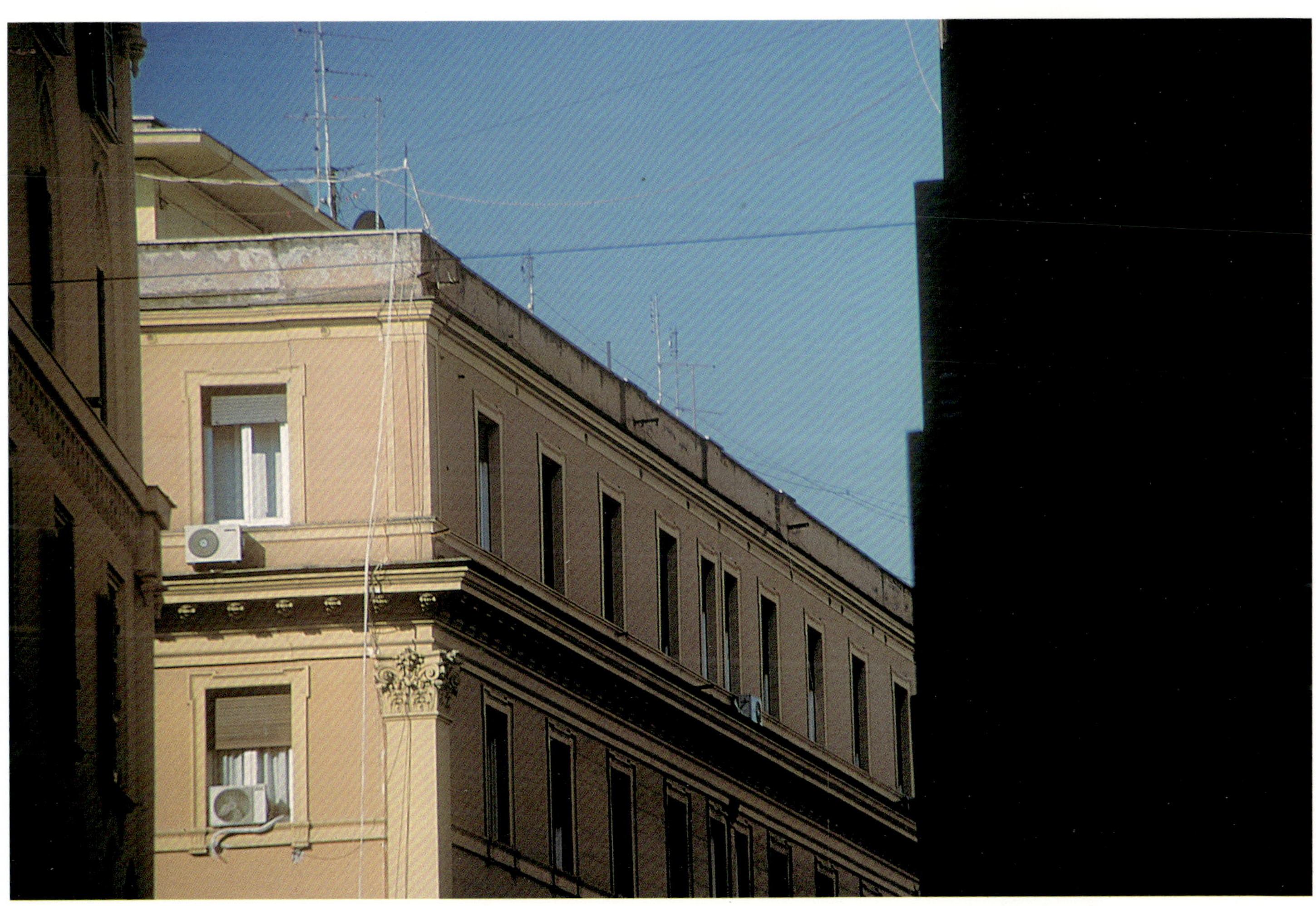

ROME, JUNE 2003

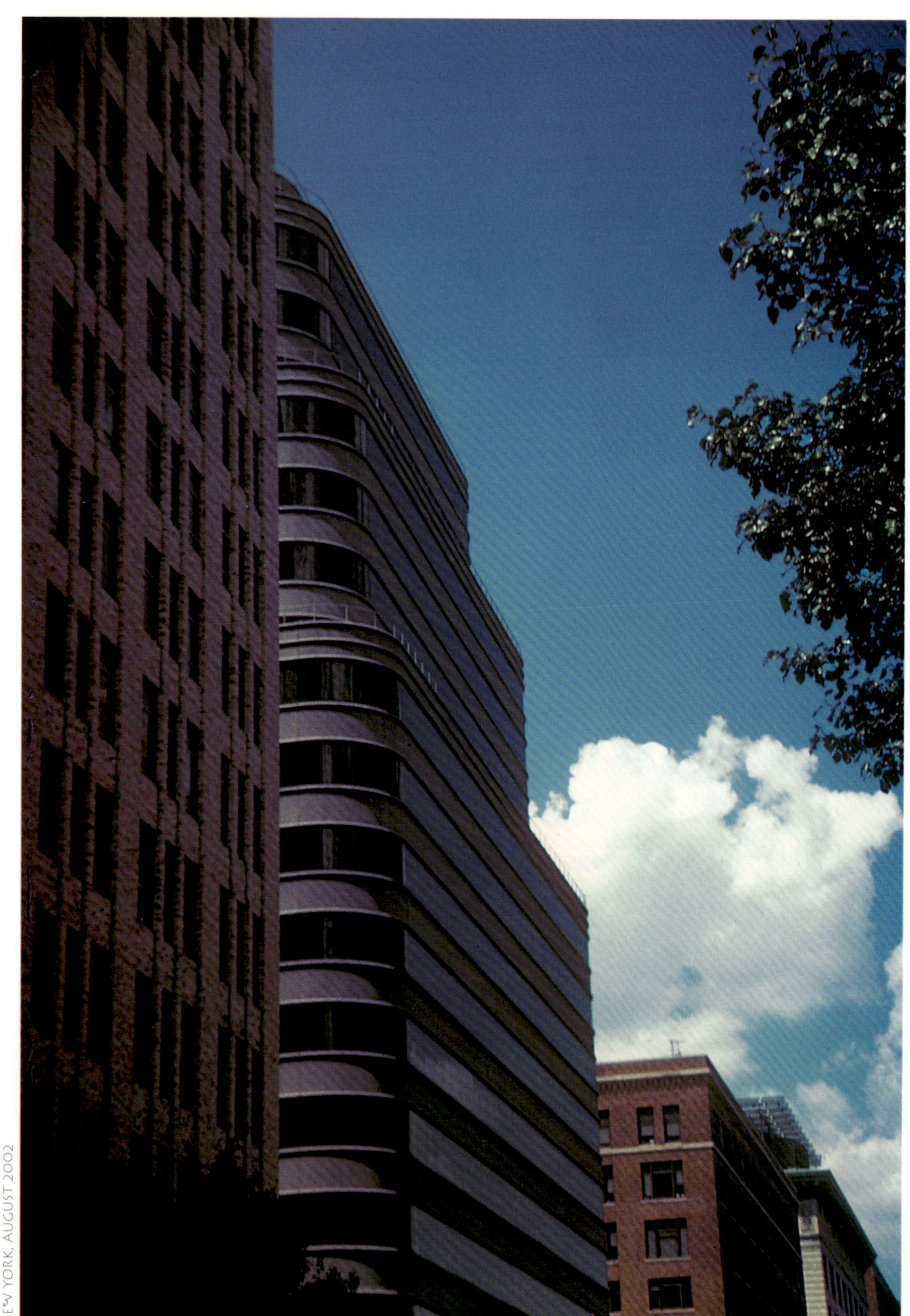

NEW YORK, AUGUST 2002

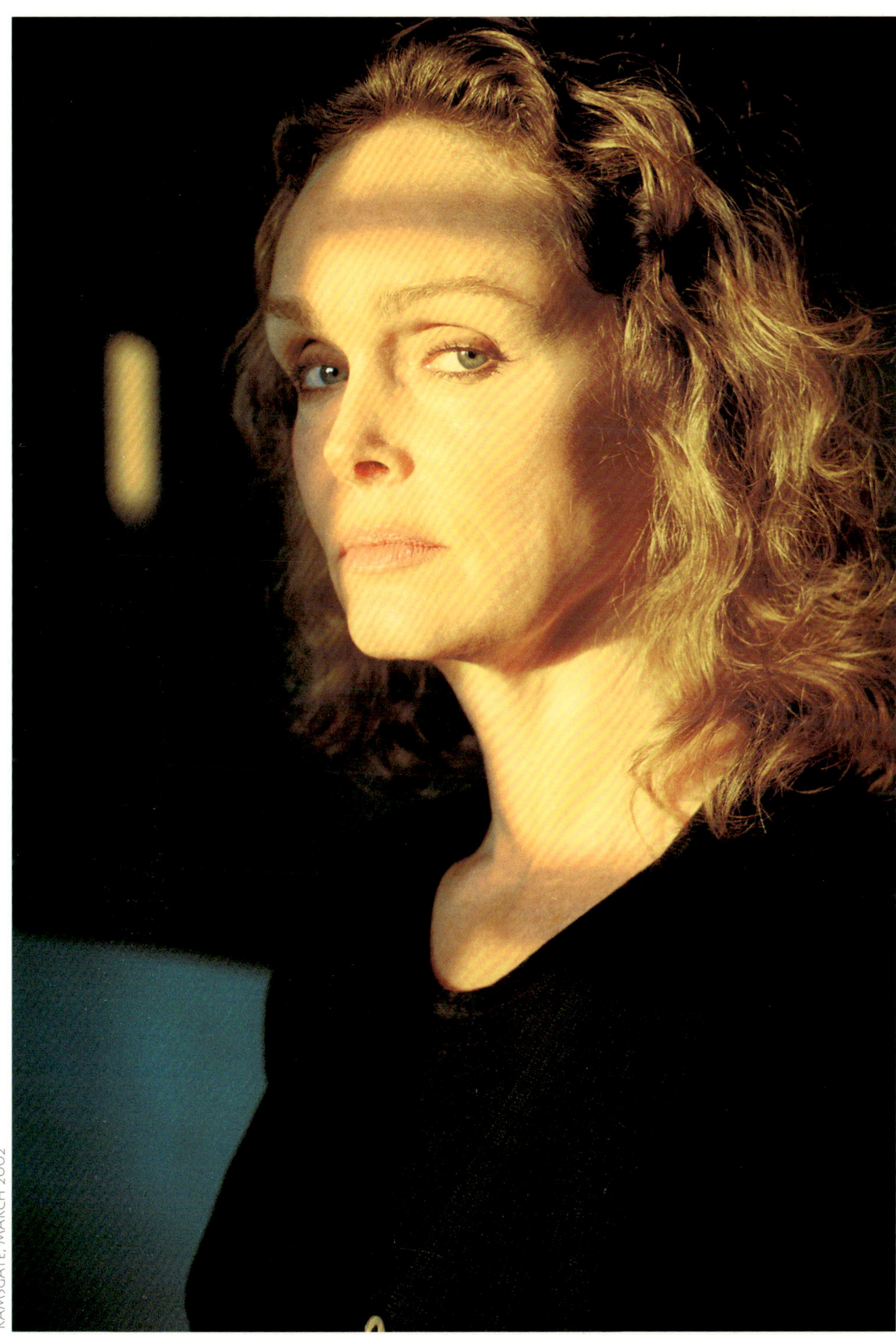

RAMSGATE, MARCH 2002

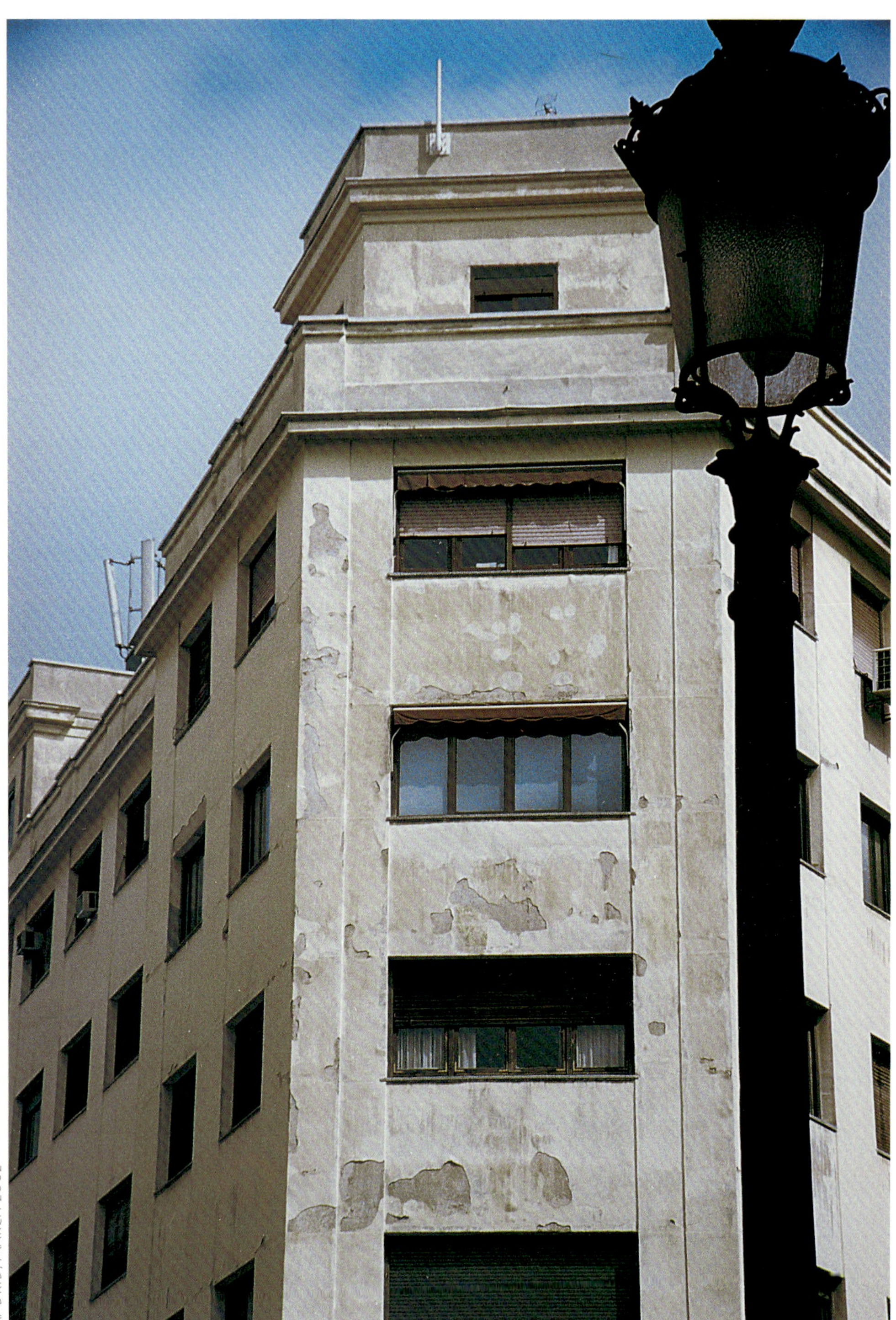

MADRID, MARCH 2002

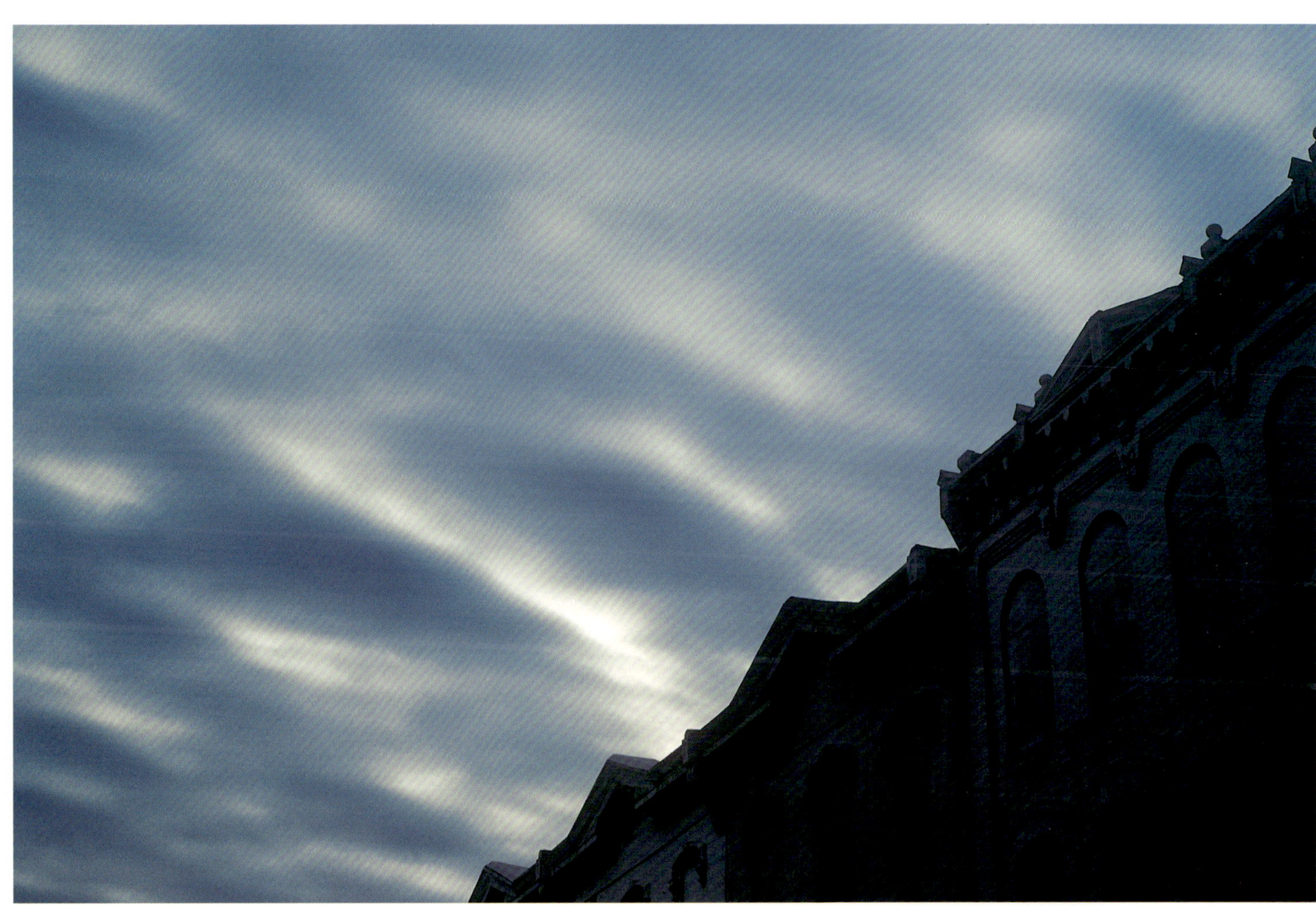

SAVANNAH, GEORGIA, JANUARY 1997

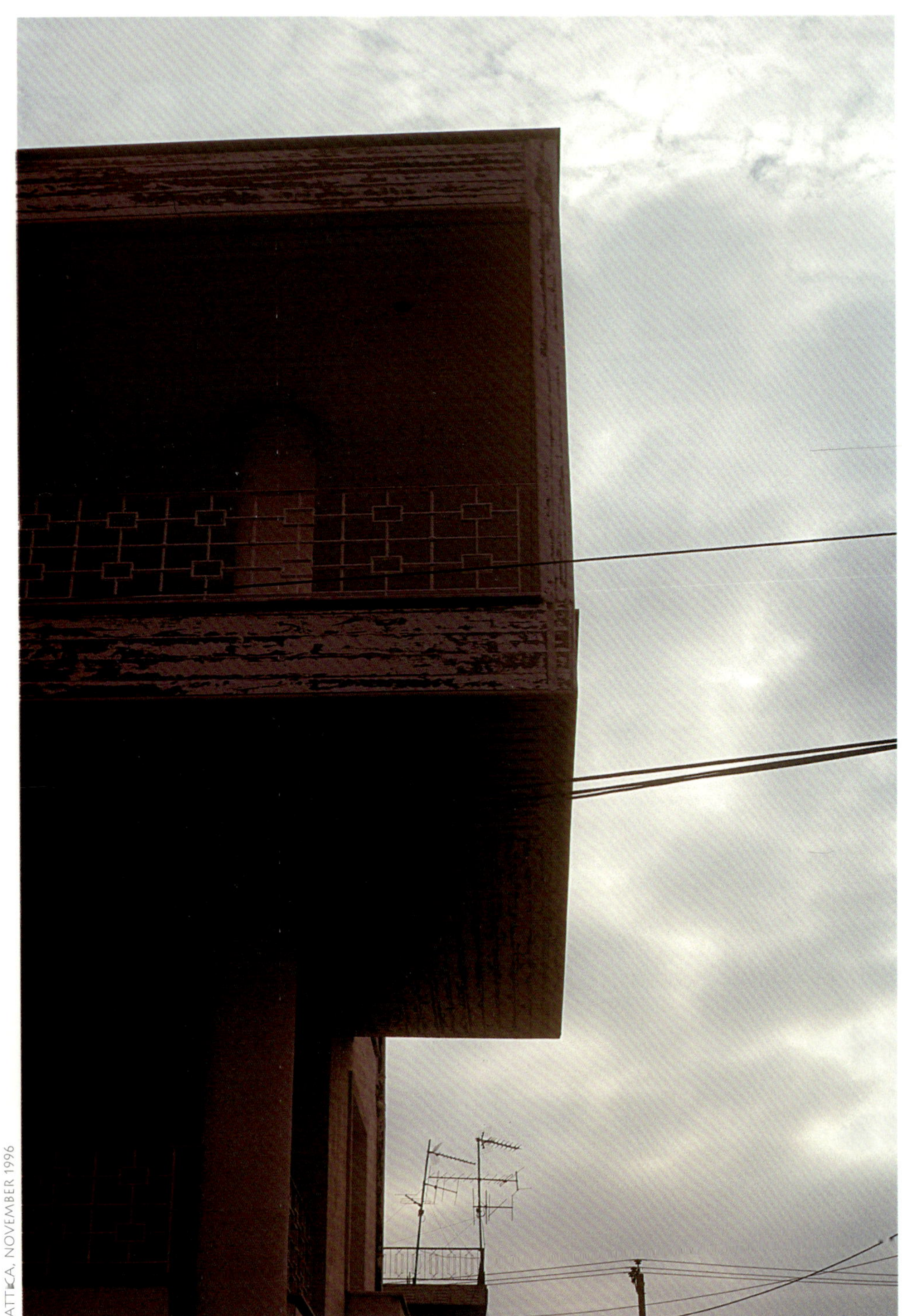

ATTICA, NOVEMBER 1996

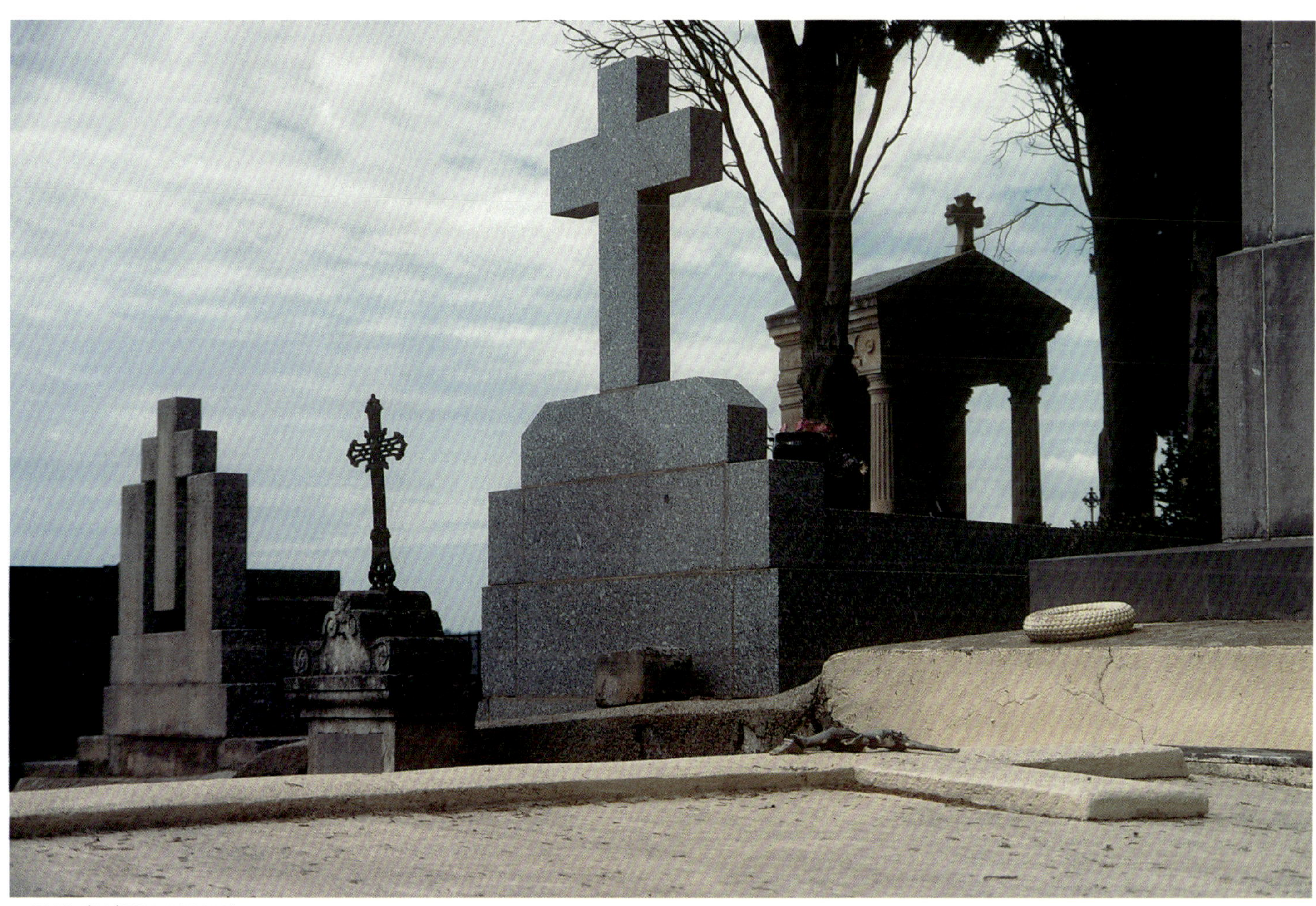

MURVIEL LÈS BÉZIERS, JULY 2003

92

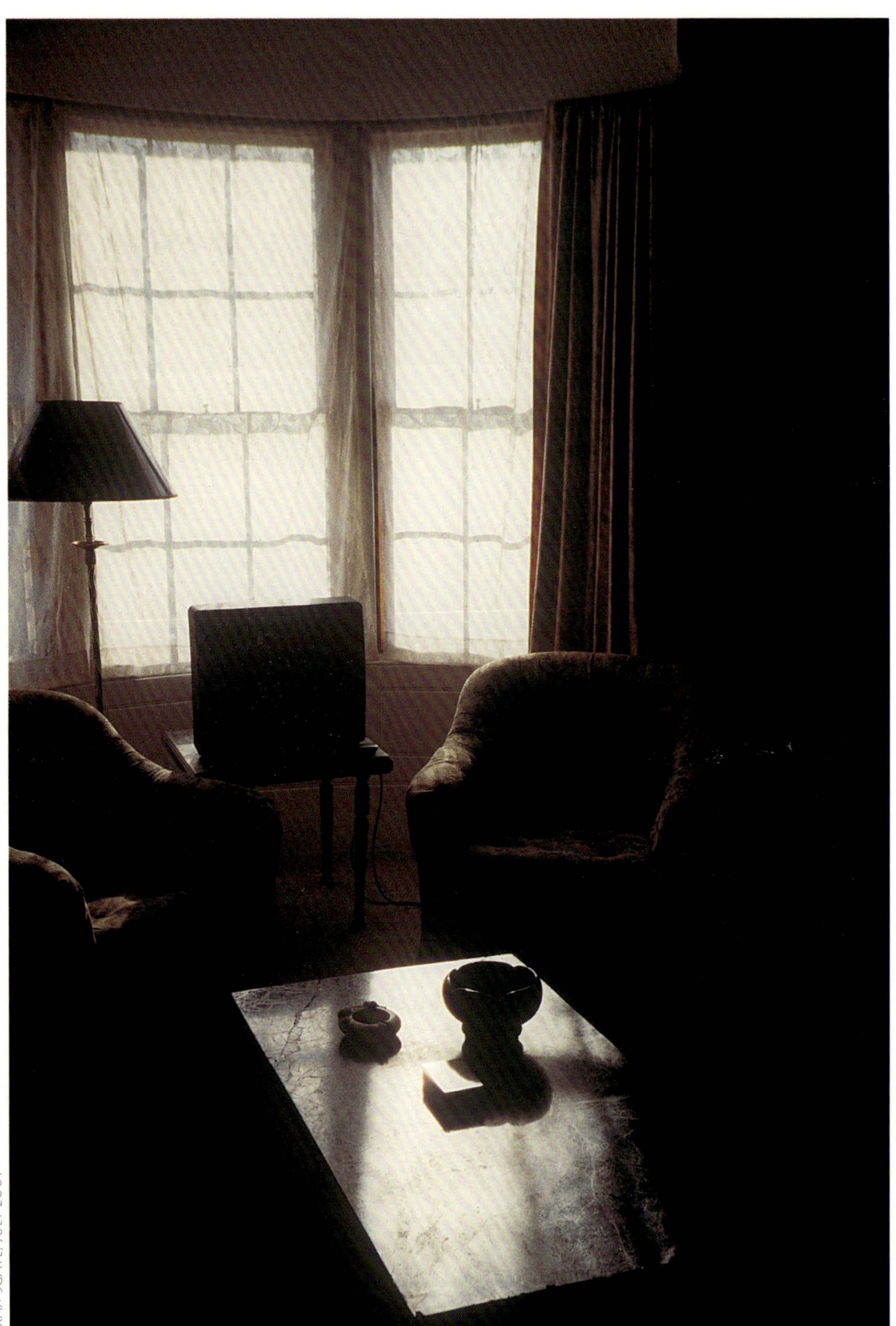

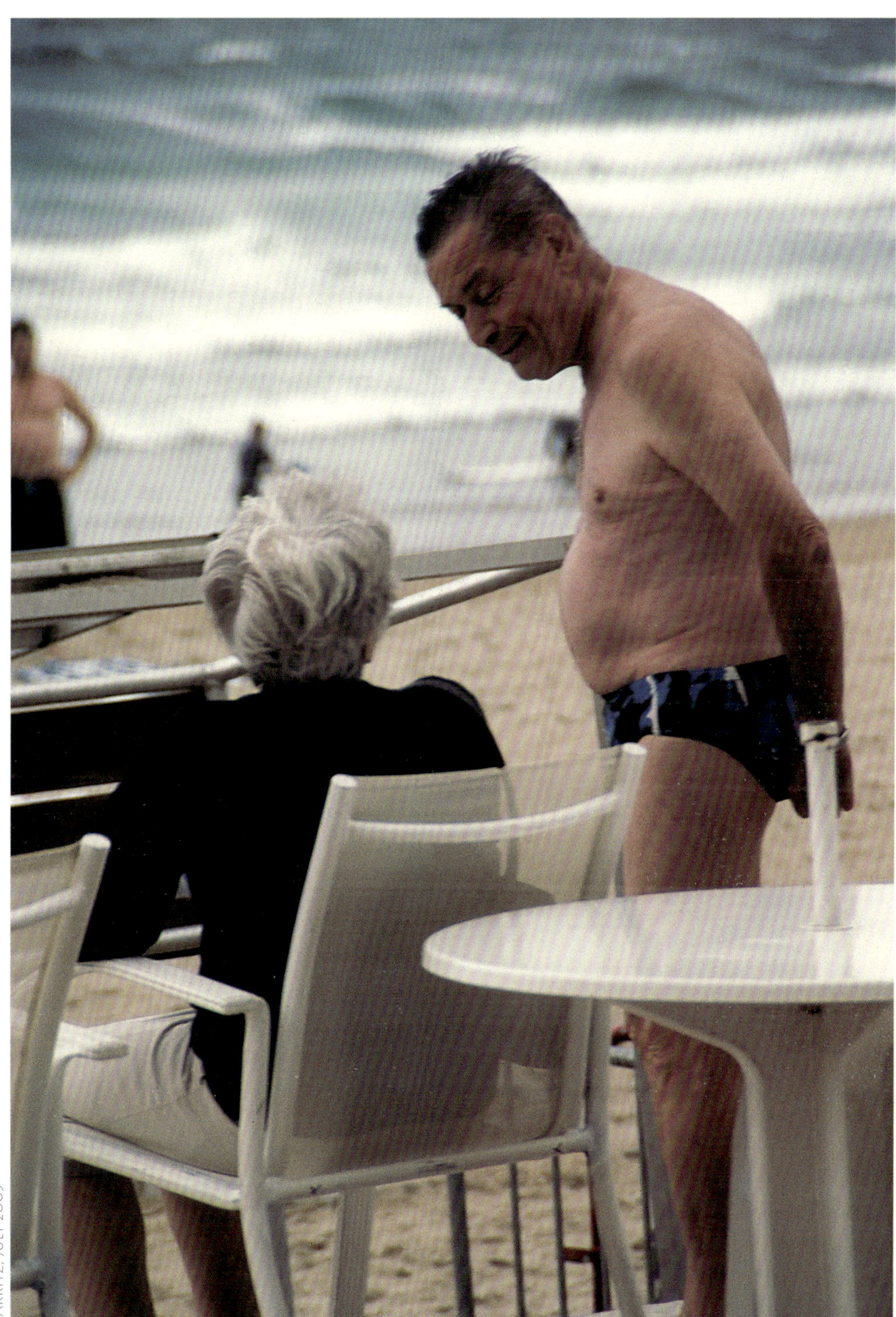

BIARRITZ, JULY 2003

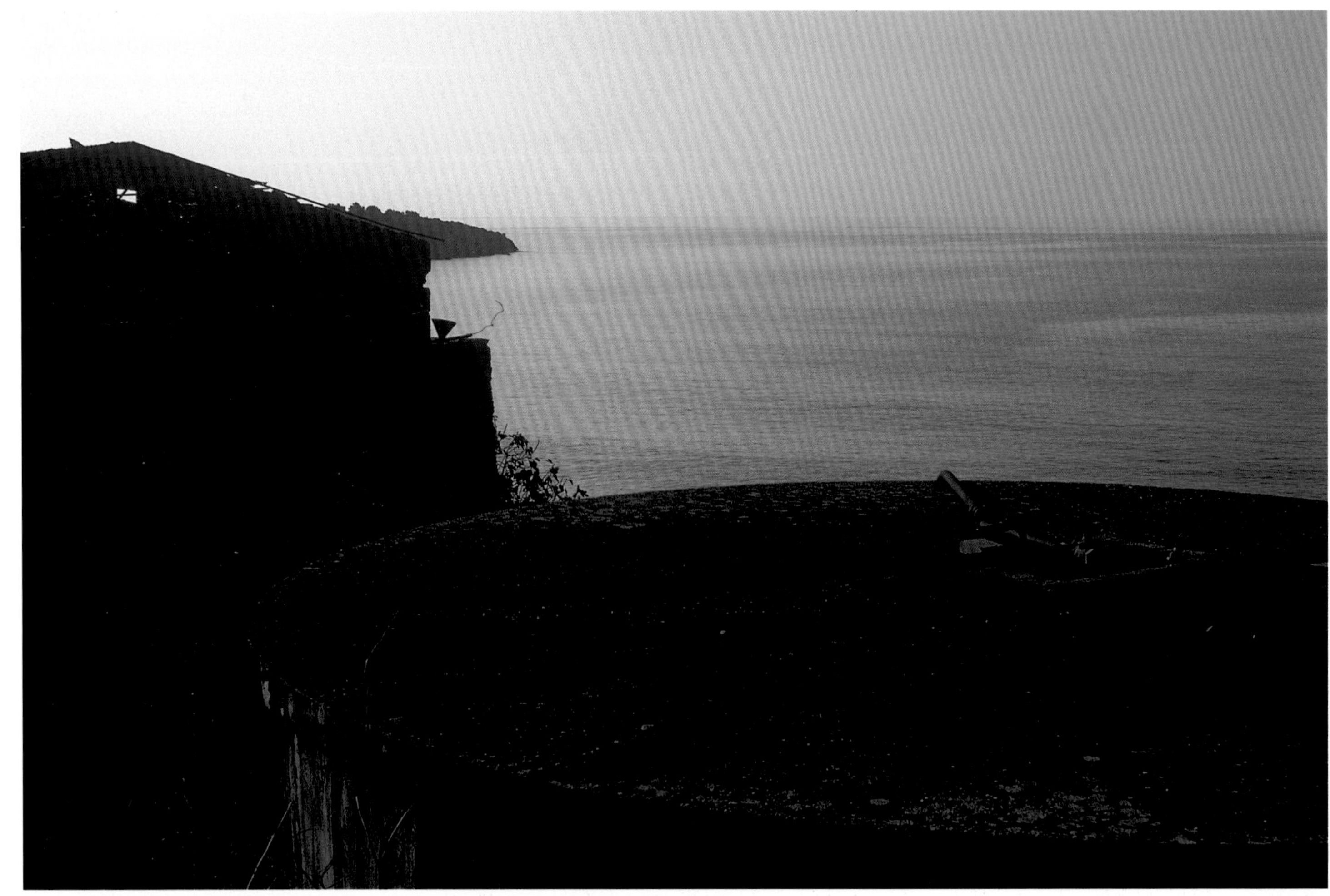

KARDAMYLI, NOVEMBER 1996

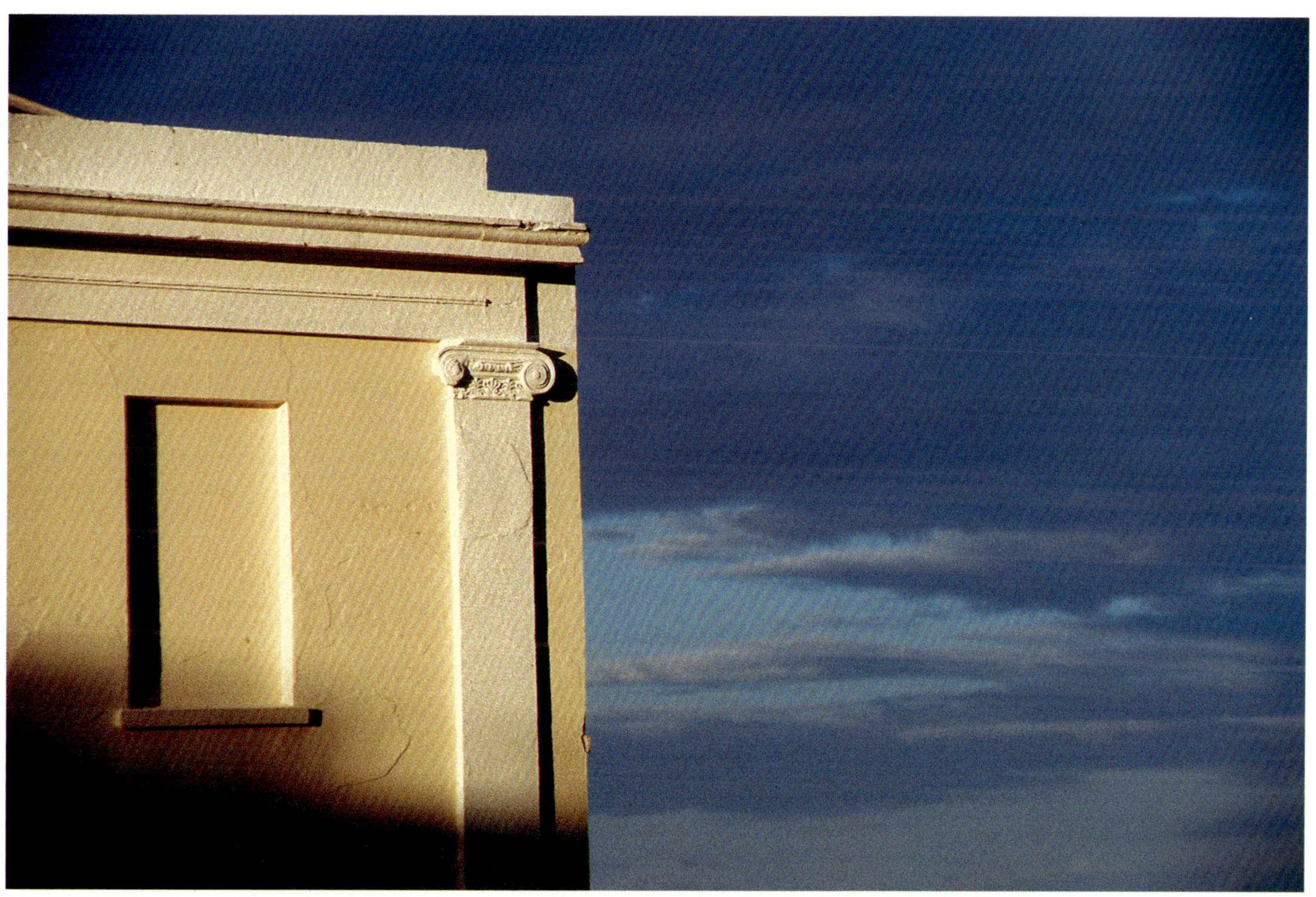

RAMSGATE, AUGUST 1998

96

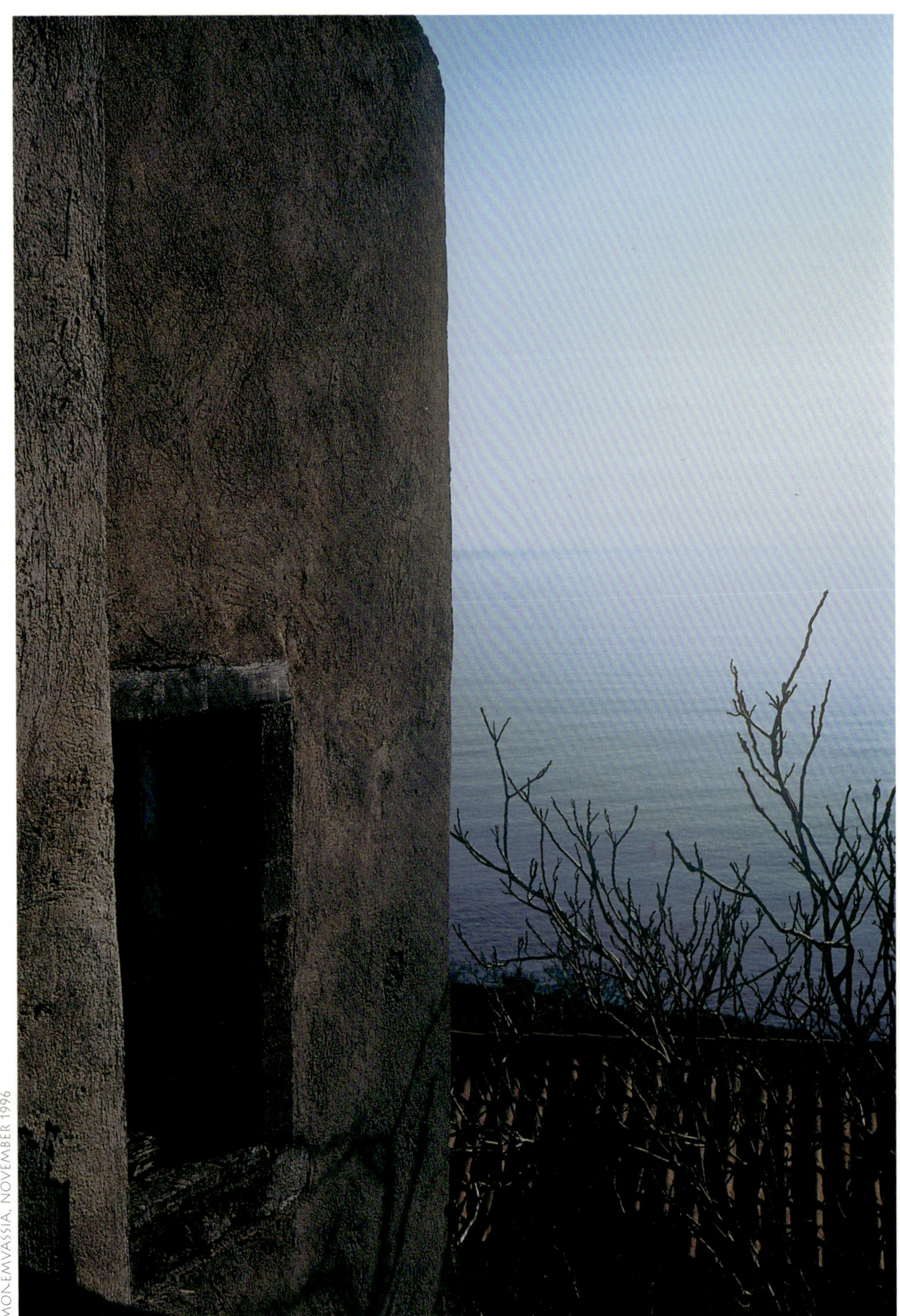

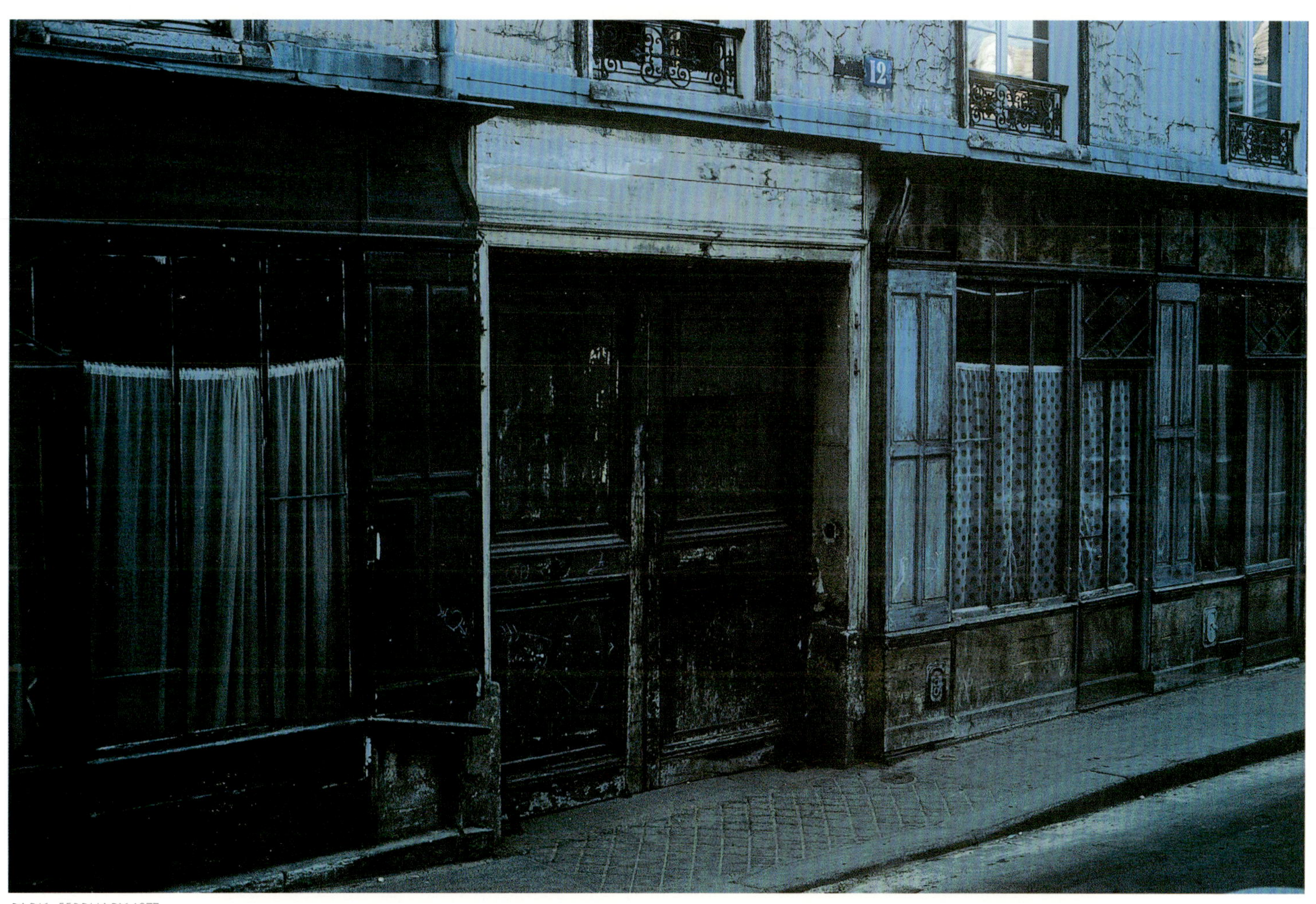

PARIS, FEBRUARY 1977

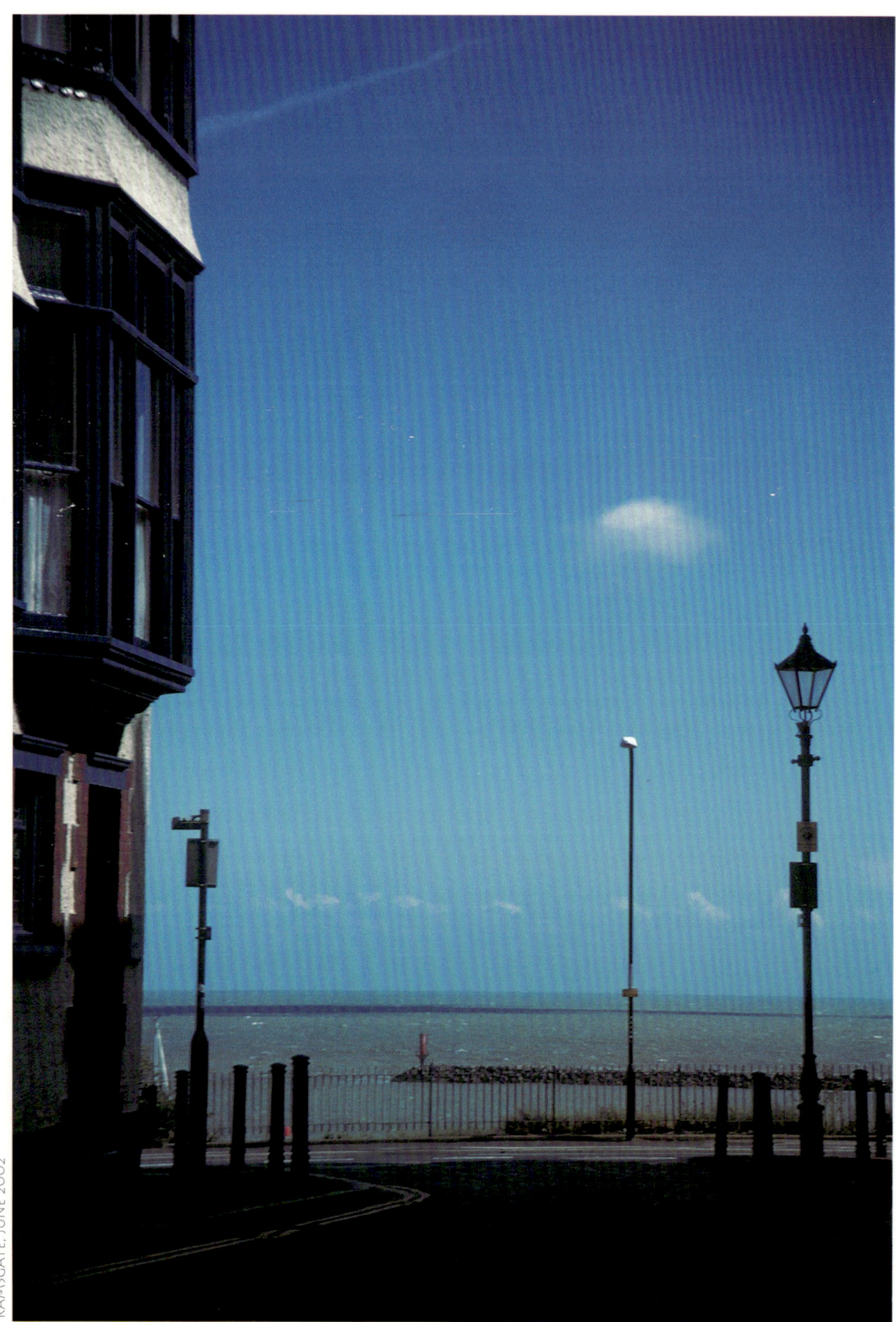

RAMSGATE, JUNE 2002

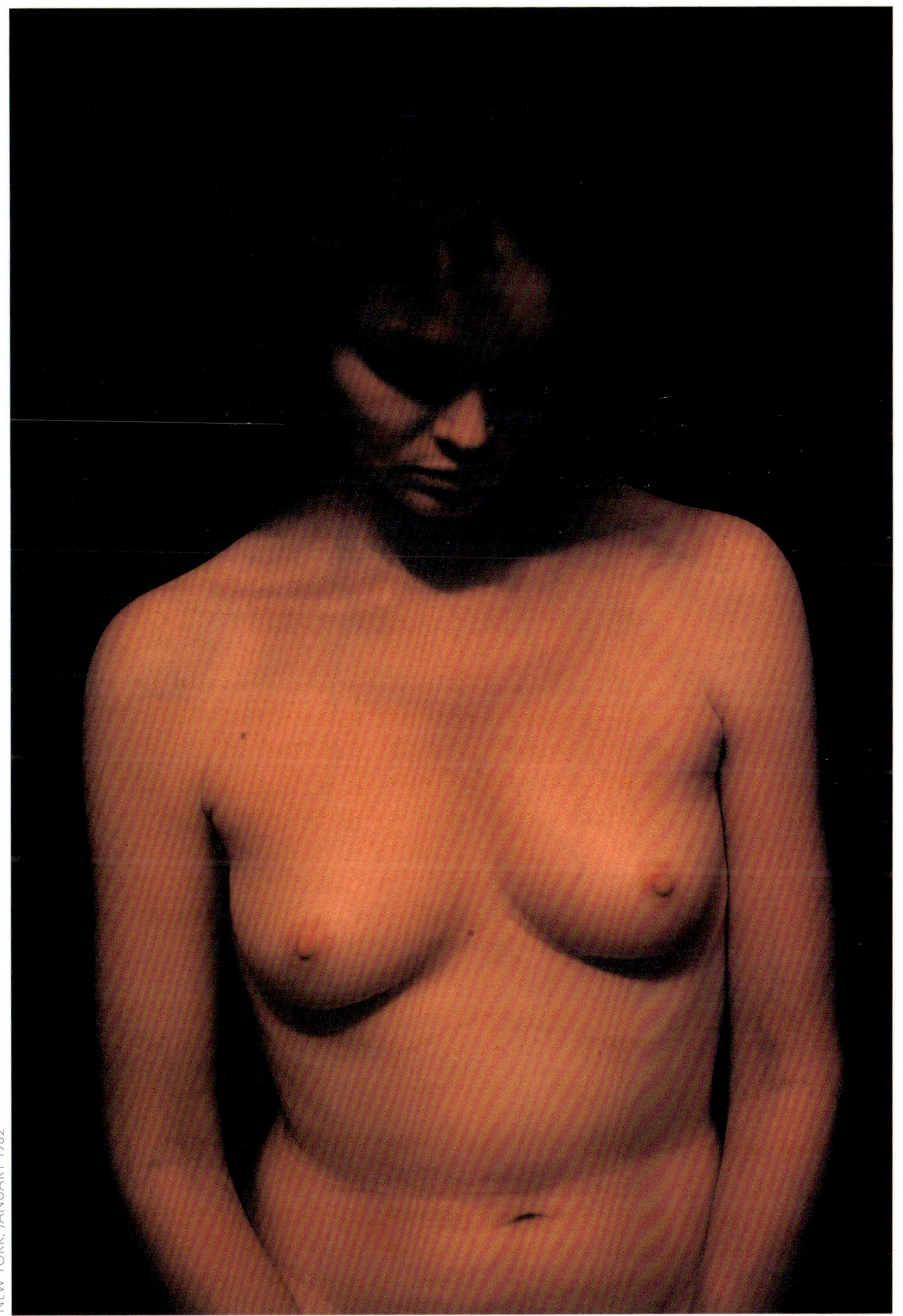

NEW YORK, JANUARY 1982

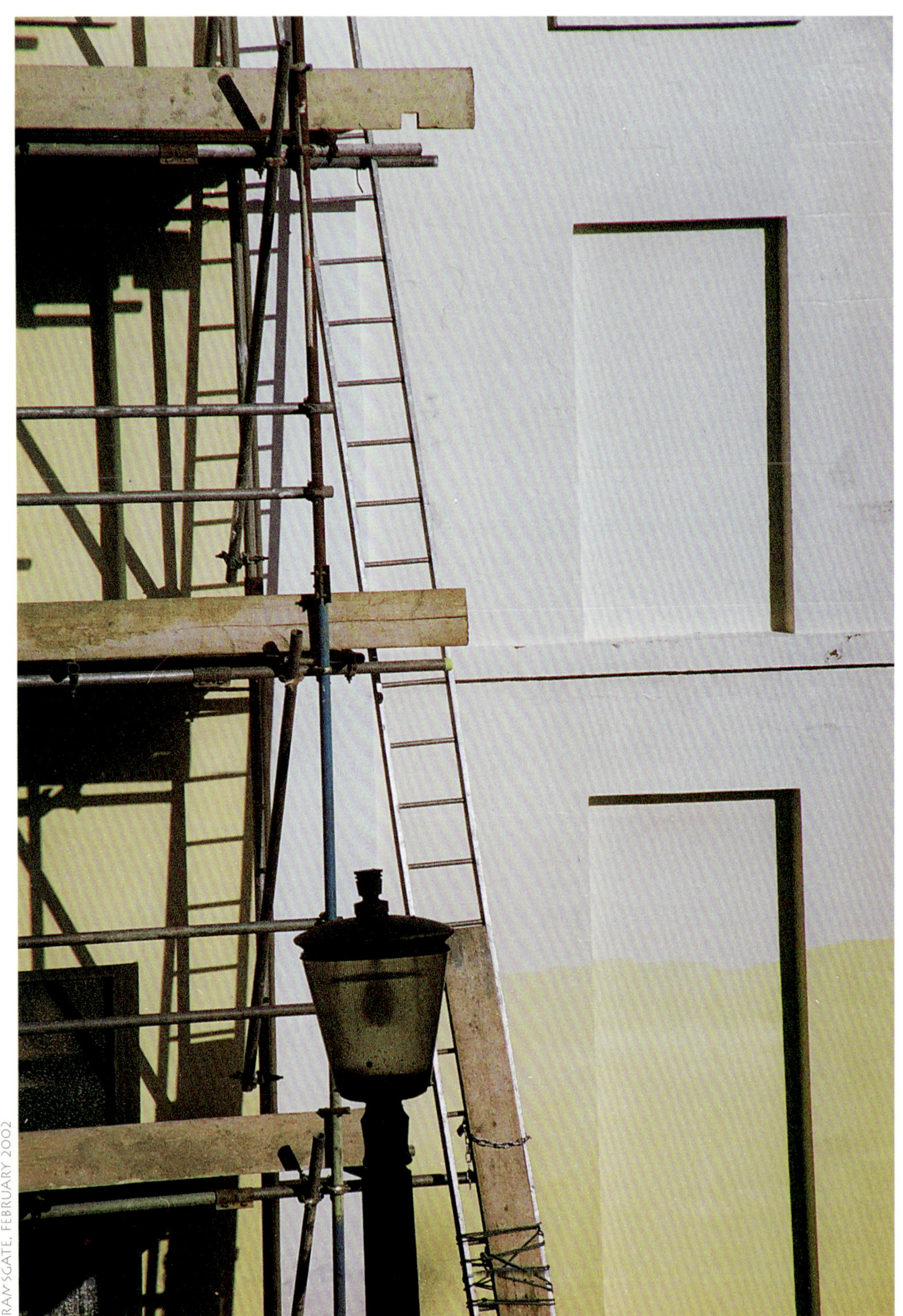

RAMSGATE, FEBRUARY 2002

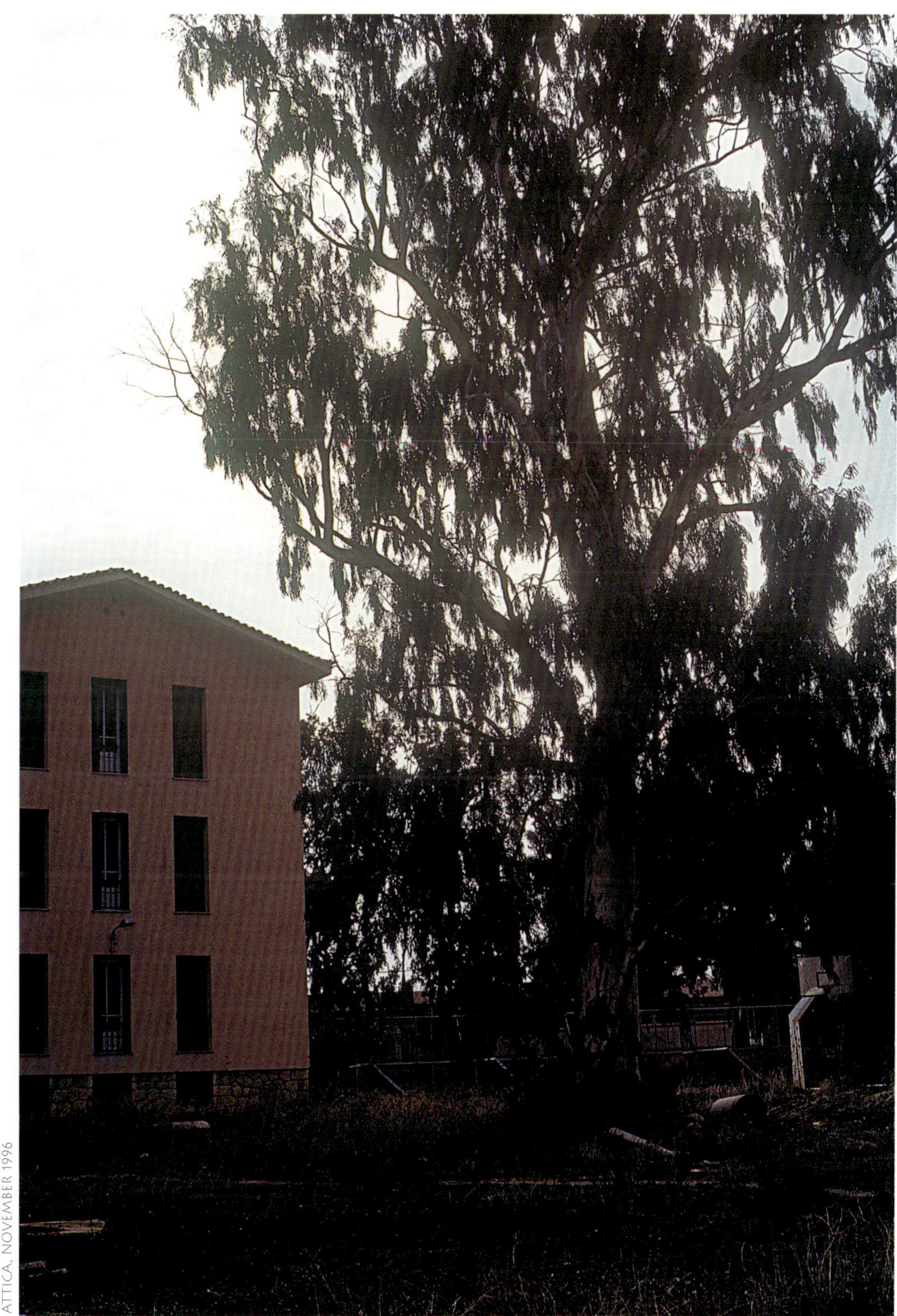

ATTICA, NOVEMBER 1996

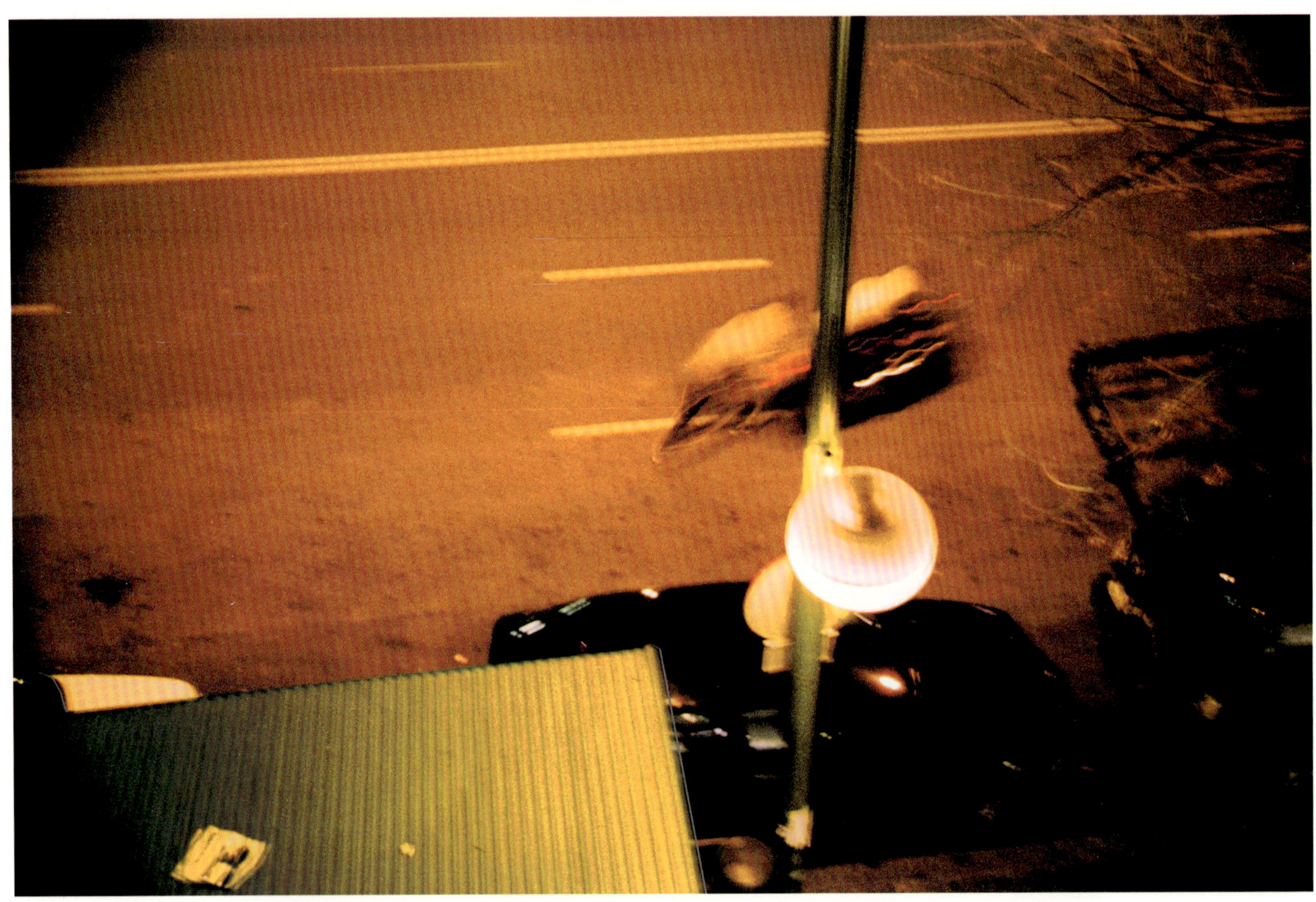

MADRID, MARCH 2002

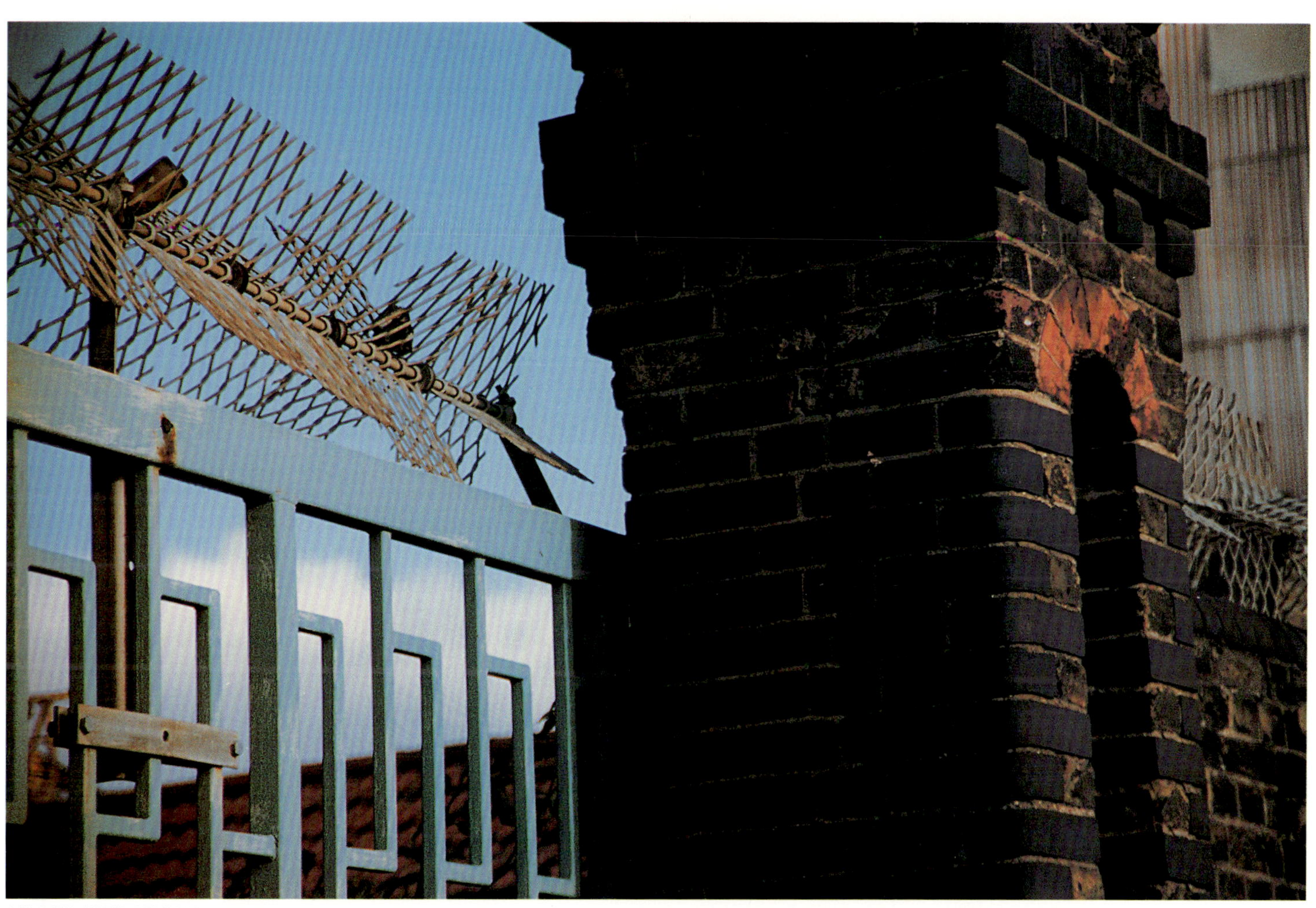

LONDON, SEPTEMBER 2002

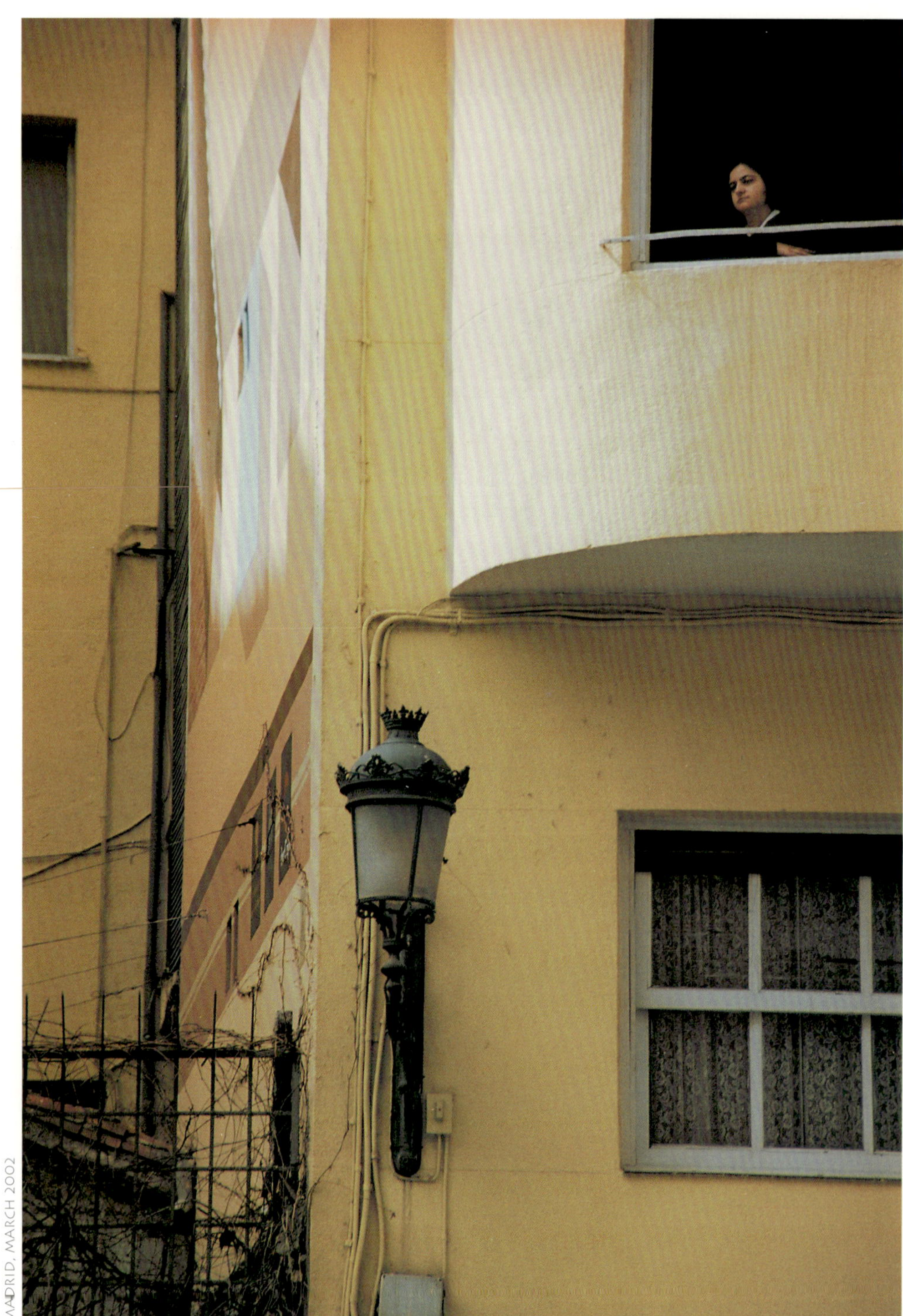

MADRID, MARCH 2002

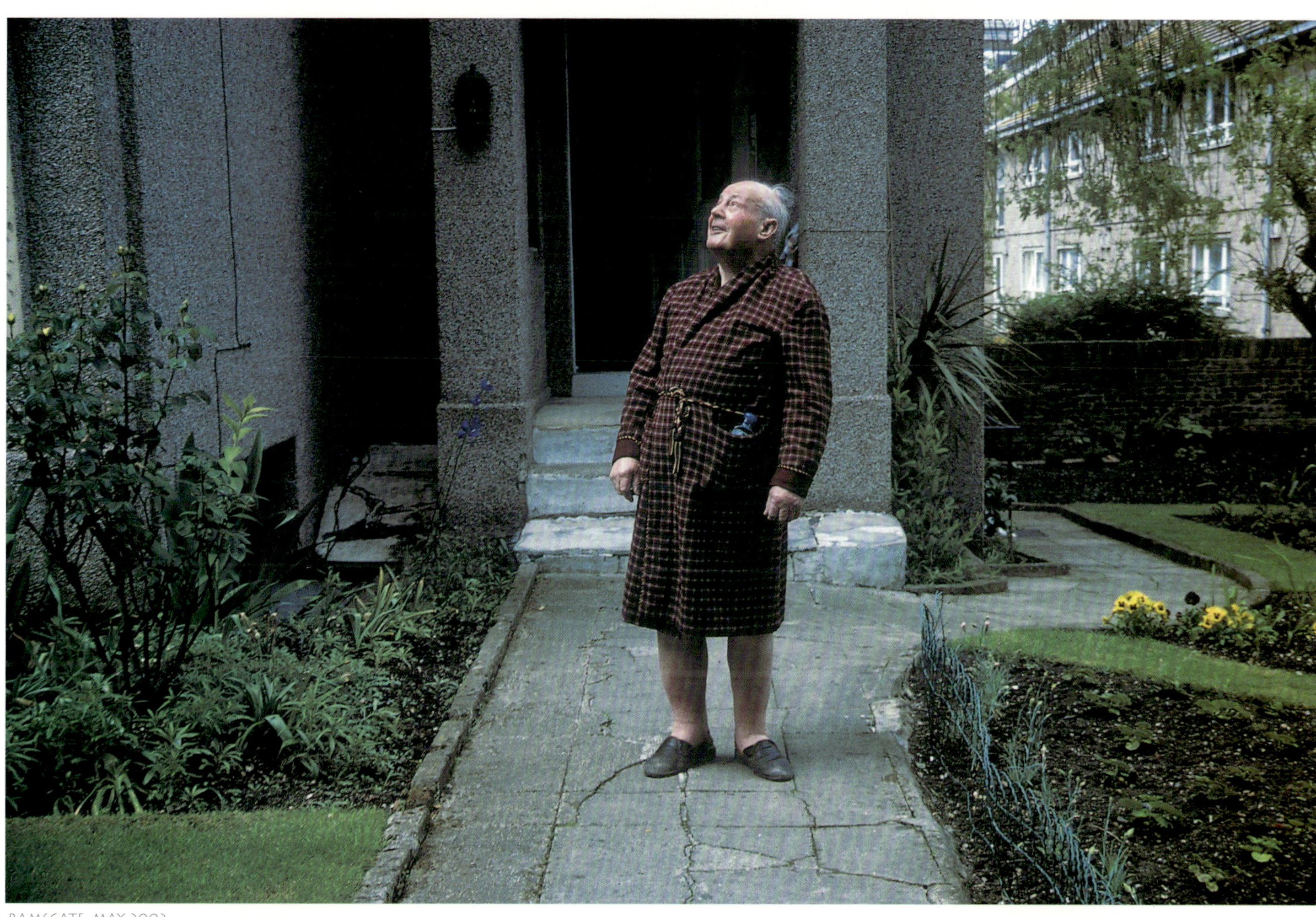

RAMSGATE, MAY 2002

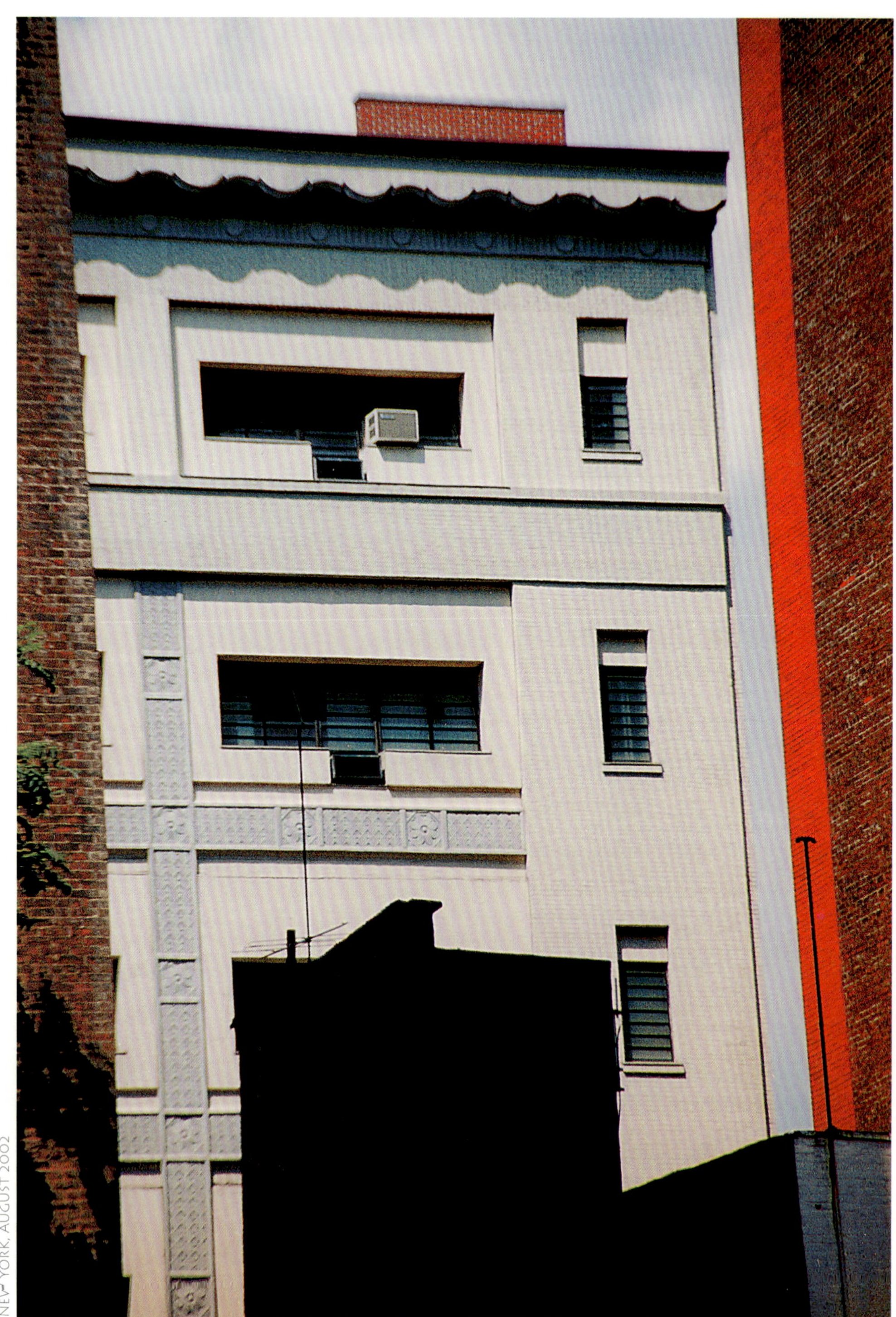

NEW YORK, AUGUST 2002

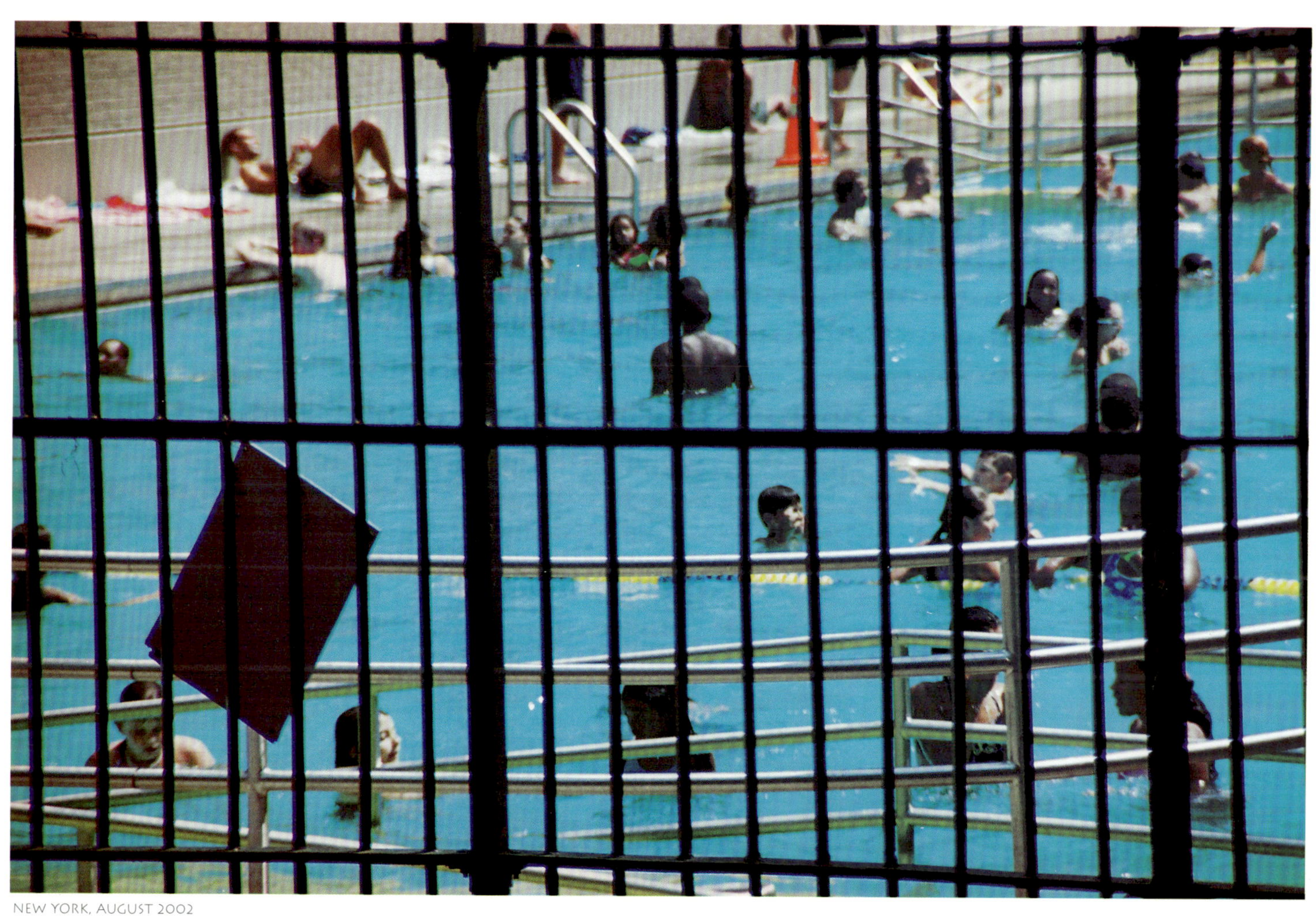

NEW YORK, AUGUST 2002

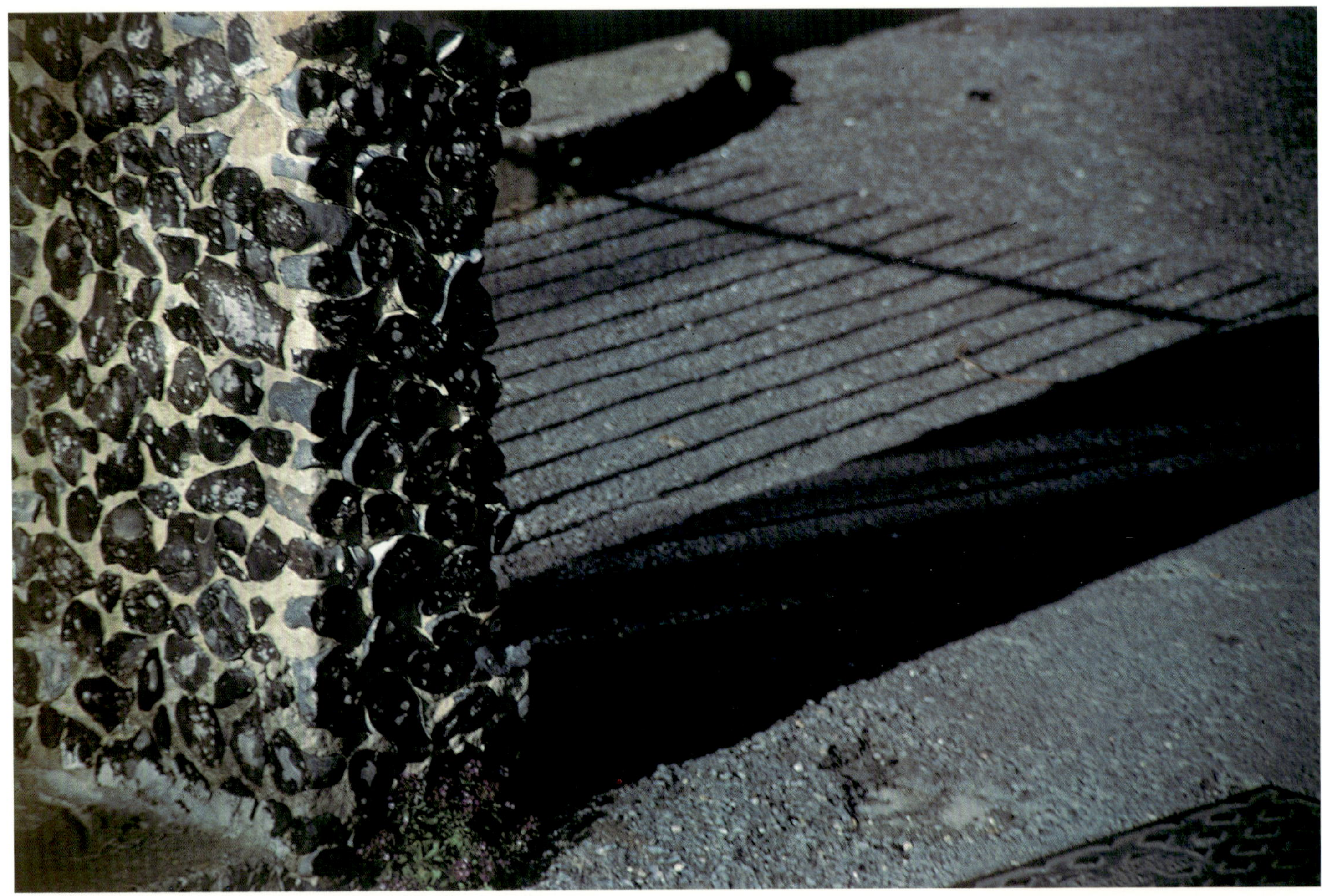

PEGWELL BAY, MAY 2002

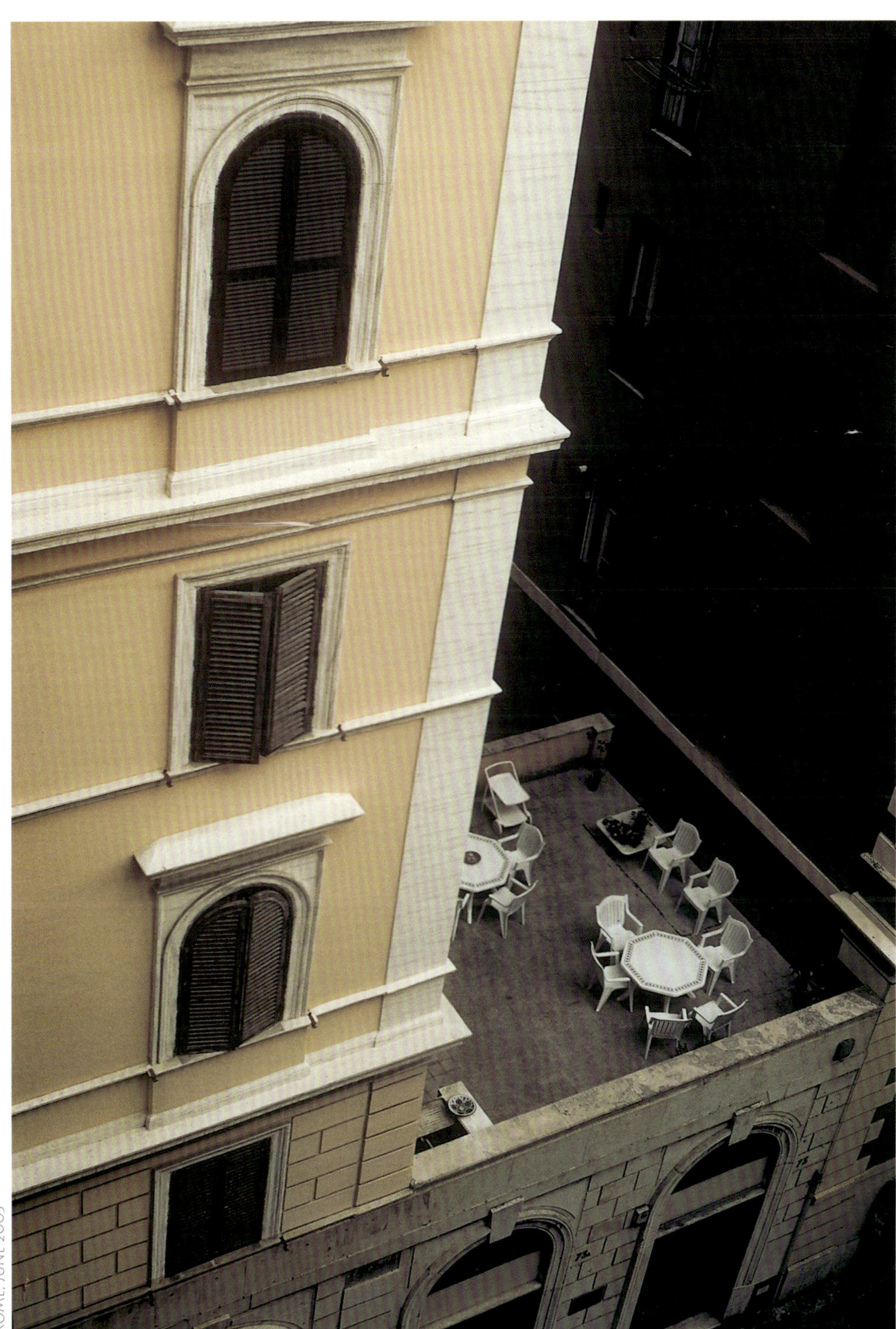

ROME, JUNE 2003

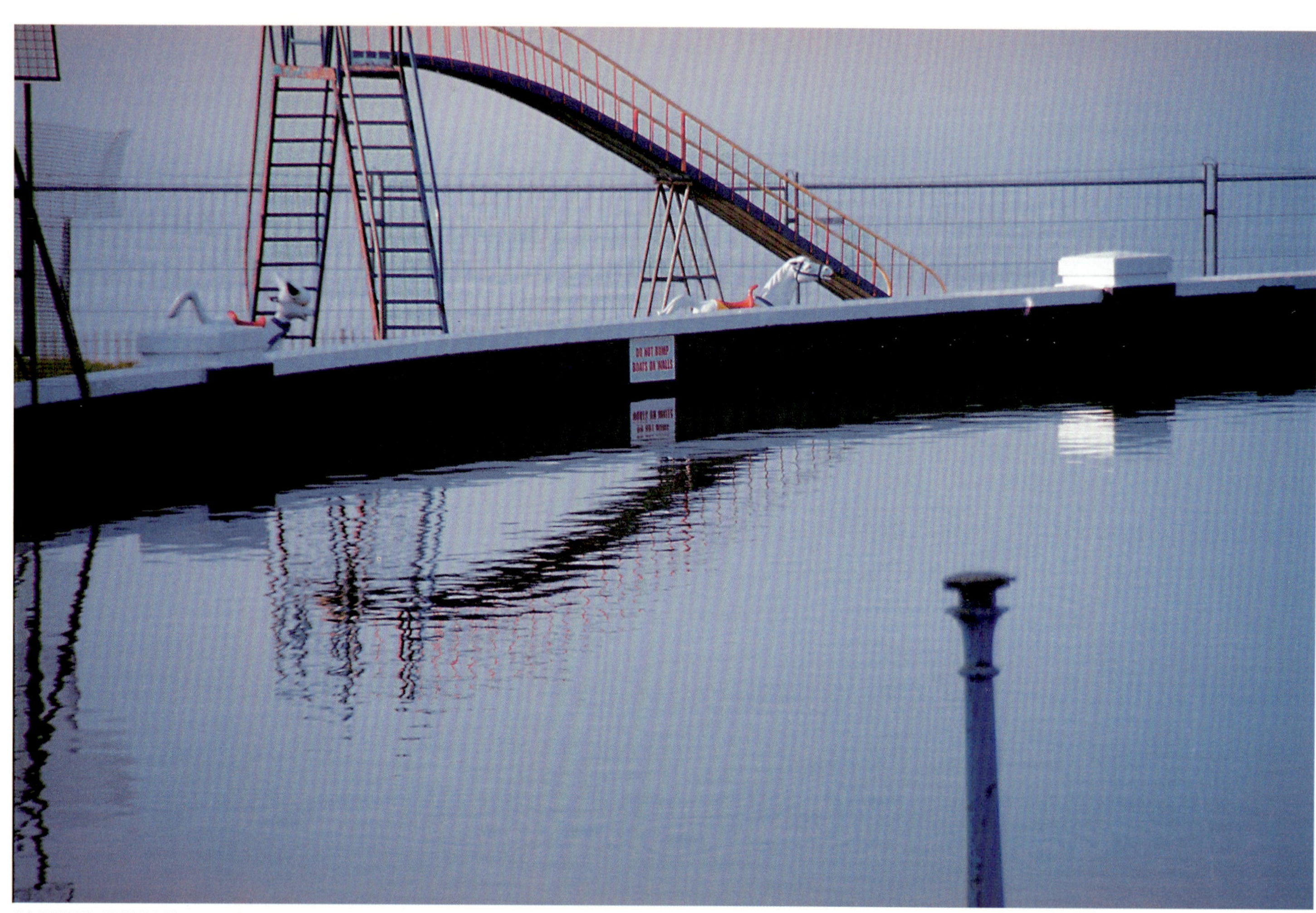

RAMSGATE, APRIL 2002

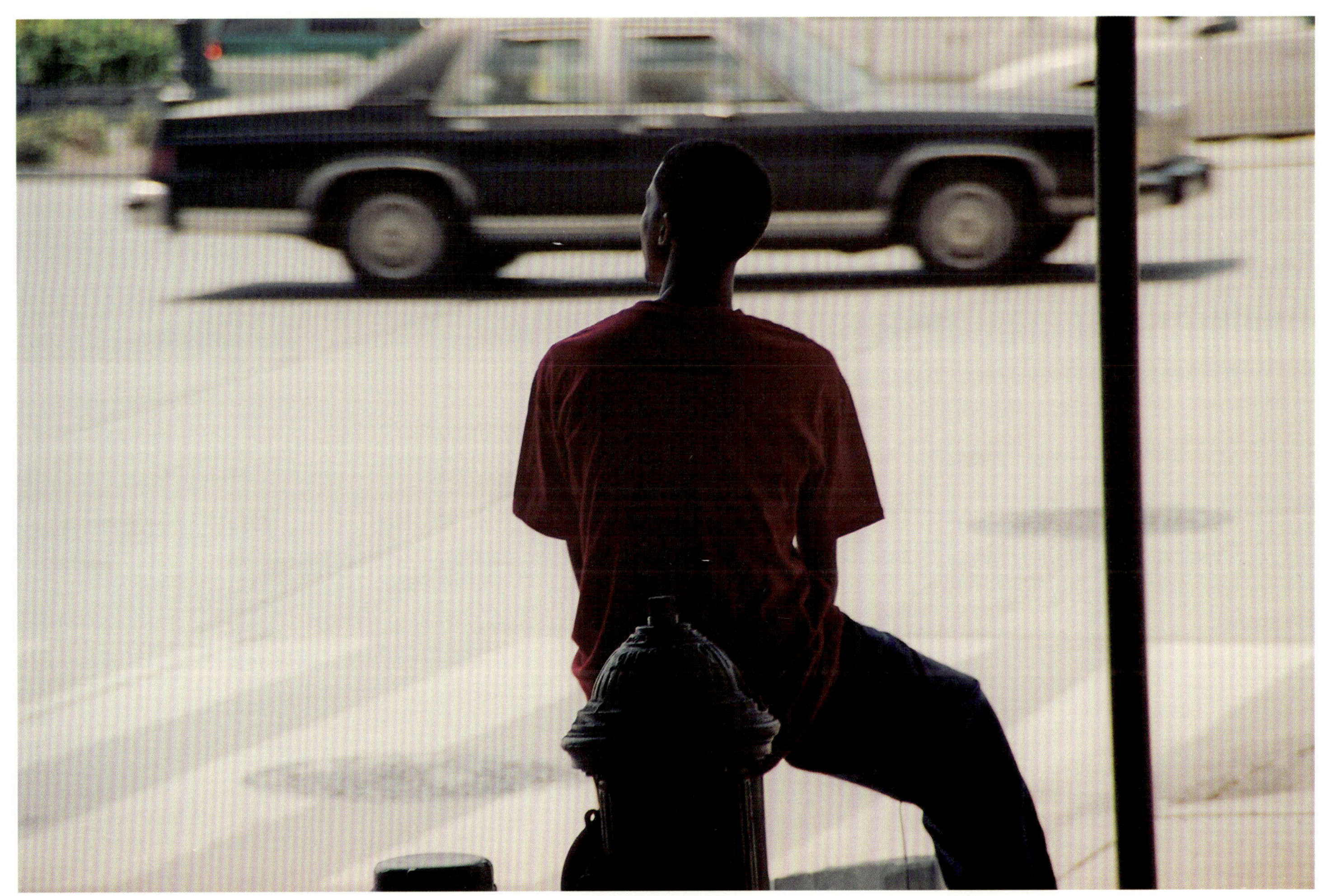

NEW YORK, AUGUST 2002

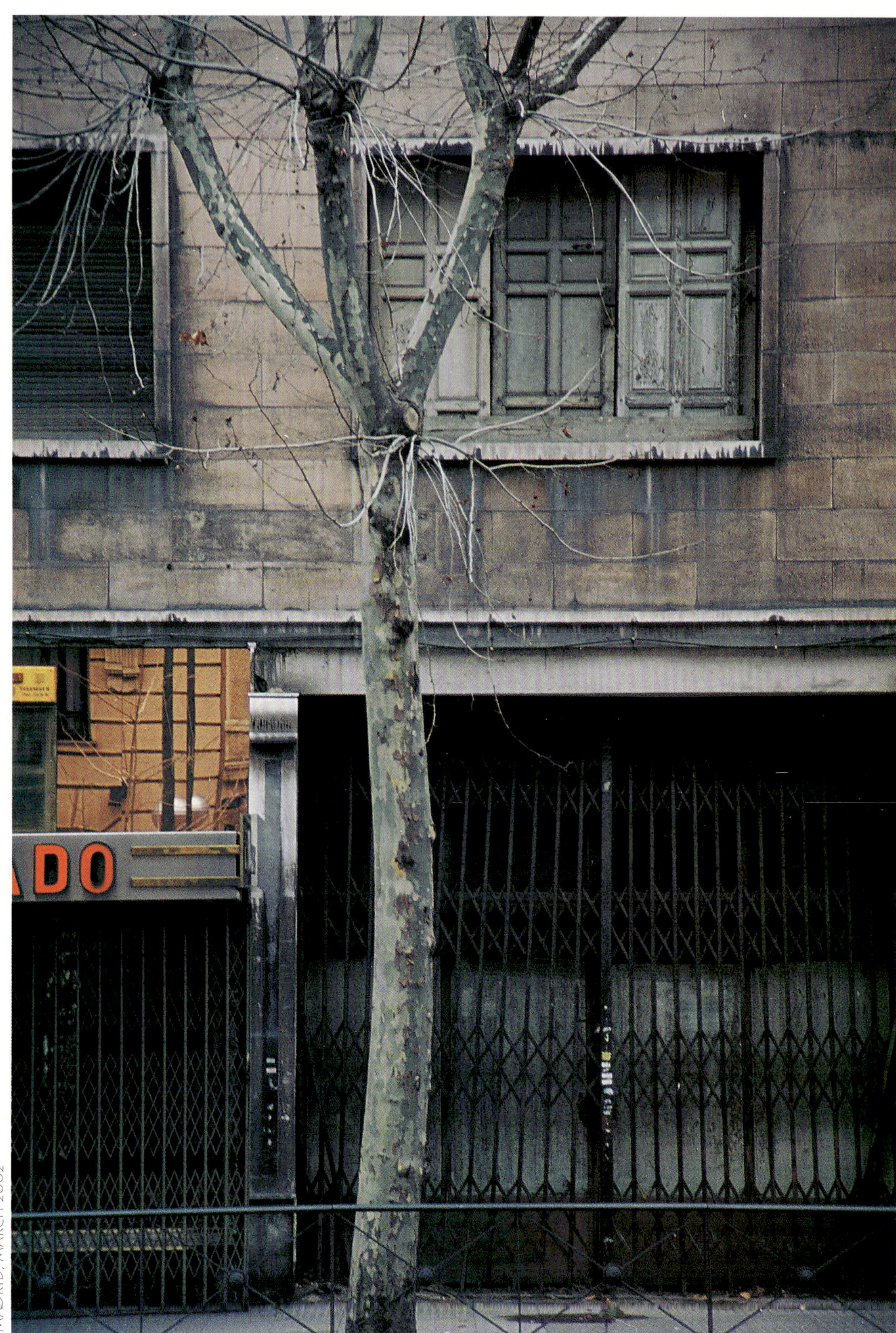

MADRID, MARCH 2002

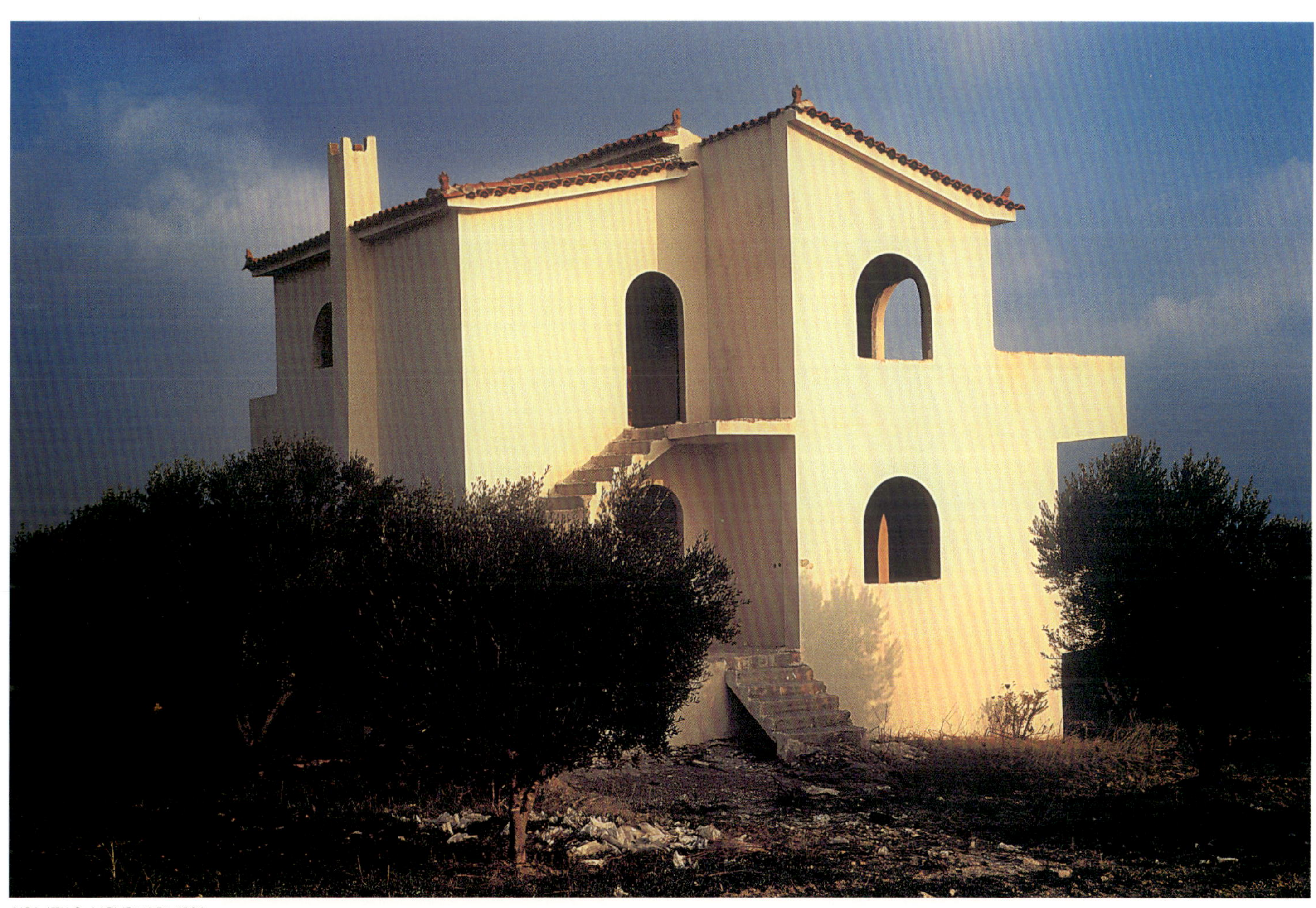

NEA ITILO, NOVEMBER 1996

114

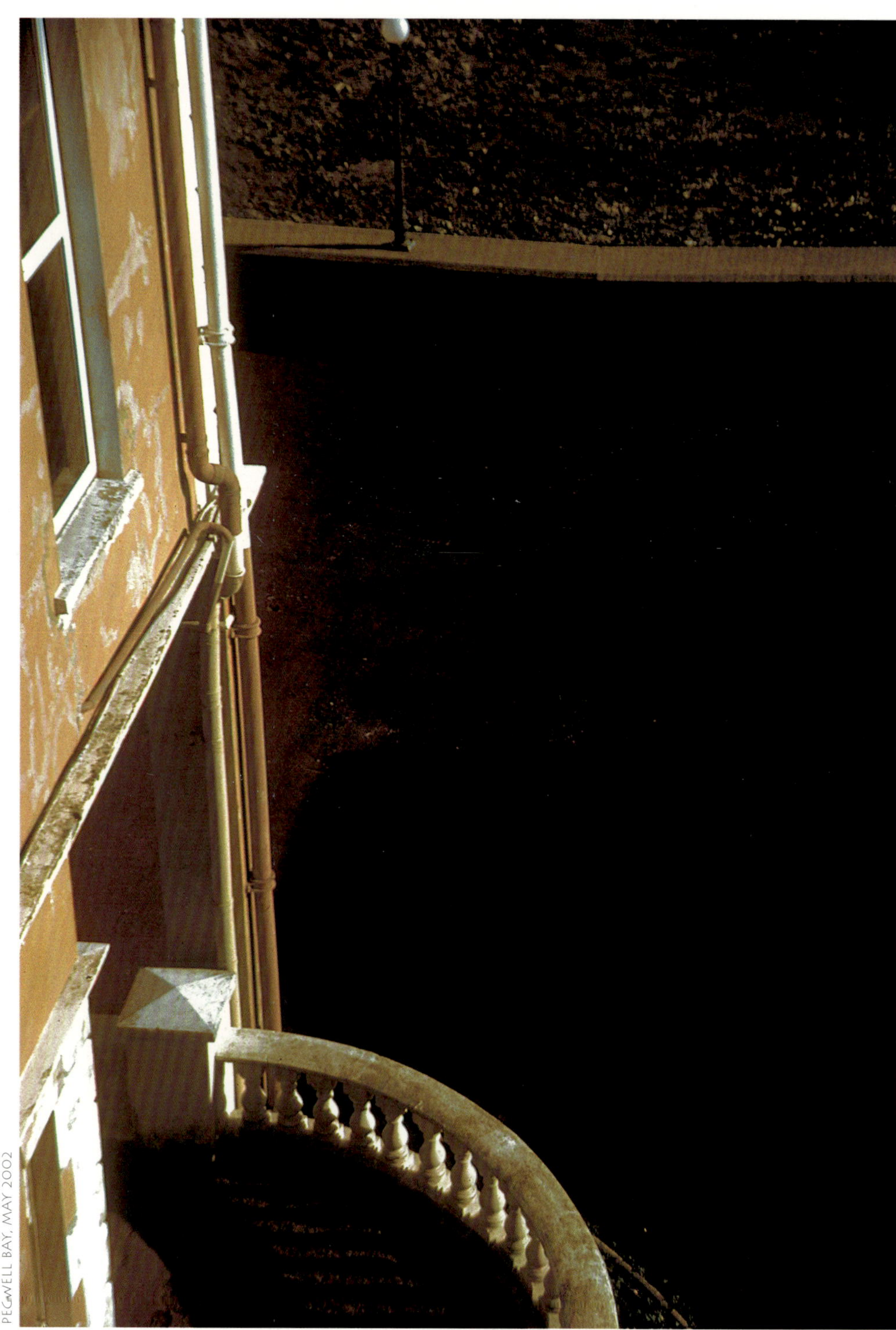

PEGWELL BAY, MAY 2002

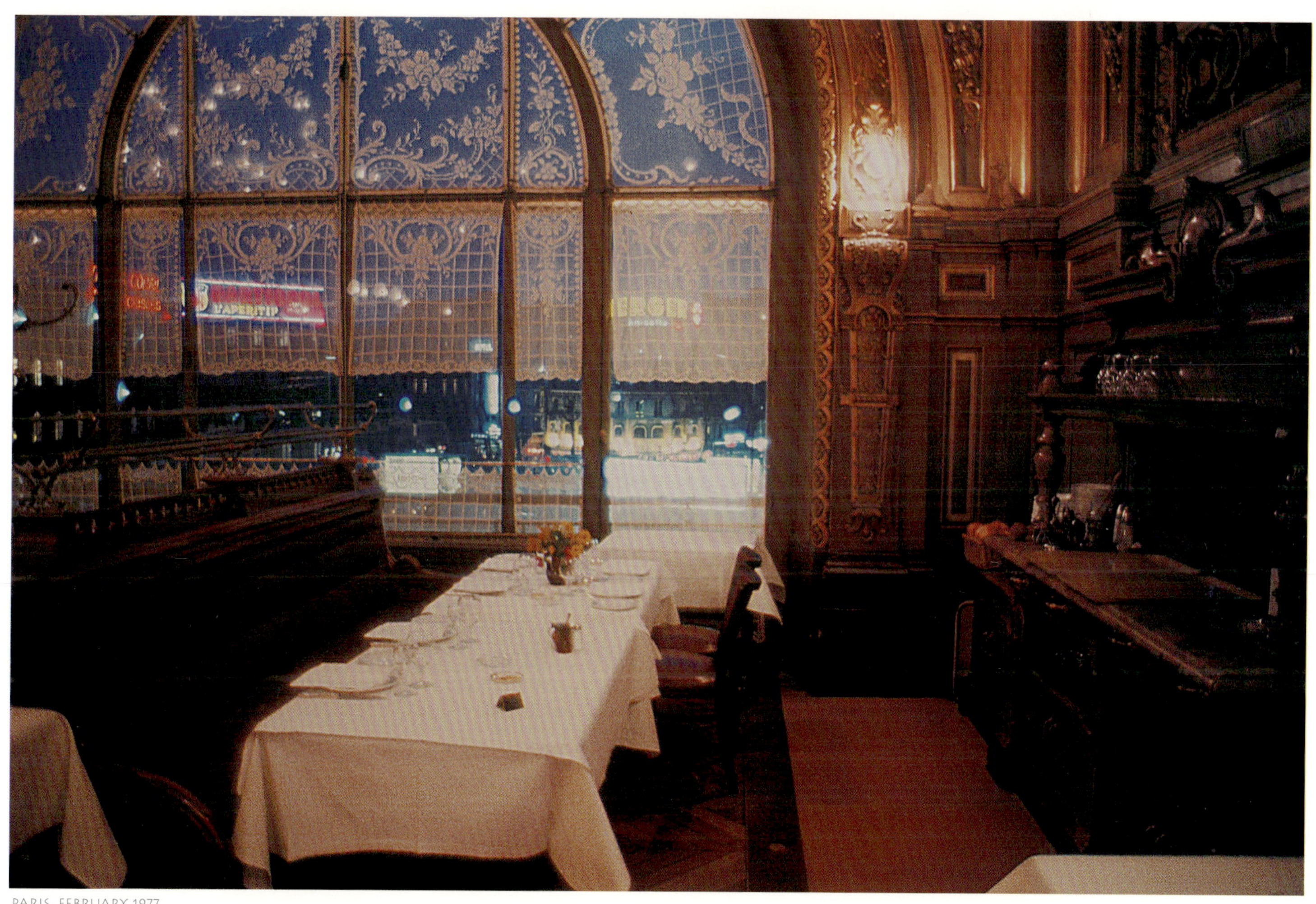

PARIS, FEBRUARY 1977

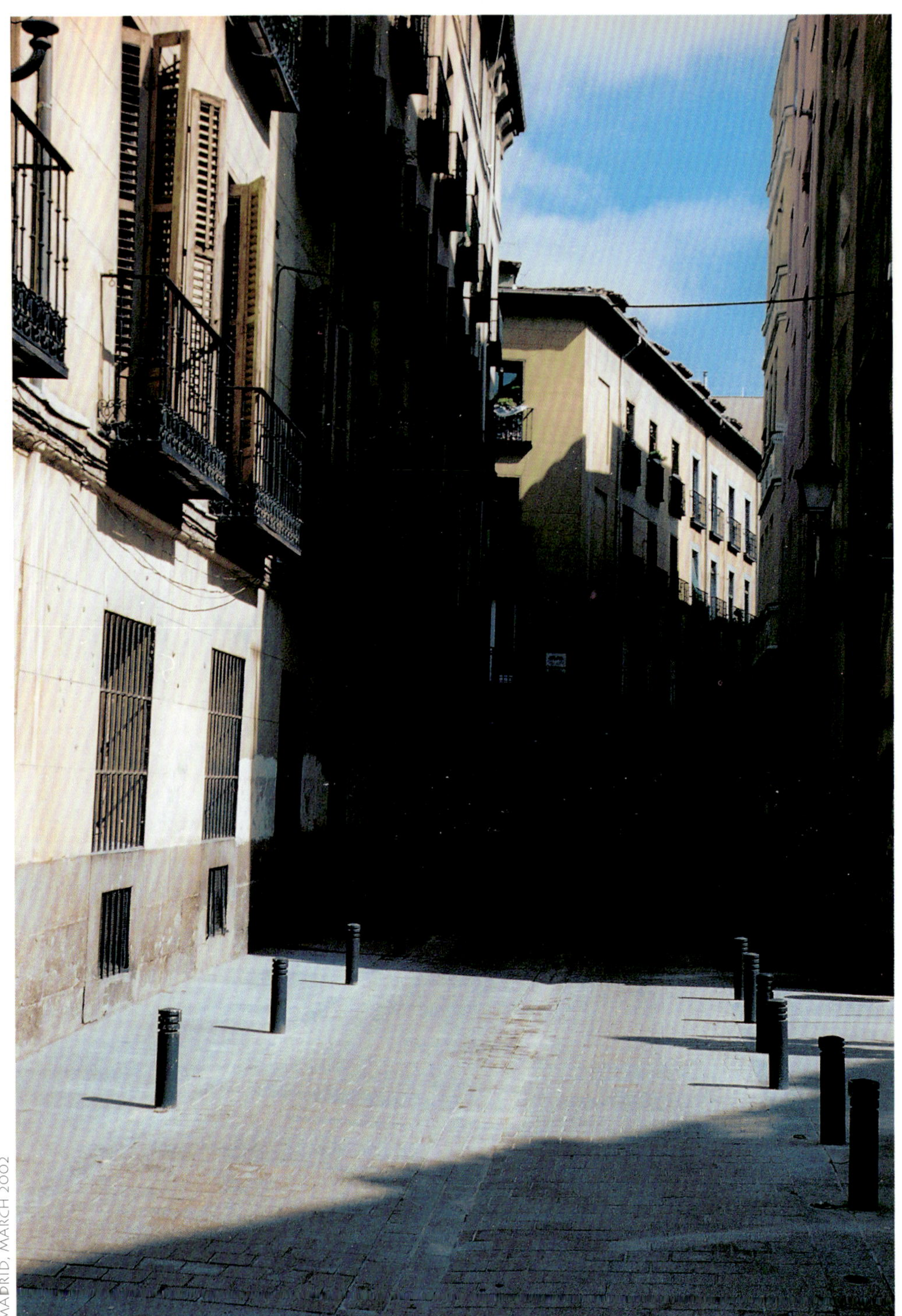

MADRID, MARCH 2002

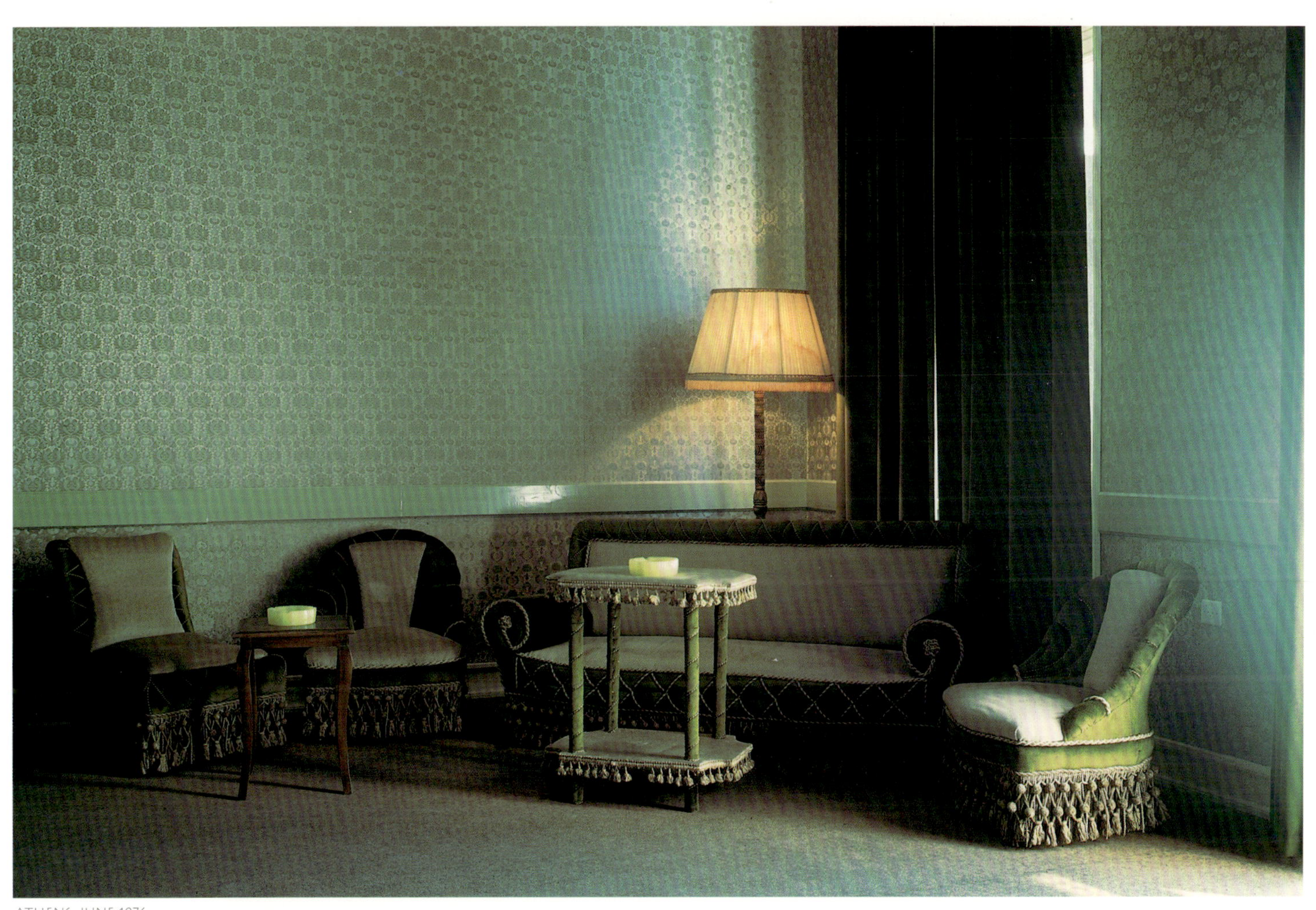

ATHENS, JUNE 1976

117

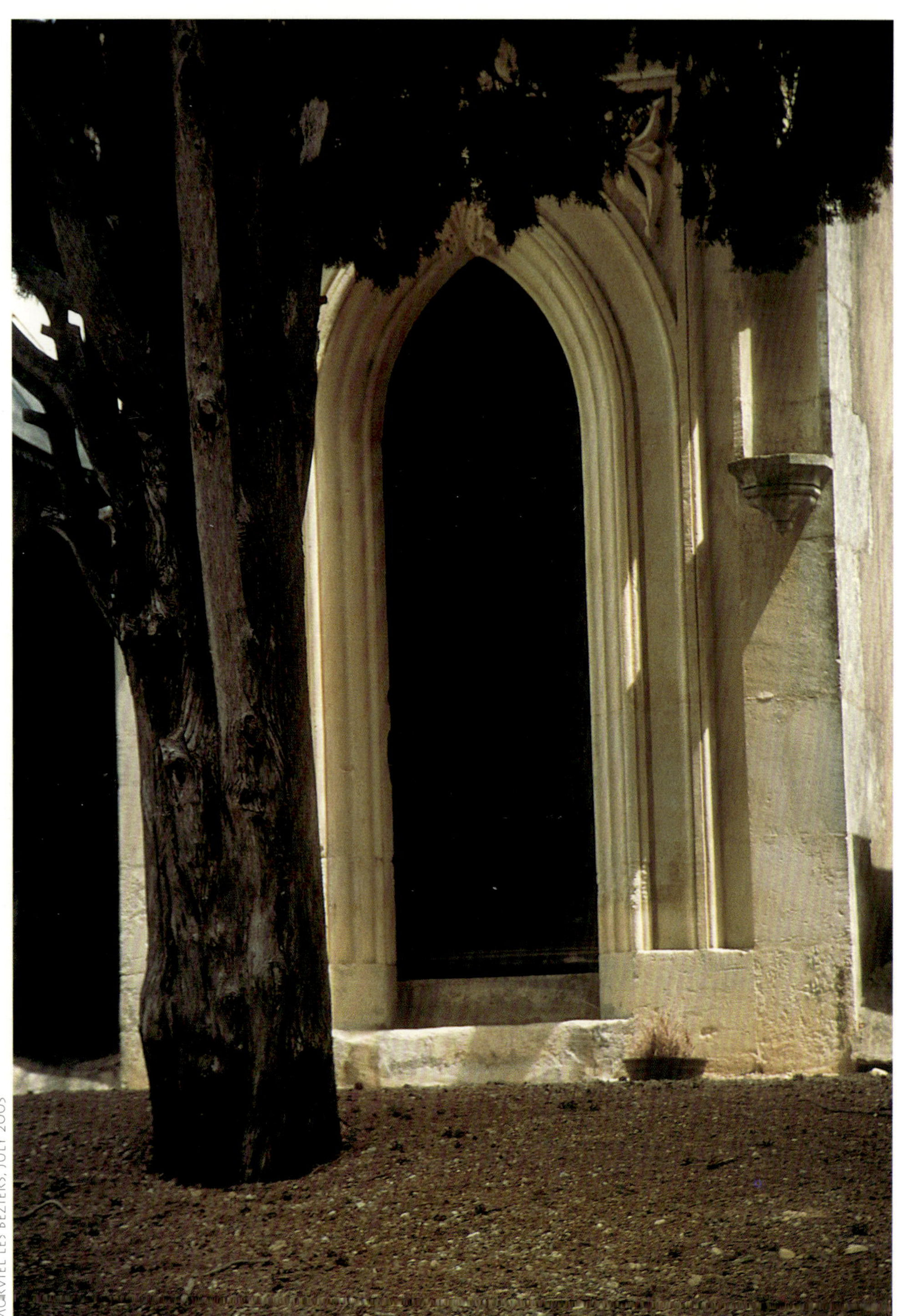
MURVIEL LÈS BÉZIERS, JULY 2003

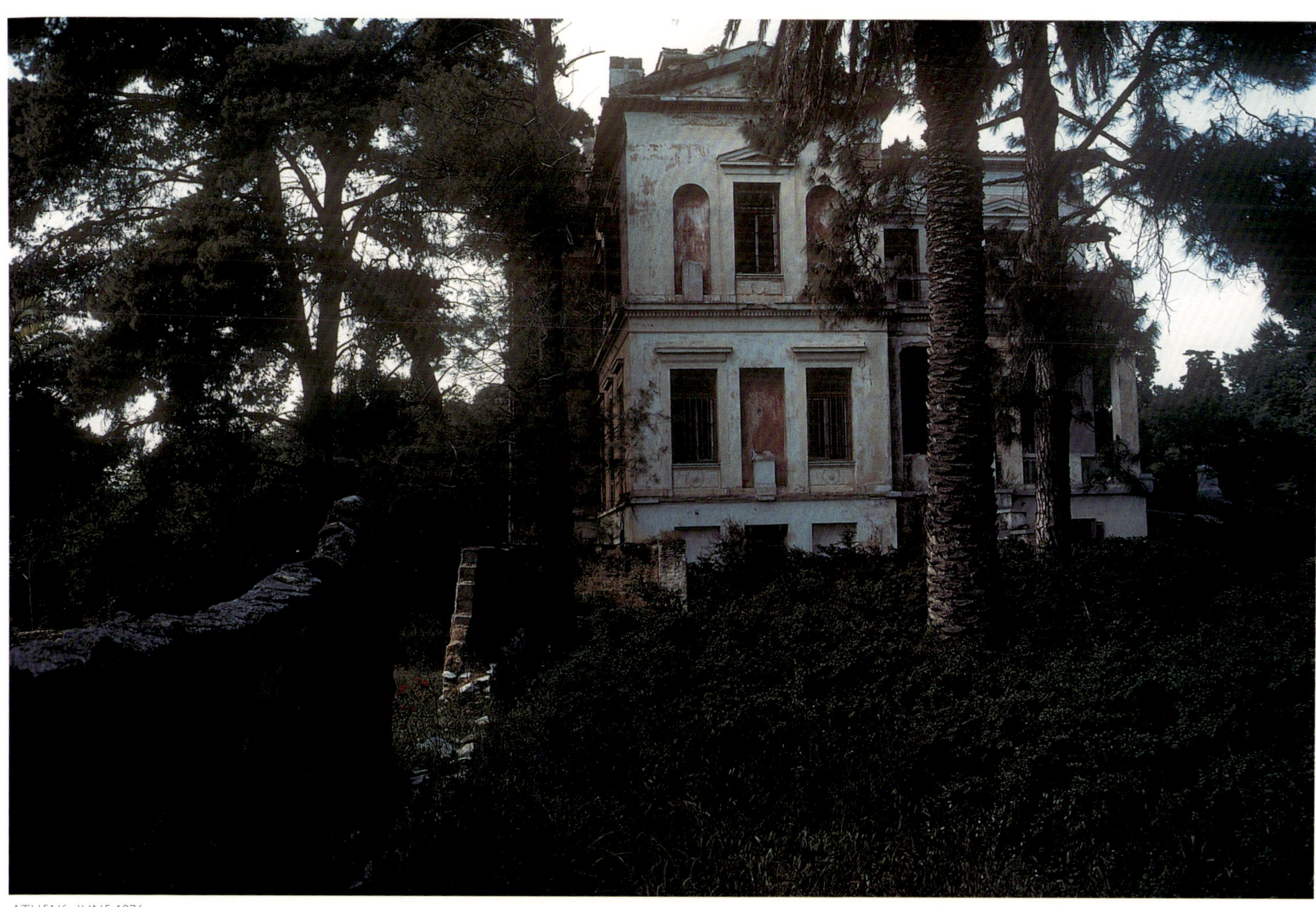

ATHENS, JUNE 1976

SOLO EXHIBITIONS

1970
Gotham Book Mart Art Gallery, New York
1972
History of Collage, Zero Art, New York
1973
Gillan Gallery, Bridgehampton, New York
1975
David Deitcher Gallery, New York
1976
Deitcher OReilly Galleries, New York
1978
Ellen Myers Inc, New York
1987
Christopher Hull Gallery, London
1988
Christopher Hull Gallery, London
1990
Selected Works 1958–1989, Hatton Gallery of the University of Newcastle upon Tyne (Retrospective)
Selected Works 1958–1989, Phillips, Glasgow (Retrospective)
Christopher Hull Gallery, London
1991
Works in Black and Grey 1978–1987, The Picture Gallery, Newcastle upon Tyne
Selected Works 1974–1990, Le Cercle Lucas-Carton, Paris
Five New Paintings, Northumbria University Gallery, Newcastle upon Tyne
Christopher Hull Gallery, London
1992
Abstract Beginnings 1962–1974, X O Contemporary Art, London
Recent Large Works, X O Contemporary Art at Vynehouse, Olympia, London (Exhibition to Benefit the Hearing Research Trust of Great Britain)
1993
The Crucifixions, Belk-Bracy Gallery, Washington Cultural Center, Beaufort County Arts Council, North Carolina
Selected Works 1967–1991, Greenville Museum of Art, North Carolina (Exhibition to Benefit Pitt County AIDS Service Organization)
1994
The Crucifixions and Selected Works, Spirit Square Center for the Arts, Charlotte, North Carolina (Exhibition to Benefit Metrolina AIDS Project)
The Crucifixions and Selected Works, Hickory Museum of Art, Hickory, North Carolina (Exhibition to Benefit AIDS Leadership Foothills-Area Alliance)
Recent and Selected Works, Gallery C, Raleigh, North Carolina
1995
Recent and Selected Works, Broadhurst Gallery, Pinehurst, North Carolina
1996
Diary of a Seducer, An Exhibition of Ink Drawings 1970–71 and a selection of recent works to celebrate the publication of the Gallery Americas Book, Carrboro, North Carolina
1997
Diary of a Seducer, An Exhibition of Ink Drawings 1970–71 from the Gallery Americas Book, Barnes & Noble, Greenville, North Carolina, touring to other Barnes & Noble stores
1999
The Crucifixions, Canterbury Cathedral, Canterbury
1999/2000
The Crucifixions, Winchester Cathedral, Winchester
2004
Michael Hoppen/Shine Gallery, London

FILM WORKS

1968
Silent Sonata, written and directed with Akira Arita, Rhode Island School of Design
1977
Le Grand Silence, written, produced, and directed by Marcus Reichert, Silver Screen Productions Inc, New York
1978
Wings of Ash (A dramatization of the life of Antonin Artaud), pilot for feature film, written and directed by Marcus Reichert, Silver Screen Productions Inc and Mick Jagger, New York
1979
Union City, written and directed by Marcus Reichert, The Tuxedo Company Inc, New York,
1991
People, production design and direction for music video by Marcus Reichert, The Cutaways, Ragin Records, Iris Sound/Metropolis Studios, Philadelphia,
1998
The Seawall Mural, design and direction by Marcus Reichert for public works fine art project, The Renaissance Project, Thanet Arts Development Office, Ramsgate, Kent, 1998

DRAMATIC WORKS

1986
Percy Lifar, a play in two acts, performed by The Hot Toddy Theatre Company (Mark Normandy, Director), The Photographers Gallery, London, 1987
1991/1993
A New Suit for Pepe, opera, book and libretto by Marcus Reichert, music by Howard Davidson

PUBLISHED FICTION

1995
Verdon Angster, novel, BurnhillWolf Book Publishers, Lenoir, North Carolina
1997
The Miracle of Fontanas Monkey, novel (a work in progress), BurnhillWolf Book Publishers, Lenoir, North Carolina

PUBLISHED WORKS OF ART

1996
Diary of a Seducer, Drawings 1970–71 by Marcus Reichert, poetry by D A Blyler, A Gallery Americas Book, Carrboro, North Carolina
2002
Full-page Marcus Reichert photograph, Modern Painters, London, quarterly issues

ART CRITICISM AND JOURNALISM

1990
'The Transparency and the Opacity', retrospective catalogue text, Reichert: Selected Works 1958–1989, Hatton Gallery of the University of Newcastle
'On Van Gogh, Francis Bacon, Picasso, Picasso and Matisse, Schnabel, Pollock, Bilbo and Artaud', Art Line International, Vol.5 No.1, London
1991
'Jack Bilbo & The Moderns', Art Line International, Vol.5 No.4, London
'They Drink to Know', The Whistler, the journal of the Chelsea Arts Club, Vol.1 No.1, London, autumn issue
1992
'Contemporary Abstract Lives', Artreports, an Art Line Magazine supplement, Vol.5 No.7, spring issue, London
1994/1995
'Investigating Sex: Surrealist Discussions 1928–32', reviewed by Marcus Reichert, The Whistler, the journal of the Chelsea Arts Club, No.8, London, winter issue
2001
'Curatorial Eyelashes', Blunt Edge 1, Peter Fuller Memorial Foundation, Forge Cottage, Newnham, Sittingbourne, Kent, April
2003
'Floating Man: The Painting of Kurt Palomaki', Palomaki: Floating Men & Pale Faces, BurnhillWolf Books, Lenoir, North Carolina

SELECTED BIBLIOGRAPHY

1970
Henry, Gerritt, ARTnews, September, New York,
1972
Coleman, A D, The Village Voice, 'Mark Reichert's History of Collage', September, New York
1975
Bell, Jane, Arts Magazine, April, New York
1976
Ellenzweig, Allen, Arts Magazine, February, New York,
1978
Florescu, Michael, Arts Magazine, April, New York,
1979
Livingstone, David, MacLean's Magazine, July, Toronto
1980
Wyndham, Francis, 'Trouble in Union City', Sunday Times Magazine, March, London
Shepard, Richard F, New York Times, September, New York
OToole, Lawrence, 'New Wave Pessimism in Anywhere, USA,' MacLean's Magazine, October, Toronto
Cagin, Seth, 'Tracking', Soho News, October, New York
Corliss, Richard, 'Black Milk', Time magazine, October, New York
1981
Jenkins, Steve, essay on Union City, Journal of the British Film Institute, autumn issue, London
1982
Von Joel, Mike, 'The Art Line Interview', Art Line International, December, London
1983
Hogue, Peter, essay on Union City, Film Quarterly, winter issue, London
1986
Newport, David, 'Mark Reichert', Screen International, July, London
1989
Warhol, Andy, The Andy Warhol Diaries, Simon & Schuster, London
1990
Hall, Charles, Arts Review, March, London,
DeSalvo, Dr Louise A, Reichert: Selected Works 1958–1989, The Act of Painting as Cabal, Hatton Gallery of the University of Newcastle
Florescu, Michael, 'Fear and Loathing & Art and Artists, Times and More Times with Mark Reichert', Art Line International, June, London
Von Joel, Mike, 'The Rewards of Endeavor, Paintings 1958–1989 by Mark Reichert, Art Line International, June, London
1991
Parton, Dr Anthony, 'Self-Amusement and Its Spectres', Christopher Hull Gallery exhibition catalogue, November, London
1992
Beckett, Sister Wendy, 'Mark Reichert's Crucifixions, Art & the Spiritual', Modern Painters, autumn issue, London
1993
Waggoner, Martha, Associated Press, syndicated article variously titled, 'Painter creates moments of agony of the Crucifixion', etc, initial appearance 19 September
Florescu, Michael J, 'The Crucifixions and Selected Works', notes from A View of the Crucifixions, Greenville Museum of Art in association with Caremark Inc, Raleigh, North Carolina
Harries, Richard (Bishop of Oxford), Art and the Beauty of God: A Christian Understanding, Mowbray, London
1994
Bloom, Ken, 'Marcus Reichert: Crucifixions', New Spirit, Spirit Square Center for the Arts Publication, January/February, Charlotte, North Carolina
Perryman, Thomas R, 'Marcus Reichert: The Crucifixion Series and Selected Works', Canvas, July/August, Hickory Museum of Art Publication, Hickory, North Carolina,
1996
Schwartz, David, Film Noir Neo Noir, American Museum of the Moving Image Publication, August, New York
1998
Kuspit, Donald, 'The Crucifixion according to Marcus Reichert', Modern Painters, winter issue, London
1999
Barber, Stephen, Artaud: The Screaming Body, Creation Books, London